URBAN BANKERS
COALITION
is proud to present you with
this copy of

IN THE BLACK
A History of African
Americans on Wall Street

21st Annual Awards &
Scholarship Dinner

FINANCIAL EQUALITY

April 11, 2002

"And Still We Rise: Building from A
Foundation of Greatness."

IN THE BLACK

Black Enterprise books provide useful information on a broad spectrum of business and general-interest topics, including entrepreneurship, personal and business finance, and career development. They are designed to meet the needs of the vital and growing African American business market and to provide the information and resources that will help African Americans achieve their goals. The books are written by and about African American professionals and entrepreneurs, and they have been developed with the assistance of the staff of *Black Enterprise,* the premier African American business magazine.

The series currently includes the following books:

Titans of the B.E. 100s: Black CEOs Who Redefined and Conquered American Business by Derek T. Dingle

Black Enterprise Guide to Starting Your Own Business by Wendy Beech

The Millionaires' Club: How to Start and Run Your Own Investment Club—and Make Your Money Grow! by Caroline M. Brown

The Black Enterprise Guide to Investing by James A. Anderson

Against All Odds: Ten Inspiring Stories of Successful African American Entrepreneurs by Wendy Harris

Take A Lesson: Contemporary Achievers on How They Made It and What They Learned Along the Way by Caroline Clarke

Wealth Building Journal: A Day-by-Day Journey to a Brighter Future, a Better You by the editors of *Black Enterprise* magazine

Forthcoming:

Bridging the Digital Divide: Strategies for African American Entrepreneurs by Bernadette Williams

IN THE BLACK

A History of African Americans
on Wall Street

Gregory S. Bell

John Wiley & Sons, Inc.

Published by John Wiley & Sons, Inc., New York.
Published simultaneously in Canada.

This publication is designed to provide accurate and authoritative information in regard to the subject matter covered. It is sold with the understanding that the publisher is not engaged in rendering professional services. If professional advice or other expert assistance is required, the services of a competent professional person should be sought.

ISBN 0-471-40392-X

Printed in the United States of America.

10 9 8 7 6 5 4 3 2

In loving memory of
Travers J. Bell, Sr.
"We'll get there, Grandpa."

Preface

ALTHOUGH MY NAME IS THE ONLY ONE TO grace the cover of this book, I am in no way the only person who deserves credit for its completion. As every author knows, the publication process can be complicated and all books are the result of many people's labor.

I must first thank my parents. My late father's imagination, determination, and ambition will always serve as an inspiration to me as I try to fulfill my promise.

My mother's unselfish support will always be the foundation for me as I pursue my goals.

I would like to thank a few people who took time out of their schedules to speak with me when I was just a college student interested in the subject. I will never forget when investment banker Wayne A. Seaton took me to lunch at the Harvard Club in 1999. It was an extraordinary educational experience, and there is no doubt that Wayne will be in the next chapter of this history. Another person who stands out is Tony Chapelle, publisher of *Securities Pro* newsletter who talked with me that same year and shared his thoughts on countless subjects.

I would like to extend my heartfelt gratitude to the investment bankers, asset managers, stockbrokers, politicians, and other people who agreed to answer my questions and be interviewed for this book. To accomplish this, I took calls from people at 7:00 A.M. and conversed with others after midnight. I talked with some while riding in their cars, to others as far away as South Africa. I must thank them all, as well as the numerous assistants, secretaries, and media relations people who arranged these interviews.

I solicited advice from many historians on the responsibilities and goals of chronicling a history book. Dr. Juliet E. K. Walker, professor of history at the University of Texas at Austin, was particularly helpful in helping me avoid potential impediments.

I am grateful to the staff of Earl G. Graves Ltd. who went out of their way to help me overcome occasional obstacles. Most notably, I want to recognize Caroline V. Clarke, editor of the *Black Enterprise* book series, who enthusiastically welcomed an outsider like me into the *BE* family.

Last but not least, the staff at John Wiley & Sons will forever have my appreciation. As a first-time author, I was lucky to be working with such a talented group of individuals. Two people deserve special recognition. My editor, Airié Dekidjiev, was a supportive and marvelous source of knowledge as I learned a process that had been foreign to me. This book would not have happened without her extraordinary ability and encouragement. I would also like to thank her assistant Jessica Noyes, who has probably received more e-mails from me than from anybody else in her life. I am grateful that my constant pestering never annoyed her; her timely and informative responses were always helpful to me and this project.

GREGORY S. BELL

Contents

INTRODUCTION

I N THE LATE 1960s, A BLACK CHILD STOOD ON the corner of his street only hours removed from a riot that had ravaged his neighborhood. He was about 10 years old and small for his age, but he loomed surprisingly large against the backdrop of burned stores and fallen buildings. Among the crowd of locals, policemen, and firemen was a reporter whose assignment was to write a front-page story summarizing the social unrest that had been building for decades. He asked the child what he thought about the turmoil that had transformed his community from the familiar to the unrecognizable. After pondering the question, the child answered as only a youngster can, bashfully but bluntly sincere: "There ain't a problem that we have that money can't solve."

The words of that child capture the essence of this book and the story I set out to tell because they represent what many consider to be the final frontier of social justice: economic equality. Monetary power can influence social and political power in ways that other resources cannot.

History has shown that many factors have encumbered the economic opportunities available to African Americans. Yet, despite many challenges and odds that at times seemed insurmountable, many people have taken on the fight for economic equality. Money is not important because it can procure nice cars, clothes, and accessories; it is important because in our capitalist society, economic emancipation is essential in implementing true and substantive change. Wealth will not cure all of society's ills; however, monetary power can influence social and political causes in ways that other resources cannot.

It is appropriate that the simple statement of a child can accurately summarize this complicated economic movement. Wall Street itself presents many contradictions. Physically, it is a short, narrow street, but for the general population it has become an exponent of the richest, biggest, greatest, and most powerful entities. It embodies fortune making–the founding of the businesses of J. P. Morgan, Charles Merrill, Bernard Baruch, and Felix Rohatyn, among many other titans of industry. When Bill Gates wanted to expand his company, he went to Wall Street. When President Gerald Ford sought advice on how to solve the economic crisis of the 1970s, he went to Wall Street. It has been the convention center for some of the most influential people in the world, and it was only a matter of time until African Americans tried to stake their claim within its boundaries either by working in the industry or by investing their money.

Although black people have made impressive strides in other professional areas like law and medicine, progress in the securities industry has lagged behind. The majority of the events in this book took place before there was 24-hour financial networks or the connectivity of the Internet. Despite today's advancements, a complete understanding of securities remains elusive to many, especially in the African American community where resources have been relatively scarce. For a long time, there were no legacies to draw from or accomplished black financiers to encourage participation and pass on their knowledge. African Americans began their journey on Wall Street centuries behind other groups.

∞

I was exposed to the world of Wall Street early in my life because at one point or another many members of my family worked at a black-owned investment bank. It was not until college that I thought to transform my family legacy into the pages you are reading. The road to this book began in the spring of 1998 when my grandfather, Travers J. Bell Sr., died at the age of 86. My loss, along with the desire to honor his memory, served as the springboard for my immersion in the history of African Americans on Wall Street, which eventually developed into this project.

In the early 1990s, Travers Bell Sr. was attending an event sponsored by the National Association of Securities Professionals, a group that represents minorities in the securities industry. One of the speakers at this gathering was former mayor of Atlanta and NASP cofounder, Maynard H. Jackson. In his opening remarks, he said, "I'd like to acknowledge Travers Bell Sr. He may be the oldest man in the room but he is also the smartest."[1] Jackson would later say, "He was an interesting man. He was there in this industry and nobody knew it. The insiders knew it but he burst out through his son, trained him, and brought him up. Travers Bell Jr. was the Tiger Woods of this industry and his father was the daddy Woods."[2] Despite his God-given ability, Travers Bell Sr. was never able to fulfill his true potential because of the social attitudes of the era in which he lived.

Born in 1913, he came of age during the Great Depression when there were no opportunities for African Americans to participate in the country's economy. He and most of his peers confronted inequality all of their lives. Yet, my grandfather took the prevalent attitude in stride and made do with what jobs he was able to get. Among other positions, he worked as a chauffeur and a clerk in a brokerage mailroom. To support his family, he sometimes was forced to maintain two or three jobs at a time.

While in his later years he would serve on the boards of companies, the only goal he had during his prime years was to provide for his family. His life and work as a brokerage clerk in the 1950s and 1960s set forth a chain of events that began my family's legacy.

After my grandfather's death, I was sitting in his apartment at a celebration of his life, and next to me was a basket full of magazines. Among the *Jet* and *National Geographic* publications was a silver and black issue of *Black Enterprise*. It was the Twenty-Fifth Anniversary issue from August 1995. Since it was almost three years old, I assumed that he had saved it for special reasons. While looking through it, I stumbled on an article by Frank McCoy called "The Building of the Black Financial World." That piece changed my life.

The article rekindled my interest in the subject of African Americans on Wall Street, a subject that I had avoided for some time because of the unfortunate events that unfolded at Daniels & Bell after my father died in 1988. When I was in grade school, half of some Fridays were spent at the Daniels & Bell headquarters. This was during an era when the company was at the top of its game and the period of dire struggle was a distant memory. For example, 1986 was a milestone because Daniels & Bell finished the year by ranking in the top 20 municipal finance houses. That achievement was far removed from the 1970s when my father and his partner, Willie Daniels, made history by cofounding the first black-owned member firm of the New York Stock Exchange. Despite this monumental accomplishment, the firm struggled during the bleak 1970s as social and economic factors worked against them. Unfortunately, as was representative of much of the black financial community of that time, disagreements often hindered what could have been accomplished together. Willie Daniels left in the mid-seventies, leaving my father as chairman of a firm that eventually broke barriers for black-owned investment banks.

While the larger lessons learned in that office settled in with maturity and hindsight, as a child I experienced the excitement generated by the game of numbers and calculation. As I did the interviews for this book, I reawakened some memories about that period in my life, such as how I struggled to carry my father's heavy briefcase from the elevator to his desk and how I earned five dollars for stuffing envelopes. While these tasks were menial, the experience had a larger impact. Bankers such as Frank Raines and Jeff Humber told me that they didn't even know what investment banking was until after college. My experience was invaluable; I was able to see for myself at a young age what Wall Street was all about and that the possibilities were indeed limitless.

After my father's death in 1988, I learned intimately that Wall Street could be more than a land of opportunity once the door to it had been pushed open. I learned it could be rapacious, cruel, and unforgiving. Publications such as the *Wall Street Journal* and the *National Enquirer* preyed on the firm during its decline. This negative portrayal caused me great grief as a teenager and, consequently, I lost all passion for Wall Street.

The *Black Enterprise* issue that my grandfather had so carefully saved aroused my interest in the struggle of many people, not just my family. McCoy's piece mentioned early pioneers I had never heard of, such as Russell Goings, and as soon as I returned to school from the funeral, I researched everything that I could find on the subject. Within a few months, I had stacks of material on the subject.

While browsing in a bookstore that summer, I came across a book by Reginald Lewis, *Why Should White Guys Have All the Fun?* (New York: John Wiley & Sons, 1994) and I loved reading it. I deeply believe that the reason a book inspires a person is because it allows the readers to see themselves in it. I used to think of Reginald Lewis in association with his victories with the McCall and Beatrice deals. I read about the drive and work behind those successes; I identified with his struggle. Before those landmark transactions were his failures to acquire Parks Sausage and other companies, yet Lewis overcame those setbacks to fulfill his dreams. I was hopeful that a similar book about the broader black financial community would soon follow from the same publisher. I made a mental note and prepared for my senior year at Oberlin College.

I continued to read everything I could get my hands on and found a vehicle for spreading the story. I created "Minorities on Wall Street," a Web site dedicated to promoting the accomplishments of African Americans in the securities industry. Although its design was simple, the content was good and I received numerous warm and encouraging e-mails. Well-wishers convinced me that a great many people were seeking information about the pioneers who had broken down the walls in the financial services industry.

As I continued to educate myself about this history, I discovered that the most valuable method for understanding this precious history is by speaking to the pioneers themselves. Newspapers and magazines can only tell you so much about a person; however, I quickly found out that Wall Streeters have little time available no matter whose son you are, or how sincere the interest.

Luckily, a few of my father's peers were willing to help me understand certain time periods and the markets of the past.

As a result of those conversations in early 1999, I was invited to accept an award on my father's behalf at the first National Association of Securities Professionals New York District "Wall Street Hall of Fame" ceremony. At the head table, I sat alongside Hank Parker, former State Treasurer of Connecticut; Harold Doley, of Doley Securities; Russell Goings, cofounder of First Harlem Securities; Alphonso Tindall, securities lawyer extraordinaire; William Hayden, senior managing director at Bear Stearns; and the Honorable Denise Nappier, State Treasurer of Connecticut. It was a dream situation for finding out more about the people who so profoundly affected black history, not to mention I gave a good speech.

There is no question that my interest in this subject came directly from my family ties; however, the more I learned about this history, the more I realized that clarification and exploration were needed to correct existing assumptions. For example, it brings me great pride to read things about my father's impact on Wall Street. In 1999, the *Investment Dealers Digest* said that the late Travers Bell Jr. is regarded as the "father of the modern minority-owned investment bank."[3] I understand why this was written; however, others also deserve recognition. I deeply believe that Russell L. Goings Jr. deserves as much credit as anyone. He convinced Shearson Hammill to open a branch in Harlem in 1968. He planned to buy the firm in the future and the first man he hired was Willie Daniels. It also has been written that "Daniels & Bell's admittance to the NYSE cleared the way for First Harlem Securities to buy a spot four months later."[4] What most don't know is that First Harlem's application was approved in 1970 before there was a Daniels & Bell. First Harlem declined to buy that spot because of market conditions.

There are many people who deserve credit for the progress made in this history and don't get the proper recognition. It became my goal to give them that credit and explain how they forced change. I have had the opportunity to learn a great deal about pioneers like Frank Raines, E. Stanley O'Neal, T. M. Alexander Jr., William H. Hayden, and so many others.

I couldn't be happier that John Wiley & Sons and *Black Enterprise,* the two publishers who inspired my interest, agreed to support my efforts and produce this book.

After receiving the backing to write this book, I was soon confronted with questions that all writers of history books must face. The articles and other reference items I had gathered for years now lay before me as a massive puzzle. A story as deep as this one, with so much material, so many people and stories to sift through, makes it difficult to choose what directions to pursue and include. Essentially, this is a play with a cast of thousands, and except for a few biographies and brief paragraphs in certain books, it is a previously unexplored history. My research was rich with anecdotes and facts but poor in structure. Would it be possible to include everyone who had made a difference, from the African Americans who literally built Wall Street with their bare hands, to the pivotal people who fought for fair legislation and opportunity within the labyrinthine network of the investment banks, to the entrepreneur who set out to do it himself?

It soon became apparent that despite my greatest ambitions, I could not include every African American who ever worked on Wall Street, every story ever told, and the history behind every dollar made.

At first, my goal was to tell the story of every person who made a difference, no matter how small his or her impact was.

However, space limitations soon changed that goal. I could have listed hundreds of African Americans with some basic information like education, employers, and big deals so that I could include everyone. But that defeated my purpose of exploring *how* individuals accomplished their goals. Reginald Lewis's book focused on both his successes and his failures, giving me a point of reference to judge his accomplishments. I wanted to do the same with my book by digging deep into stories. I was forced, when constrained by space, to focus on specific individuals. So I was also forced to make tough choices that inevitably meant certain people or aspects received less attention. Although I regretted having to make these painful decisions, all of them reflected my quest to tame this constantly expanding history.

I would be misleading if I said that I had no help in deciding which stories to pursue. I did have the final say and translated these choices from thought to print. However, this history in many ways chose itself as three themes found the spotlight. This trinity of important themes forms the basis of this history: *social power, political power,* and *financial power* working together for progress.

To successfully depict the cooperative influence and work among these arenas, I decided early on to look at the majority of this story through the eyes of entrepreneurs. My own legacy made it a natural focus for me, and I could more deeply understand those who decided to go it alone. I have also been influenced by the remarks of such luminaries as Earl Graves, who insists that ownership is key. That belief is fitting on Wall Street because stock and capitalism are all forms of ownership.

While there are many inspiring and important stories of black people within the corporate financial industry, milestones within the major firms have lagged behind that of entrepreneurship, for plenty of complex causes. As discussed later in this book, the first registered black-owned broker/ dealer emerged in 1952. In contrast, the first black partner in a major investment bank wasn't named until 1985. The first black-owned firm became a member of the New York Stock Exchange in 1971, the first in its 179-year history. It wasn't until 30 years later that an African American was selected to head a major financial firm. Change on Wall Street does not happen because of social concerns, only because it makes financial sense. Within the firms, there is still a long way to go. In recent years, all of the major investment banks have formed diversity departments to address these problems.

My purpose is to promote the work of the many who have contributed in the fight for a truly color-blind market. While some like Reginald Lewis and E. Stanley O'Neal have gained great attention for their successful work, the early contributions of others like Philip Jenkins and John Patterson remain unknown to most. Although their results may not have had as big an impact on the bottom line, they served as an important foundation for the significant strides made in this movement.

However, I did not write this book with blinders on. Like any panoramic history, this story describes many setbacks. Some of them even fit the definition of tragedy because of misfortune, bad business decisions, legal trouble, or the simple limits of mortality. No matter what group is under scrutiny, a fair account inevitably uncovers the movement's pitfalls and struggles. Still, an overriding theme of progress and achievement drives this story, and those same goals are responsible for the barriers that have come crashing down.

This history spans centuries when traced to those who built the financial district, through depressions and bull markets to the current players. I have tried to present a fair portrayal of that time period while knowing that more stories could be told about the past and that the future holds many stories yet to be told.

In the end, performance determines success. While some African Americans have failed on the Street, there have been many who have pushed the limits of what is possible. They are to be revered, and yet many continue to work in virtual anonymity. It is these people who deserve monumental recognition for their labor in the world of high finance and are the heroes in the fight for a truly fair and equal marketplace.

Many times during this process I have been asked if African Americans have made great strides on Wall Street. I have contradicting answers. If you look back into history and see where we started, the answer is yes. If you went back in time and told the slaves their descendents would be involved in billion dollar deals, I am sure they would have been happy. However, if you consider the current participation of African Americans relative to other groups, the answer is no. The combined participation of African American firms in the year 2000 accounted for less than 1 percent of all transactions. Diversity in the upper ranks of the major firms is still disproportional.

1

THE BEGINNING

I N THE LATE 1950s, A BLACK STOCKBROKER joked, "The only Negroes on Wall Street before us were either sweeping it or shining shoes on it." Although the quip was made for laughs, it concealed a somber tone of unfulfilled promise. The joke was based on truth. No African American had ever come close to reaching the status or wealth of even the most average of securities professionals. No African American had been in a position with enough influence to shape and embolden the industry and, consequently, the world. But the joke also belied the truth. In fact the first blacks began to work within the securities industry in the early twentieth century.

It is not surprising that the black stockbroker who told this joke, or the generations of black financiers who came after him, knew little about the first African Americans on Wall Street. In one of the biggest industries in the world, a business synonymous with structures of grandeur and people of prestige, the first African Americans on Wall Street barely registered on the map. Traditionally, this business was a patrician profession that ran along the lines of a good-old-boy network. In this exclusive world, deals were made in backrooms and social clubs, institutions that were closed to all outsiders—nobody

17

was more rejected than minorities. Whereas some whites could disguise their social background and education, most people of color could not easily hide their origins and were immediately branded as second-class. African Americans had been trying to engage in the securities industry since the early nineteenth century. Yet, they met with stiff resistance.

Wall Street had come to symbolize capitalism and big business because many of the leading brokerages and investment banks claimed it as their home. Underlying each day's activities, the shares traded and deals made, was a power structure that was based on relationships. Legacy and heritage were important aspects of the business, providing access and credibility. Nowhere was this embodied more than in the Street's most recognizable name, J. P. Morgan, who was the son of a banker. Because tradition was paramount, African Americans had no way to enter business on the same levels as their white counterparts simply because blacks had no legacy. Their fathers or friends were not working with securities, and their mere appearance caused waves of unease. This is especially unjust because their ancestors literally helped to build Wall Street. Because of the extreme social attitudes that have permeated throughout American history, those builders and their descendents were unable to profit until the twentieth century in the very arena they constructed.

This injustice became more than folktale or legend in June 1991, when construction workers excavating a site in lower Manhattan stumbled on a "Negro Burial Ground" which is believed to hold more than 20,000 African slaves. The discovery was one of mixed emotion. Archeologists and historians alike were delighted to uncover a priceless map of the past; however, it is sad that these slaves were never recognized for the work they did.

It is believed that African slaves were brought to the Dutch colonial city of New Amsterdam (now New York City) in

1625. Like modern times, the area was a center of financial activity due to its access to ports and other waterways. The slaves were brought from Africa to do the physical labor in this prospering city. In addition to building roads and other structures in what is now lower Manhattan, slaves also built the world famous Trinity Church.

In the mid-seventeenth century, New Amsterdam's economy was booming and, fearing an attack from New England, the Dutch decided to build a wall to shield them from any attacks by land. A log wall that was more than 2,000 feet long was built. Despite its enormous stature, the wall proved to be useless when New Amsterdam was invaded by English troops from the sea. As a result of the invasion, leadership changed; the region was now headed by James II, Duke of York, and the town's name changed from New Amsterdam to New York. The large wall was demolished in 1698. However, its memory remains. The area in which it once stood was named Wall Street, soon to become the hub of deals and capitalist activity.

Slaves were treated just the same as other commodities such as lumber and fur and were traded in similar fashion. James II was a major player in British slave trade. Soon, a slave market was established on the East River and Wall Street, and designated as the city's official exchange ". . . place where Negroes and Indians could be bought, sold, or hired."[1]

As New York City grew into its current role as center of the financial world, African Americans were predictably locked out. Blacks were traded on Wall Street during the 1700s, and the institutionalized attitudes did not change by the nineteenth century. African Americans also lacked the education or experience with money to successfully operate in the then nascent securities industry. Therefore, the first participation with stocks and bonds came, predictably, from the client side.

Black ownership in equities can be traced back to the early 1800s. Records and folktales reveal emerging black professionals trying to master the rules of investing. The New York African Society for Mutual Relief is believed to have owned $500 in bank stock. Around this time, Stephen Smith, a lumber merchant from Pennsylvania, was the largest shareholder in a thrift named Columbia Bank. Stock ownership also thrived in the South. Marie Louise Panis of New Orleans, Louisiana, owned almost $50,000 worth of stock in Citizens Bank of Louisiana. A commission broker from the state of Louisiana, John Clay, also held a few shares in companies. Although the story cannot be verified, it is believed that in the pre–Civil War period, an African American tried to buy a seat on the then young but flourishing New York Stock Exchange (NYSE) only to have his offer rebuffed.

The denials and limitations within the big corporations and institutions, such as the NYSE, because of racism and segregation, led many ambitious but realistic African Americans in the early twentieth century to build thriving businesses within their own communities. This philosophy sparked one of the greatest successes of this period among people of color. Strangely, this explosion of capitalism developed miles away from lower Manhattan in Tulsa, Oklahoma. This site was home of the development that would later be known as the *Negro Wall Street*. Although the town had nothing to do with New York's Wall Street, the label described the tremendous growth and development of business within the 35-block radius known as the Greenwood District.

Like many regions throughout America in the early 1900s, Tulsa was divided by segregation. While some areas were hindered from substantial economic development by these Jim Crow policies, others were not. Many communities drew from their own talents and resources to create and build thriving businesses within their boundaries and Tulsa led this movement.

Tulsa's saga promotes the best in self-reliance and talent that black Americans have to offer. These were universal and successful themes that would apply later in all businesses, including the securities industry. Ironically, what drew the best out of these individuals was the harsh reality of segregation. Restricted from hair salons, supermarkets, restaurants, and other white-owned business establishments, the black residents of Tulsa built their own. Other black communities spent their dollars at white businesses, despite being viewed as inferior. In contrast, the people of Tulsa realized the power of ownership. Because black shop-owners provided all the needed services to cater to the black community, all monies and investment stayed within the community and it blossomed. In that 35-block span, there were 1,500 black-owned businesses and houses, including 10 millionaires and many families with substantial savings.

Perhaps that progress was too successful for the attitudes of that time, because racism wiped out all of that development and hope on a spring day in 1921. Hearing a rumor that a black man was accused of sexually assaulting a white woman (a charge of which he was cleared nearly 70 years later), a mob descended on the town and set it on fire. Thus the Tulsa Race Riot of 1921 started. Millions of dollars were lost in damages and, more important, hundreds of lives were taken in the melee, bringing a sudden end to the Negro Wall Street. A sterling symbol of black self-reliance and success was destroyed, never to fully recover.

As Tulsa burned, other important black businessmen were founding, growing, and running their businesses in other black communities. Although they might not have known it at the time, these pioneers served two purposes: First, and most obvious, they were filling a need by giving their black communities products and services. Second, their

21

example inspired the generations that followed, encouraged their pioneering spirit, and taught them that seemingly impossible goals were possible.

Arguably, the most influential black entrepreneur of the twentieth century was Arthur Gaston, the Birmingham, Alabama, native who, starting with $500, increased his wealth to between $30 million and $40 million. He founded the Booker T. Washington Insurance Company in 1926 selling policies to black steelworkers. With vision and a legendary work ethic, Gaston used the insurance company as the foundation of an empire that included Citizen Trust Bank, hotels, and radio stations. Other early black business luminaries included Alonzo Herndon, a former slave who founded Atlanta Life Insurance; John Merrick, A. M. Moore, and C. C. Spaulding, cofounders of North Carolina Mutual Life Insurance in 1898; and Madame C. J. Walker, the hair-care products mogul. Even though these people did not work directly with securities, many early African Americans who worked on Wall Street would credit them with helping to develop a capitalist framework in which to think and dream.

The end of a revered business community like Tulsa and the lack of other thriving black business districts like it exposed the need to succeed within the existing aggregate power and economic structure. Both the riot's force and integration in the Northern cities underscored the fact that for black Americans to work in a system where whites made the rules and had most of the money, it would be necessary to learn how to work with them. The high-finance industry was one of the biggest targets and, consequently, one of the toughest to penetrate. Educational resources were scarce, and not many African Americans were prepared to work with securities. Nor were brokerage firms willing to give them an opportunity—the same opportunities afforded some whites with a similar lack of preparedness. So rarely was that the case that, in the early years of the century, only one lone black man was on record as working with stocks—W. Fred Thompson. He is believed to be the only African American broker who worked with securities in the early twentieth century. He began his work in 1903. Black Americans needed time to master how to play the games that others created, as well as to find people who were willing to play with them, regardless of color. That would not always be easy.

In 1920, the securities industry was about to embark on an unprecedented boom. That period for the industry was unlike any that had come before it. Cutting-edge businesses, such as the automobile and radio industries, helped to provide a deep universal confidence that eventually developed into the Roaring Twenties. A soaring stock market lured everybody, from the elite to their butlers, into investments that seemed as guaranteed as any speculation could be. The financial district maintained an air of invincibility as people jumped into the market without regard to caution or risk. Investors relied on tips and rumors as heavily as if they represented careful analysis and strategy. History would later assign this period a label of recklessness and manipulation, but for the people working in those years, it was pure magic. Significant black participation in the markets began in this euphoric environment when white legends like Joe Kennedy and Bernard Baruch made their fortunes in this market.

The entrance of black speculators, such as H. R. George, the Jones brothers from Chicago, and others, into this boom started a theme that was common among the first few generations of African Americans on Wall Street. With whites in control and racial tensions high, during the first half of the twentieth century minorities did not have the clout or resources to push open any doors. Instead, they could enter only when the gatekeepers gave permission. The reasons were both financial and emotional. During bull markets, more positions were available because brokerages were expanding, hiring, and focusing less on expenditures. In addition, bosses and owners were happier when stocks were rising. It was hard to find a broker who was not beaming with uncontrollable glee after earning huge sums of money. It was when the fortunes turned and people were glum that African Americans would find out how far they had really come on Wall Street. If the old adage that blacks are "the last to be hired, first to be fired" is any indication, such times would bring disproportionate pain.

However, even during the high-flying 1920s, the days of working in white-owned broker/dealer firms were still a few years away. The first African Americans documented as having substantial successes in the business came, as others did, in the Roaring Twenties. The money was enticing and it seemed as if nobody could lose. Everybody from chairmen of corporations to shoeshine boys were whispering tips and rumors, all of which seemed to pan out. Diving into the middle of this action were black speculators who did not have any clients; rather, they engaged in proprietary trading, meaning that they were investing for their own accounts.

Perhaps the most recognized was H. R. George, a Harlem resident who carried himself with a flamboyance and boldness that separated him from most. According to *Ebony,* there is a legendary description of him driving through the uptown streets in his long, sleek Packard, which at the time was the most popular car.[2] Supposedly the automobile had sleeping accommodations similar to those of a train, as well as an icebox located within arm's distance of the front seat so that he would not be inconvenienced when retrieving a snack. He used this car to travel between the two offices he maintained, uptown in Harlem and on Wall Street. He would often order his two secretaries to ride with him so that he could continue his dictation. He soon acquired the reputation as the richest black in New York.

George earned his fortune, as speculators do, by taking daring positions in investments. They take above-average risk to earn above-average returns, usually in one big coup, unlike brokers who earn their living from the commissions received with each transaction for a client. In the bull market of the 1920s, the business was not nearly as regulated as it is now, which resulted in greater manipulation and, consequently, more money. Many "pumped and dumped" easily manipulated stocks, those with little volume, and were rewarded with extraordinary returns.

It was in this scheming business that H. R. George earned the majority of his money. His attitude fit the times so perfectly that he was given the nickname the Black Wolf of Wall Street since it took the attitude and instincts of an animal to come out on top in this sea of mistrust and two-faced businessmen. At one point, the deals and investments in which George was involved were believed to have been valued in the millions.

Other black speculators were Edward and George Jones from Illinois. The Jones brothers were more famous for their "day job" than their securities positions. They were policy operators who ran "wheel games" in neighborhoods throughout the south side of Chicago. It is rumored that at their peak, the brothers were earning $15,000 a day. A stylish pair, they spent much of that money on luxurious goods and services. However, $1.6 million of it was deposited in commercial real estate that resulted in ownership of a Ben Franklin store. Other investments were securities, a natural move because many have always considered Wall Street to be a sophisticated numbers racket. At the height of their success with this endeavor, they owned more than half a million dollars' worth of equity in companies like General Motors and American Telephone and Telegraph.

Their success, as well as that of the stock market, came crashing down in 1929. In just two days that October, the newly formed Dow Jones Industrial Average fell more than 22 percent. The brokers who jumped off buildings or were sleeping on cots in shelters after losing their homes were the physical reminders of booming bank accounts that had vanished. Within a few devastating days, fortunes that investors had built with sweat over many years were wiped out.

Among those left with only their broken dreams were H. R. George, the Jones brothers, and the few other black speculators of the period. H. R. George was thrown into bankruptcy. The Jones brothers' securities holdings were wiped out as well. Years after that, problems with the IRS and mob-related problems that are inherent in the numbers racket soon forced the pair out of Chicago. Although these speculators were destroyed by the extraordinary circumstances of the Crash, they provided a historical lesson that would be revisited time and again in the decades to come. Despite great success, black financiers could count on the rapid arrival of great obstacles.

With all of the chaos of the Crash of 1929 and the subsequent Great Depression, the first stage of black participation on Wall Street ended quietly. This was not unexpected because their names and successes were not familiar to African Americans beyond their neighborhoods. From a historical perspective, in that age with few communicative mediums, these speculators did not inspire others to learn or enter the business. Nor were there opportunities to work for anybody other than themselves. Jobs at white-owned firms were not available to people of color in the early twentieth century. That certainly did not change during the Depression when white fathers could not afford to employ their sons, let alone black people. Wall Street was a battered and bruised place. The same people who had skipped along the sidewalks in euphoria, dressed in top hats and expensive coats a few years earlier, were now slumped over in despair wondering how to survive.

Because opportunities were closed in the major brokerages, a handful of black-owned securities firms opened. The R. T. Bess Company opened in 1923 and continued on into the Depression era. Another firm named the Evanita Holding Company began in 1934 and its president, John J. Gundles, operated it. He raised initial start-up capital of $10,000 by selling its stock at $10 a share. Within a year, 75 investors had signed on, and in return, Evanita issued a 5 percent dividend to all shareholders.

Not all those who expressed interest in the firm were accepted. Many indicating the little experience with securities that most blacks had during those Depression years were rejected. "[Gundles] stated that the Evanita had turned down dozens of prospective investors who were under the impression that they were going to get rich overnight," the *Amsterdam News* wrote in 1935. "The only persons admitted to membership in the company, he said, are individuals who realize that they are taking chances."[3] A testament to their hard work, the firm survived those terrible times by investing in companies like Pullman Company, Chase National Bank, and National Biscuit Company. However, the firm eventually closed in 1943. Ironically, this was a few years before an unprecedented boom in the securities business. As the United States emerged from World War II triumphant and with renewed spirit, social attitudes in the industry improved and doors opened.

The first African American registered stockbrokers and salesmen entered Wall Street in the late 1940s. (Unlike the days of W. Fred Thompson, all stockbrokers were now forced to register with the National Association of Securities Dealers [NASD], which was formed in 1939, hence the importance of the word *registered* when sifting through history.) In this pre–Civil Rights movement era, blacks were not hired because of any social motives. Reverend Martin Luther King Jr. and the now famous boycotts and sit-ins had yet to enter the national dialogue; there was no hint that the action reflected a larger effort of inclusion or other diversity initiatives. Rather, hiring this handful of African American securities salesmen was simply a business decision.

The black middle class was growing as educational opportunities increased the number of lawyers, doctors, and other accomplished black professionals. Brokerages sought to attract these investors by hiring people who reflected their background.

Exactly who became the first registered black securities salesman is unclear. Two men, Thorvald McGregor and Lawrence L. Lewis, were each credited as being the first in two different black newspapers in 1949. This confusion is understandable considering that Wall Street was not something most African Americans cared about at that time. It was not as if the entrance of these brokers sent waves throughout the country. However, the local papers, as well as broader-based black publications such as *Jet* and *Ebony,* promoted this push within the financial industry.

McGregor's Wall Street career began in the summer of 1949 at the age of 40. Born in the Virgin Islands, he spent his young adulthood in the Marines. After his service tenure, he entered the import-export business until he was hired by the Wall Street firm Mercer Hicks. One of its officials is said to have commented on the hire, "We hired him simply because

we feel he knows how to make money," a progressive statement for the time, whether it was true or not.[4]

Unlike his peers, Lawrence Lewis had spent the majority
of his working life in the securities industry in a number of
positions. In his early twenties, he became a clerk in a San
Francisco firm called J. Barth & Company. He advanced to increasingly more responsible positions like assistant and then
member of the accounting arm, but he was prevented from
achieving his ultimate goal of brokering on the Street. Seeking employment as a stockbroker, he moved to New York City
because that is where the financial industry was concentrated
at the time, and the opportunities were better. Brokerages
were not distributed nationally as they are today; most of
them were in New York. After a search of 120 firms, he finally found one—Abraham & Company—that was willing to
hire him. Although he was brought in to expand the firm's
client base, Lewis also "made it clear that he did not wish to
be limited to Negro customers."[5]

Lewis's determination was quite appropriate, as other endeavors would later reveal. Although many approached the
black investing market with great optimism, they soon learned
that it was tougher to crack than even they had imagined. Perhaps the greatest attempt to attract black investors during this
period was a move by the brokerage house F. L. Salomon into
Harlem. There had been previous attempts to do securities-
related business there, such as the Evanita Holding Company
that tried it and failed. Hoping to defy history, F. L. Salomon
opened in Harlem in the summer of 1950.

The company was a member of the NYSE, and its
founder, Lewis Salomon, decided to open offices on 125th
Street shortly after hiring its first black salesman, Abraham
Cowing. The two men met shortly after Cowing's graduation
from Hunter College. After they hit it off, Salomon set up
some introductory courses for Cowing at Francis I. DuPont

Company, another brokerage. After Cowing completed those courses, the two men put together the plan for the Harlem office.

They set up shop in the Hotel Theresa. Located on 125th Street, it is a Harlem legend that was once one of the most successful lodging institutions in the city. By the time F. L. Salomon moved in, segregation was falling and the hotel's star was on the decline. It was in this space that Cowing sought to make an impact and, in some sense, recapture a taste of the Theresa's past glory.

The new venture confronted a black retail market that was not interested in the brokerage's products, a theme that will apply throughout this history. The foundation for this resentment was the severe economic inequality that divided America. Despite the growing middle class, the majority of African Americans still lived below the poverty line. With little discretionary income or knowledge about securities, most were indifferent to F. L. Salomon's presence in Harlem. Therefore, the task before them, as well as the generations of brokers that would follow, was to break through the substantial barriers that had been building for decades.

One of his methods to debunk myths or other impediments that would provoke African Americans' caution toward the stock market was to advertise using laypeople's terms. "You use electric lights daily, then why not buy in the company and share in its profits?" he would often ask. It made sense to try to sell folks on the idea of buying ownership in the businesses that they already used, but few saw the logic of his reasoning (or if they did, they refused to follow through with it). The F. L. Salomon Harlem branch closed after just three months. When asked why it failed, an official of the company said, "Negroes aren't investment conscious yet because they have not had the experience. Stock trading is still foreign to the majority of Negroes."[6] Yet, an *Ebony* article from the time went further in expressing the complicated feelings of African Americans, indicating that some of the conflict derived from lingering perceptions of slavery: "Some believe the failure is due not only to lack of investment knowledge by Negroes but also the desire of Negroes with money to go directly to Wall Street to buy stocks rather than to a Jim Crow office in Harlem."[7]

When some in the black community questioned the motives of their kind who worked in white-owned firms, entrepreneurial pursuits seemed like the logical solution. In addition, ownership brought freedom from the internal politics in offices. Breaking into the securities industry as an entrepreneur in the 1950s was difficult and unusual, which is why Norman McGhee's move was historic and important. In 1952, he created McGhee & Company, which is widely believed to have been the first black securities firm to obtain an NASD license. Rather than go through the hassle of dealing as a subordinate, he chose the founder's path. Often dumbfounded, people would ask him why he risked opening this strange thing called a brokerage. McGhee's answer would almost invariably be, "Why not?"

His work with stocks and bonds was symbolic of many of the early pioneers who would follow him with their own black securities companies. They were college-educated and maintained a business background outside Wall Street. With few openings in the white-owned firms and the problems inherited by working those companies, they simply began their own businesses as they entered the middle stages of their lives.

McGhee was born in 1895 in Austell, Georgia, located approximately 30 miles outside Atlanta. Its composition prepared him in many ways for his future life in business: The majority of residents were white. His father was a minister, and education was stressed in his middle-class family. His

brother was a college professor and his sister a school principal. Norman's interest in education led him to Howard
University, where he received his bachelor of arts degree, as
well as his law degree in 1922. During this period, he got
his first exposure to the world of business, working for Dr.
Emmett J. Scott, Secretary of the Treasury of Howard University. After three years, he left the job to pursue law in the
North.

The difficulties that plagued blacks in his home area motivated McGhee to move to Cleveland, Ohio. "He moved to
Cleveland to escape the South and give himself a better opportunity," says his son and former employee, Norman
McGhee Jr.[8] There, he set up his own law practice and eventually branched out into other areas of business. Along
with serving as a consultant to the Empire Savings & Loan
Company, he ventured into his most profitable business
area—real estate.

Whereas most Americans viewed the Great Depression as
a great calamity and watched their estates and property sink
in value, McGhee saw it as an opportunity. In the late 1930s,
he founded Citizens' Realty Management Company to profit
from the turmoil. It was in circumstances such as these, when
the storm was wild, that McGhee's personality served him
best. His former secretary, Dorothy Horton, described him as
a serious and intense individual. Such a demeanor allowed
him to withstand the risks of real estate investments during
this period of despair. As people in the Cleveland area began
to lose their homes to pay off creditors, McGhee, with his connections to banks, was willing to take these assets off their
hands. "He was able to get these houses for no money down
and pay off the mortgages with the rent," his son remembers.
His endeavor expanded so much that, at one point, his company owned more than 100 properties, which he soon leveraged to enter the securities industry. "On Saturdays I used to

just collect rent and that is how he developed his money to go into the stock business," explained Horton.[9]

McGhee's prosperity in real estate was part of a series of successes that allowed him to travel in an elite circle of doctors and lawyers who exposed him to wealth and the power of investments. Also, his second wife, Dorothy, came from the wealthy and socially prominent Cook family of Washington, D.C. Perhaps his most valuable and influential experience was his work on the fiscal board of an organization named after Phyllis Wheatley, an eighteenth-century black poet. "By working at the fiscal board at Phyllis Wheatley [Association], he got some insight into the value of investments," says Horton.[10]

With this insight, McGhee constructed a philosophy that served as the foundation of his firm. He applied his stoic demeanor to his efforts to expose the serious economic challenges that faced African Americans. The *Cleveland Press* depicted McGhee as "a new type of leadership that will undertake to awaken the masses of Negro people to the wisdom of setting aside a part of their earnings for future economic security."[11] To accomplish this goal, McGhee & Company opened its doors in 1952. After obtaining an NASD license for $25,000, the firm was free to engage in business with the public. The question now became, who were they going to do business with? After friends and family had given their accounts to the firm, all efforts to expand beyond that base would be difficult. Ninety-five percent of the investing public, most of whom where white, would not dare transfer their investment securities to a so-called Negro firm, especially one without a track record. The African American retail market was full of opportunity, but that potential would not develop without struggle and persuasion.

To put it simply, the black market was not interested in stocks and bonds, as evidenced by the failure of F. L. Salomon's Harlem branch. Relative to other Americans, blacks were poorer, less trusting, and more reluctant to put their money into investments. For good reason, Wall Street appeared to be an all-white game, and in some sense, enveloped in a haze of uncertainty. Add to that the tension of the times, with their brothers and sisters fighting for their civil rights throughout the country, and the stock market was not at the top of many black Americans' agendas.

Still, McGhee was going to try and build a securities business for himself. His venture would never do well in terms of profits; his son said, "We never made a hell of a lot of money."[12] However, they were successful in drawing many originally uninterested people into the perimeters of finance.

To overcome the obstacles that encumbered his expansion, McGhee went through traditional advertising promotional channels. He was able to profit from his relationship with Cleveland's black newspaper, the *Call & Post*. Like so many black newspapers that were developed to inform growing urban populations, such as the *Amsterdam News* in New York City and the *Los Angeles Sentinel* in California, the *Call & Post* was the main source of black news in Cleveland. McGhee began his work at the publication as an editor with the *Cleveland Call* before it merged with the *Post* in the 1920s. Two decades later, with his brokerage firm set up, he began to produce a weekly column detailing the basics of investing and securities. He also used this forum to advertise his firm, encouraging all readers who sought further information to join a weekly class held at McGhee & Company offices. There, "he got people to invest in days when people didn't know a thing about it and weren't educated," says Dorothy Horton.[13]

McGhee began to organize small investment clubs in Cleveland, Ohio, as well as in other places where the company maintained offices such as Illinois and North Carolina. He would also travel to local YMCAs to orchestrate six-week investment courses. These gatherings set the stage for McGhee to stand before large groups and passionately argue his opinions about the black American's place in this country. "The time is here and now that the Negro must assert himself through participation in the industrial enterprises which have produced the greatness which is America's by becoming owners in larger measure in the share representing control of American industries," he once said. "The avenues of financial democracy are less difficult to travel and lead more directly to equal consideration and acceptance than any other road."[14] The result of these sessions was enlightened people, as well as new customers.

The black public were not the only people who needed education. McGhee's brokerage needed trained office workers. Some of those hired had little background when it came to securities; however, after some prodding and lessons, they were able to perform for the company. Dorothy Horton, who had worked as McGhee's secretary, was sent to school to take finance courses. "I became cashier and learned the terminology and how to keep the records properly because the SEC would come investigate," she explained. "One of the gentlemen from the SEC was kind enough to come down and show me how to do it."[15] Salesmen also did not have brokering experience according to McGhee Jr. They came in from the marketplace; they simply transferred from the client side, or took the lessons learned in one of his classes to the highest levels. The implementation of a full-time staff of about 10 people helped to sustain the black brokerage as it attempted to build lasting revenue streams. However, it would not be alone for long.

Another firm called Special Markets, Incorporated, also originated during the 1950s. Unlike McGhee & Company, this firm planted its roots in the heart of the financial district. The firm was announced in 1955 as "the first black-owned and -operated brokerage on Wall Street."[15] Its distinction from McGhee

& Company was one of semantics because *Wall Street* was not meant to symbolize the securities industry, but rather the actual street itself.

Even that terminology was a tad misleading because the office was at 92 Liberty Street, two blocks from Wall Street. Later, the title would be changed to "the first black firm located in the Wall Street area." That decision wasn't determined by rent costs, available locations, or other considerations; it resulted from the attitudes that the firm's mere presence inspired. "We tried for three months to get a location on Wall Street but nobody would rent to us,"[16] said cofounder and president Philip M. Jenkins in 1967.

Jenkins was the firm's driving force throughout its life. An extremely interesting and gentle person, Jenkins was better known in the New York area for his work with clocks than stocks. Born in 1898, he grew up in Bristol, Connecticut, and graduated from Temple University. He had stints in a variety of professions, for example, educating fellow African Americans about retail selling during the Depression. Throughout his life, however, his main hobby was antique clocks. So interested was Jenkins in the subject that he produced and was host of a New York radio show called *Tick Tock Time*. This interest in clocks led to one of his most valued relationships. Decades later he met then Georgia Governor Jimmy Carter while visiting the Governor's mansion as a member of the National Association of Watch and Clock Collectors. His interest was so rabid that, beyond just touring the grand structure that day, Jenkins was able to get his hands on and repair some of the mansion's old clocks.

In 1952, Jenkins settled on the securities industry as a profession. He began as an account executive at a brokerage called B. G. Phillips and Company and quickly moved to a managerial position at Baruch Brothers and Company. His success and reputation were so renowned that the now defunct

Sepia magazine dubbed him "The Wizard of Wall Street."[17] That reputation carried back over into the business world when he was named to the board of directors of the Mutual Investment Company of America. He is believed to be the first African American to reach such a position in an investment company. It was after this run of successes that Jenkins cofounded Special Markets.

Unlike McGhee & Company, the founders had substantial experience working at white-owned firms, at least in the context of the time. The word *minority* was an important part of the firm's initial business plan because they targeted groups beyond the African American market. They sought to market their services to Asians, Hispanics, and other ethnic minorities who were outcasts on most Wall Street client lists. To get business, Jenkins sought to hire salespeople who spoke the native languages of potential investors.

Even though their strategy ventured into these diverse areas, it was always their intent to keep the head of the firm black. The principals all were black. Jenkins' right-hand man at the start was John T. Patterson Jr., a tall, driven man who also had experience in the business. A graduate of Lincoln University, he worked as mutual fund salesman during the day while obtaining his law degree at night. Prior to joining the firm, he had racked up more than a half million in mutual fund sales. Earle W. Fisher, who like Jenkins had worked at Baruch Brothers, was the secretary. Naundin J. Oswell, a former official with the Queensbridge Houses, became the treasurer of the new company.

The original intent was for the firm to act as a brokerage: Find people who were ignored by the other stockbrokers, teach them about the capital markets, and execute their selected stocks. That strategy, though it seemed logical, turned out to be nothing more than a gilded dream. "Our market—the Negro market—just wasn't sophisticated enough to justify the expense," reflected Jenkins.[18] Despite the growing population of middle-class black New Yorkers, inexperience and nescience with the stock market deterred most from even attempting to purchase individual securities. Beyond the mere ability to make an educated decision about the prospects of a particular investment, there was also no real effort on the part of the black market to venture into speculation. Black families who rose in class and fortunes in the 1950s generally were satisfied with their holdings, and determined to keep them. After enduring the years of economic depression, and with memories of the 1929 stock market crash still vivid, most people were content with the conservative returns from savings accounts. African Americans also tended to spend more to upgrade their living standards. All these factors exposed the flaw in the firm's initial business plan. Even more telling were the absent profits. These circumstances led Jenkins to shift strategies and concentrate solely on selling mutual funds.

The change of strategy for Special Markets reflected a trend that was sweeping through the industry. The 1950s saw dramatic growth in the size and influence of institutional investors such as pension funds and mutual funds.

Jenkins saw mutual funds as the best investment for African Americans. These funds did not demand the financial sophistication otherwise required to maintain an individual portfolio and they were less risky. Professionally trained managers made the decisions imperative for investing money.

Another firm that strongly believed in mutual funds emerged two years later: Patterson & Company. The similarity between the firms is not surprising because it was founded by ex vice-president of Special Markets John T. Patterson Jr. The now defunct black newspaper *New York Age* proclaimed it as "the most publicized and well known of the Negro firms . . . Wall Streeters consider Patterson & Co. one of the more progressive young firms."[19]

Patterson got his ambition from his parents who owned stocks in addition to their tailor shops. "John always said that he wanted us to get our piece of the pie," says his sister, Carol Patterson Lewis. "Once he started selling mutual funds, my parents started buying from him on his recommendations and that money put me through college!"[20]

At the time of his company's founding, Patterson was 31 years old and had an enormous body of accomplishment. His career in the investment field began in 1952 at the First Investors Corporation while going to law school at night where he established himself as a masterful mutual fund salesman. He was awarded the Highest Volume Cup award for writing $127,000 worth of business in a two-month period. The following year he received First Investors Corporation's Distinguished Salesman Award. "He was the best salesman," says Lula Powell-Watson, who briefly worked at the firm. "He was very competitive, but had a way about him whether it was business, friendship, or social that was very likeable."[21] Such success led him to dream and then achieve higher aspirations. First was his stop at Special Markets; then he moved on to head the corporate finance department at a white-owned firm named McDonald Holman & Company before he founded the firm that bore his name.

Beyond the obvious personal goals involved in this venture, Patterson acknowledged the broader good of black activity in the capital markets. "I believe the Negro's salvation lies in finance, and more of us becoming owners and managers of capital," he once said. "The NAACP and the Urban League have done a tremendous job in opening up new doors for us, but as we push further ahead and the areas of segregation narrow, it's up to us to find new opportunities."[22]

The company set up shop at 250 West 57th Street and had other small offices in Washington, D.C., and Baltimore, Maryland. Although most of the firm's employees, both salesmen and supporting staff, were black, 40 percent of their customers were white. A major product of the firm was research in the form of an Investor Information Department headed by Marguerite Belafonte then wife of Harry Belafonte. Visitors at the firm commented, "Not only did we see account executives busy on the phone taking orders or selling prospects for appointments, but several were diligently studying textbooks and manuals. Said the firm's general manager, R. Franklin Brown, "Our clients depend on our knowledge in a very important area—investing their money!"[23]

Firms like McGhee & Company, Special Markets, and Patterson & Company, were small but important symbols of possibility on Wall Street. Although the owners' wallets did not reflect great success, the mere existence of these firms was a subtle indication of the progress being made. And this progress even extended beyond gender lines at a time when women were outcasts in the business despite having successfully filled men's jobs during World War II.

In 1953, Lilla St. John became the first black woman to pass the NYSE exam to work for Oppenheimer & Company. At the age of 25, she quit her career as a singer and television host in Milwaukee, Wisconsin, to enter the business because she found it "utterly fascinating."[24] Such successes were the foundation for growth, albeit slow growth, in the turbulent 1960s. In this decade, African Americans would continue to expand their firms; and in light of the social struggles, the major firms would respond with their own initiatives.

2

COLD CALLING

FOR BLACK AMERICANS—PERHAPS, FOR ALL Americans—the 1960s will always be synonymous with the Civil Rights movement. The sit-ins, protests, and boycotts in the name of social equality rightfully dominated the nation's attention then, and the pages of history forever. With their work during those years, leaders like Martin Luther King Jr., Malcolm X, and Andrew Young marked a place in the hearts of millions, as well as in this country's history. When weighted against the efforts and heroics of this movement, it is little wonder that the continued progress of minorities on Wall Street, albeit slow, received little attention. However, even though the financial district and the South were worlds apart in style, priorities, and goals, the two could not help but affect each other under the umbrella of one grand American vision. The turmoil generated from the enormous unrest gradually forced the biggest brokerages to confront their own attitudes. While not all of them reacted or adjusted in meaningful ways, the bottom line was that more African Americans acquired positions in the most prestigious firms.

Although there was some correlation between the protests and the highest ranking executives' efforts to hire more African

Americans, the mood on Wall Street in those years compared with the distress in the rest of the country vividly illustrated the differences that still existed. While riots were erupting, while demonstrators were fending off attacks by dogs and fire hoses, and while hippies were preaching peace and love, Wall Street experienced its greatest bull market. Even though world events often affect the mood of investors, during a few years in the 1960s, the profits earned were simply extraordinary. As they sat in their penthouse suites and corporate jets, Wall Street moguls were literally and figuratively above it all.

Most of Wall Street had little to worry about while the stocks kept going up. The 1960's bull market was even more prosperous than the market of the Roaring Twenties. However, these riches were not a continuation of the Go-Go years, but a rapid recovery from the economic scares of the decade's early years. The stock market had stalled in 1960, the first year in the post–World War II era when it failed to make significant progress. Sell-side sentiment grew stronger until bottoming out in 1962 when the Dow Jones Industrial Average (DJIA) experienced its worst losses since the Depression. There were a lot of bond losses and retrenchments. Yet, the market was able to shake off the doom and gloom in time for a run of gains. Interest rates began to drop and the DJIA topped 1000 for the first time, before settling in the 900s in 1968.

After decades, if not centuries, of succession and nepotism on Wall Street, the rebellious children of the 1960s rebuffed all tradition of the previous generations. The graduates from Ivy League schools were not flocking to Wall Street as they had before because, other than the government, the Street was the ultimate sign of the Establishment. The students of Columbia and Dartmouth who were storming deans' offices were not going to be sitting at trading desks the next year. Beyond the symbolism of such actions, the tangible result of this shift was that opportunities were opening up in the major firms.

Branches of brokerages were opening up all across the country creating a greater demand for bodies just as the supply was decreasing. This development along with the changing attitudes of the younger generation led to an explosion of black participation within these firms. (Not to get carried away, there were only about 60 black stockbrokers in the industry by the decade's end. However, that represented about a 600 percent increase from the 1950s.)

There was a big difference between the two decades in the firms that were hiring blacks. The brokerages that employed African Americans in the 1950s, such as F. L. Salomon and Abraham & Company, have faded into distant memory. During the 1960s, black salesmen would find positions in Merrill Lynch and Bache & Company (now Prudential Securities), houses that have endured into the twenty-first century. Many of the firms were also beginning to feel the social pressures of the times. "These wirehouses now felt that they had to take action before action was taken against them" says a stockbroker from the period.[1]

In January 1965, Merrill Lynch, by far the biggest and top-ranking securities company at the time, hired its first three black stockbrokers. Its founder Charles Merrill, had revolutionized the brokerage business and retail business in the same manner that J. P. Morgan had changed the investment banking business. When the company announced the hires, the move made headlines as an example of a new era of social responsibility.

For African Americans, it was another sign that opportunities were growing—Merrill Lynch was the king of Wall Street. It had won the throne because of its brokers, and now three African Americans were among them—Harvey Thomas, Forrest Tomlinson, and George W. King Jr. To put their presence in perspective, they were the only people of color out of 2,550 account executives. Thomas and Tomlinson had some background with numbers and finance. Thomas had worked in the accounting arm of the New York City Fire Department, dealing with pension funds and insurance companies. Tomlinson graduated with a degree in finance from New York City College before working for the Welfare Department.

The last of the three, George King, had never even dreamed of working on Wall Street. "I never thought a career in finance was possible,"[2] he recalled. King graduated from Maryland State College in 1958 with a degree in construction. From there, he joined the U.S. Navy. In 1964 when his tenure was up, he was 28 years old and desperate for a job. He chose to settle in New York because, as a bachelor, he felt there was no better place to be. To make that happen, he sent out resumes to as many companies as he could find ranging from his background in construction to the uncharted waters of finance companies. As luck would have it, Merrill Lynch was looking for people who had just finished military service.

King, like Tomlinson and Thomas, took the aptitude test given to every applicant at that time, and they all seemed to do well. They were hired. Thomas and Tomlinson were assigned to work in Merrill Lynch's main office at 70 Pine Street. King went to work in a branch office at 295 Madison Avenue.

The irony of this development for King was that he had just secured a position with the biggest and arguably most powerful brokerage house in the world, yet he had no idea what he was getting himself into. "At the time, I didn't have a clue as to what a stockbroker did," he explained laughing. "I knew they were obviously in the finance industry but as far as I was concerned, a stockbroker sat there all day, reading the newspapers and people came to him and bought stocks. I did not realize that you had to go out and get the clients!"[3]

He learned otherwise in Merrill's required training course that all brokers took to meet the necessary regulation requirements. However, a course or the written word can teach you only so much, as the fledgling brokers were about to find out. Sometimes, strategies and common sense do not pan out, as many earlier black stockbrokers had discovered. "My manager told me, 'Since you're black, why don't you go get some black clients?' So I spent my first month going door to door and got nothing, not one account."

In contrast to the decade before when a salesman like Lawrence Lewis could receive a substantial percentage of his business from black retail investors, the times had changed. The Civil Rights movement was now at the forefront. People were focused on the sit-ins, protests, boycotts, and other demonstrations of the day and saw little value in stopping to invest in the traditional retail securities relationship. As cities burned and black Americans died for the most basic rights, Wall Street was not at the top of their national agenda and that shift was reflected in the changing attitudes of potential black clientele.

Even so, the sheer brand name of their firm enabled the three men, like brokers in other well-known firms, to secure accounts with wealthy white investors in places as foreign as Long Island. King's first client was with the president of a division in a large company. He acquired the account over the telephone, simply because he worked for Merrill Lynch. Race was never a factor, at least not until clients started meeting with him, but some fellow employees gave African Americans fantastic support. "There was a woman I had been dealing with and had talked with on the phone a few times and she asked if she could come in and meet with me and I said fine," recalled King. "When she walked in, she said, 'Can I see George King?' The receptionist pointed to me and the woman just stared. She went into the manager's office and demanded that she be assigned another broker. Then my manager said, 'If you don't want to do business with him, then we don't want you as a client.' I'll never forget it."[4]

Another leader in this area was Bache & Company, the second largest brokerage house, with a retail network of about 1,800 brokers in over 100 branch offices. During this period, it recruited a handful of black brokers. President Harry Jacobs credited his predecessor for pushing for this change. "It was Harold Bache who sought to recruit more black stockbrokers," Jacobs says.[5] In addition to Dennis Barron and one or two others who had been hired the decade before, several talented blacks entered during the 1960s. Paul Haywood was one of the first in 1961 and would stay for four decades. Two other hires during those years—Willie Daniels in New York and Harold E. Doley in New Orleans—would later rise to prominence. But, perhaps the black man with the highest position was Wylie H. Whisonant, who served as the manager of Bache's branch in Rockefeller Center. After graduating from George Washington Law School, he joined the company's Washington, D.C., office in the early 1960s and then was promoted to New York. There he supervised 28 white brokers, serving in that position until he moved to American Express in 1975.

The success of many black brokers during this period proved that they could perform if given the chance. In many ways, being an account executive was the best business for African Americans at the time. First, it did not require the kind of education that it took to be an investment banker, a blessing because blacks typically lacked the resources or opportunities to undertake such schooling. Second, in those days, 90 percent of all brokerage business was handled through the U.S. mail and over the phone. Often, the big brokerages would assign clients. In such circumstances, skin color meant nothing; only the words, strategies, and ideas mattered. That is why a meeting with a client raised fears in the black financial community. Many dreaded such events simply because it was uncertain how a client would react to knowing that his money was in the hands of a black man. Sometimes, the clients would drop the black broker, no matter how much money had been made or how sage the advice.

Firms like Merrill Lynch and Bache & Company wanted to hire even more African Americans during that period but were not able to find many qualified applicants. By "qualified," they usually meant college graduates, and those young professionals were not flocking to Wall Street. "After all we had been through in America, all of my friends wanted security," said one broker. "They wanted the safe salaries that government and educational positions provided. Most wanted nothing to do with a commission-based business like brokering because it was too risky."[6]

In the 1960s, a small group of black women also entered the business. One standout was June Middleton who worked for a firm called Hornblower & Weeks-Hemphill. It is believed that when Middleton entered the field in 1964, she was the only black, female stockbroker who worked for a New York Stock Exchange firm. She attributed her position to education and exposure to the business when she was a child. The only black child in a Manhattan public school, her class read the stock market tables every day, and learned how to interpret the figures and their movement. Social limitations afflicting both African Americans and women impeded her immediate fulfillment of her career aspirations. So she entered the business in the only way she could, as a secretary at another NYSE-member firm called Cohen, Siminson & Company. During her time there, she was allowed to take the registrations exam and she passed. Although her first year in the business, 1962, was the worst in decades, she persisted, first moving to an over-the-counter firm, then to Hornblower & Weeks-Hemphill. So rarefied was her presence in the firm that observers mentioned her wardrobe or that she removed her earring when talking on the phone as often as they commented on her performance. Still, she used her unique status to her advantage, saying, "A woman can get an investor's ear more quickly than a man. After all, many women handle the finances in their family."[7] As far as race in her business, she claimed half her customers were black and insisted that they were no different than others. "Some are traders by instinct. Others are more conservative. But, they all want to make money."

The black woman on Wall Street was rare, but often more successful than one might think. As Special Markets moved into the 1960s, a second force emerged, Wilhelmina B. Drake. She served in several roles for the firm. She was Director of Women Activities, a member of the board of directors, and corporate secretary. She was instrumental to the firm's ability to continue on and pay the bills in what was not a very profitable business. Shortly after its founding, Special Markets' goal shifted from creating riches to survival. After more than a decade in business, Drake said with pride and a touch of lament, "We haven't achieved our goals but we are still here."[8]

Part of the reason that the firm remained alive was its success with the female market. So heavily weighted was their success predicated in that group that at one point Philip Jenkins estimated that they accounted for 90 percent of the firm's clients. "It's a part of the socioeconomic pattern of Negroes," Jenkins explained in 1967. "The Negro community for many years has been a matriarchy."[9]

To lure in this market, Drake created "Women's Day on Wall Street" in 1957. It became an annual event, drawing many potential clients, editors of publications, and others. Each participant received a tour of the New York Stock Exchange; lunch at Antlers, a well-known restaurant; and a lecture by Special Markets' principals about the power of investing in mutual funds. Their pitch was that investing was an important way to save for children's education, the purchase of a home, travel, retirement, or business. Jenkins, whose youthful face was enormously disarming, also had an ability to talk in laypeople's terms using everyday analogies. "We are financial physicians," he once declared at a conference. "Just as the doctor prescribes for human ailments, we prescribe for physical ailments."[10] Such analogies were helpful in bringing in accounts including their most important and notable, the Alpha Kappa Alpha, a sorority for black women.

The belief of Special Markets, Patterson & Company, and McGhee & Company in mutual funds was part of a larger movement on Wall Street. The industry was seeing the institutionalization of assets in the form of mutual funds, trusts, and other professionally managed groups. Many remembered the ramifications of their irrational exuberance before the 1929 Crash, and the subsequent Great Depression; and they sought trained investors to handle their money. Trusts catered mainly to the wealthiest class and were maintained mostly by banks.

The emerging power from all of these institutions was the pension fund. The gathering strength of unions soon changed the attitudes of U.S. corporations about caring for workers once they retired and left the workforce. As conglomerates and corporations grew during this period of prosperity, the workforce expanded; these two factors account for the explosion of pension funds. Mutual funds emerged as the choice for the middle class because it was the best of two worlds. These investors aimed for safe returns with the potential of substantial upside.

While Special Markets' claim to fame was being the first black securities company in the financial district, Wall Street got its first black firm in 1960 when H. L. Wright & Company moved into 99 Wall Street. The brokerage's selection of home base was eerie because the building would in the future house notable African American companies such as TLC Beatrice and Daniels & Bell, and would stand next to the offices of E.G. Bowman.

In the Wall Street tradition, H. L. Wright was named after its founder, Harry L. Wright. The firm was unique in that its main ambitions lay beyond the brokerage business in the areas of corporate finance and underwriting.

Wright graduated from Tuskegee Institute with a degree in business administration. After taking a few graduate courses at Columbia University and the New York Institute of Finance, he entered the workforce as a fiscal officer of the U.S. Department of Agriculture. He also served as a research analyst with the New York State Banking Department and the U.S. Department of Justice. Perhaps his most prestigious fiscal position was serving as comptroller of the United Negro College Fund.

Harry Wright's work on Wall Street began in 1954. Unlike most of the African Americans who were focused on retail investors, he entered the business on the institutional end, investing for the growing pension funds and trusts. Soon he was named the manager of his institutional department, and then went on to manage a branch of Eisele & King, Libaire, Stout and Company in the Hotel Theresa. Opening in 1957, it failed as previous attempts before it had.

Its failure freed Harry Wright of any obligation that would have encumbered his attempt to create a viable financial company in the form of H. L. Wright. At first, the company's activities seemed to concentrate on the traditional brokerage area. However, Wright soon launched an ambitious plan that received some attention from black publications. In September 1961, he announced the formation of a four-person corporate finance department that aimed to help provide capital to "small and medium-sized Negro-owned businesses."[10] So grand was his plan that he not only aimed to do such financing in New York, the Northeast, or even throughout the United States, but also sought to expand to Africa, British Guiana, and the West Indies. In this announcement, Wright claimed that he had negotiated a deal with a major, white-owned bank that would supply the firm with the credit necessary to accomplish these plans. Those dreams, however, proved to be too big for the time and faded away shortly after the initiative began. A little more than a year later, in December 1962, the firm was awash in red as losses piled up, depleting its operating funds. Its NASD license was expelled when capital fell below the allowed limits.

Around this time, the McGhee firm was growing. At its peak it maintained about 10 salesmen to pitch the value of investments to the public. All the clients were black. Those among the elite circle, who had some experience investing in the market, used the firm as a brokerage to buy individual stocks. Those who were in the game for the first time tended to use it as an intermediary to put money into a mutual fund. After a decade of providing this service, the firm's management decided to stop being the means and instead be the end. In 1966, the Everyman Fund was created. McGhee's philosophy was conservative, reflected in a portfolio of mostly blue chip stocks. At its height, the firm had approximately $200,000 under management. This was supposed to be the precursor to great success. In the late 1960s, Norman McGhee Jr. went to New York in search of partners to provide support for the fund and what was to be Everyman Management Corp. After many negotiations, he purportedly secured a deal with the then Bache & Company, for a $400 million credit. However, when the United States entered a recession in the 1970s, the financing fell apart as did this phase of African American entrepreneurship on Wall Street.

The 1970s brought difficult times to the stock market. McGhee & Company had never been financially strong. The *Wall Street Journal* reported in 1955 that its monthly revenue topped out at $10,000 a month, leaving little room for much profits.[12] McGhee Jr. affirms, "We were always under financed." After years of enormous economic expansion in the post–World War II era, Wall Street hit a storm, and the firm was unable to stay afloat. After 18 years, the doors to the Street's first black brokerage quietly closed its doors. Patterson & Company went out of business in the early 1960s and John Patterson went to work at Bache until 1965 when he branched out with other plans including the founding of the Southern Bronx Overall Economic Development Corporation (SOBRO).

Special Markets also faltered in 1970. Years later when looking back at the firm, Philip Jenkins acknowledged that it achieved little economically; instead, he counted his greatest contribution as some information he told the Securities and Exchange Commission (SEC) about organized crime members who had tried to bankroll him. Such was the end of the first phase of this history. In its place, a new group of black financiers sought to break through into the greatest Wall Street institutions.

3

THE BIG TIME

IN JULY 1968, THE MEDIA RECEIVED AN AN-nouncement for a press conference. The alert went out to the financial writers who relay the daily market activity and information about companies to the general public. In many respects, this press conference included the usual players and settings. Sitting next to the podium was Robert C. Van Tuyl, chairman of Shearson Hammill & Company, one of the five largest brokerages in the business—they were often in the news. On the agenda were the usual topics—securities, investors, and business. There were, however, a few striking differences. For starters, this meeting did not take place at the New York Stock Exchange on Wall Street; instead, it was held on 125th Street between Lennox and Fifth. Last, the man who spent most of the time at the microphone talking and engaging the press with answers was not Van Tuyl, but a burly black man named Russell L. Goings Jr. Goings announced that after two years of negotiation, Shearson Hammill had agreed to put one of its branches in Harlem.

The well-publicized creation of this Harlem branch, which would later become First Harlem Securities, the second black-owned member firm of the New York Stock Exchange, symbolized the new attitude of this generation of African

American brokers. The first black firms operated on the fringe of the financial community by catering to a market of minority retail investors that the elite brokerages largely ignored. The black entrepreneurs who surfaced on Wall Street in the late 1960s aimed to create companies that would work *within* the mainstream of the securities industry and compete for its most lucrative businesses. They were determined to break into the old boys clubs, including the New York Stock Exchange, where many of the Street's elite fostered connections and made deals. As social change swept through American cities, it appeared that Wall Street would have to adjust accordingly and if it did, a few entrepreneurs were ready to capitalize on it.

The origins of what would become First Harlem Securities can be found in the frustration and opportunity that has led many risk takers to start companies. Most blacks in the industry believed that managerial positions in white-owned firms would be closed to them for the immediate future. Although they had made tremendous progress since first setting foot on Wall Street, dramatic changes in management were not yet possible. The obvious solution was to work in a black-owned firm, a proposition many dreamed of, but few thought feasible. Although the available opportunities for African Americans seemed limited and restraining, they also brought financial security. Not many were willing to jeopardize their own capital or reputation in risky ventures, especially during the uncertain times that had ruined Special Markets, McGhee & Company, and many others.

During the late 1960s, Wall Street was littered with the detritus from hundreds of broker/dealers who had to close shop or merge with other struggling firms because of the moribund economic conditions. Established firms like Hayden Stone and

Goodbody & Company were saved by the *Crisis Committee,* a group formed by the NYSE to deal with faltering brokerages. Others like McDonnell & Company could not be saved and were forced to liquidate their assets. Even such august investment banks as Merrill Lynch and Morgan Stanley were treading water during these years and only survived because of shrewd management and deep pockets.

It was a terrible time to start a brokerage, let alone a black brokerage that would have to endure additional burdens beyond the realms of finance. The failure of any black-owned firm working under the watchful eye of the financial community would simply confirm the Jim Crow attitudes that still permeated some offices throughout the Street and the country.

With all the obstacles that stood in their way, it was a wonder that anybody had the courage (or stupidity, depending on your point of view) to create a bigger black firm than those that had just failed. Still, a few men were so filled with ambition and frustration that they were willing to take the gamble. One such person was Willie L. Daniels, an institutional salesman, who had spent a decade on Wall Street working at several firms, constantly searching for better opportunities. But, after years of looking, he concluded that he would never get his fair share working for others.

"If you are working for another firm, you reach a level when you become unprofitable to yourself," Daniels told *Sepia* magazine in 1972.[1] Because he was an institutional salesman, Daniels was paid with commissions, meaning that the majority of proceeds he generated went to his employer. But, if working for himself, all the proceeds from his labor would benefit him. Such discrepancies convinced Daniels that the road of independence was that path he should take. However, he could not have imagined how difficult that road would be.

Struggle was not anything new to Willie Daniels. He grew up poor in the small southern town of Valdosta, Georgia. As a boy, to get extra money, he took a job running errands for one of the wealthiest families in the town. The family happened to be involved with investments, and over time young Willie took notice and soon associated success with securities. His desire to learn big-time finance led him to Florida A&M, the black college located only a few miles from his hometown. He concentrated on finance courses hoping to land a job on Wall Street, but when he graduated in 1960, few brokerages had opened their doors to African Americans. Consequently, Daniels was forced to take a job with Francis I. DuPont Company as a filing clerk. He eventually moved up in the ranks to become an institutional salesman and went on to work at major firms like Bache & Co., Shearson Hammill, and Smith Barney. Despite his constant search for better opportunities, it was soon evident that he could fulfill his hopes only by starting his own firm. But where would Willie get such an opportunity? As often seems to happen, opportunity came knocking on his door.

The year 1968 was arguably the most turbulent in U.S. history. Two of the nation's heroes, Martin Luther King Jr. and Robert F. Kennedy were assassinated. The Democratic Convention in Chicago was marked by violence rather than policies. Riots were erupting throughout the major cities of the nation, and into the madness came Richard Nixon, who that year was elected the 37th president of the United States. While Nixon's accomplishments and intentions will forever be debated, a top priority when he entered office was to heal the social unrest of black Americans. The Voting Rights Act of 1965 gave them great political strength, and Nixon needed to extend his hand to that constituency. One gesture came in the form of the Office of Minority Business Enterprise (OMBE), which was created to increase minority business holdings, minority home ownership, and create more jobs for minorities. At the time, a majority of black-owned businesses were mom-and-pop shops—small, neighborhood stores that had little impact on the socioeconomic problems. The Nixon administration wanted to support big businesses with high profiles that in turn would bring them better publicity. Since there is no greater stage in American business than Wall Street, it seemed like a logical place to go.

Once the Nixon administration decided to back a black Wall Street firm, the problem became finding a group to support. One possibility rested in Harlem with the Shearson Hammill group. After Goings secured the commitment from Shearson Hammill, he began to recruit black brokers both on and to the Street for his office, and the first man to join him was Willie Daniels. After Goings & Company had achieved some success, Nixon's top aides reached out to talk about possible financing. After a meeting at the executive building in Washington, D.C., Goings decided not to take their offer. According to Jim Greene, the third man to join the Shearson branch, "Russell said that he did not want to go solo with government money."[2] Goings instead preferred to find investors who would not smell of federal handouts. His refusal, however, was an opportunity for Daniels to make history by bringing the first black-owned member firm to the New York Stock Exchange. He did not have the same feelings about government aid as did his colleagues and decided to leave the Shearson branch to begin working on the new firm.

With some financing in place, Daniels was well on his way to making history. He scrolled through all the names in his card file and eventually assembled a staff of "personal friends and business brothers" to support his efforts for additional resources. The failure of so many brokerages at the time was vivid proof that Wall Street is a capital-intensive game; Daniels knew that he needed more than the government money he had been promised. He paid his small staff a stipend and worked at Smith Barney to fund his employees. Their job was to research markets and statistics to show the great promise of the black market to potential investors. Knowing that they were halfway there with the financing energized his staff, but a small technicality in an old law delayed Daniels's plans for two years, and eventually he found himself alone again.

Daniels's problem resulted from an interpretation of Securities Exchange Commission (SEC) laws, the government agency that was created to regulate the securities industry after the stock market crash of 1929. After the SBA referred him to the Small Business Investment Company, Daniels soon had a deal. "They agreed to guarantee us up to $1.85 million," he later said. "But, we found that this would be violating section 12D3 of the Investment Act of 1940. So that $1.85 million would have gone down the drain without an SEC waiver."[3] Because of this setback, the team he had assembled to assist his efforts left him for more promising opportunities. In the midst of this struggle, with no end in sight, it became apparent to Daniels that having an ally would relieve some of the burden and responsibilities that weighed so heavily on his shoulders. However, the search for the right man would not be easy.

To locate the perfect partner, Daniels went back to his address file contacting many of the black brokers he knew, only to be turned down every time. Nobody wanted to take the requisite risk of such a venture. Although most African Americans in the industry felt they did not get their fair share, they also realized that relative to their brothers and sisters suffering throughout the United States, they had it pretty good. Daniels kept plugging along until one rejection included a suggestion. Bache & Company broker Paul Haywood told him that he had just turned down a similar offer from a man in St. Louis who was also trying to get a firm together. His name was Travers Bell.

Travers J. Bell Jr. was born in Illinois in 1941. In direct contrast to Daniels's southern upbringing, Bell grew up against a backdrop of city streets and tall buildings on the south side of Chicago. Like most of the kids in his neighborhood, he had no aspirations of working on Wall Street; it just was not something that black people did. After high school graduation, Bell was unsure about his future and short of money, which provided the perfect opportunity for his father to reel him into the securities industry. Bell Senior had always tried to get young Travers interested in the stock market and got his son a job as a messenger at Dempsey Tegeler, a Midwest brokerage house where Senior worked as a clerk in the operations department. At the time, Dempsey Tegeler was one of the most powerful investment houses outside of New York. An experience on young Travers's first day, convinced him that Wall Street was where he wanted to spend his career.

In a story Bell often repeated, he described how he was told to deliver a briefcase across the street to a company called H. N. Billesby. On his way over, Bell looked into the briefcase and saw what appeared to be meaningless crumpled papers. After completing the walk to his destination, he met the specified man to give him the briefcase and in return received a check for $175,000. "My eyes went boiing!" Bell later said. "I thought that this guy was paying me for paper!"[4] Assured that the securities business was the path to fortune, Bell signed on full-time as a messenger. However, unlike most other blacks who had preceeded him in that position, he did not stay in the mailroom for long thanks to Jerome Tegeler, cofounder and the driving force of the firm. One day, he approached the young messenger and sat him down for a chat. "Travers, I wanted to help your father but I couldn't because nobody was ready for that yet," Tegeler opened with. "However, I don't care anymore and I am going to do something many people are not going to like, I am going to teach you this business."[5]

Tegeler deservedly had a reputation as a demanding, bullish man. His nickname, "Jerry the Great," fit his tyrannical style and emperor-like stature. However, he had a generous side to his personality. In the 1950s, Dempsey Tegeler employed an African American named Richard Thomas who also began in the mailroom. Soon Thomas expressed his desire to become a broker, and with Tegeler supporting his efforts, he became the first black account executive in St. Louis. Likewise, Tegeler saw a spark in Bell that suggested the youngster had the potential for bigger things. Tegeler's son, Tim, who worked at Dempsey Tegeler during the same period, said Bell's rise had to do with performance, not race. "To him [Jerry Tegeler] people were people, no matter what their background. The only thing that counted was their ambition. If they had that, he would help them. And Trav had that as was obvious by his career."[6]

Because Bell put in many long days and had a mentor to look out for him, he moved up quickly. Dempsey Tegeler constantly acquired companies, and in 1963 it bought Straus, Blosser, and McDowell, another Midwest brokerage firm with 15 offices. Tegeler made Bell, at age 23, the operations manager of the whole company. He worked in the accounting end of the business until he graduated from Washington University in 1967.

After graduating from college, Bell went to work at another broker/dealer named Fusz Schmelzle, where he served as chief operating officer while building his sales and trading experience. All along, he was determined to have his own firm one day. "The one point that outweighed everything else was that as a black man I had this unusual opportunity to learn the securities business and that knowledge just was not with anybody else black. I had an obligation to exercise that knowledge. That was really the triggering point. I felt it was more than me."[7]

One day while sitting in his office, Bell reached across his desk to pick up the ringing phone.

"Travers Bell speaking," he yelled into the receiver.

"Mr. Bell, this is the most important telephone call you have ever received," Willie Daniels said.

"Mister, have you considered that it might be the most important phone call you ever made?" Bell replied.

Soon afterward, Travers Bell was in New York to meet Willie Daniels at a Broadway play, *The Wiz*. The idea for Daniels & Bell, Inc., was born.

At first glance, Daniels and Bell were striking opposites. Daniels's southern charm and warm persona stood in direct contrast to the cautious, cold nature Bell had developed in Chicago. It did not appear that the two personalities could work together and eventually that assessment would be proven correct, but in 1970, they put aside all differences in pursuit of their common goal. But the obstacles in their path were considerable. "Every time we would feel like we solved a problem, they would come up with a new rule that we had to contend with," Bell told the *Atlanta Journal Constitution* in 1972.[8] "One day, my partner and I were sitting there, and he started crying. He said that he couldn't take it anymore." So, filled with frustration, Daniels got out of his seat and left to solve his problem. Luckily, he had encountered a fledgling reporter a year earlier, and now he revisited him. The meeting set off a chain of events that would propel them to great heights.

In 1969, a writer named Myron Kandel, who later went on to become a legendary financial reporter at CNN, was editor of his own publication called the *Wall Street Letter*. Some of his sources had told him about a black man's attempt to get a firm together. He approached Daniels hoping to get a good story, but their conversation convinced him not to print it. "I spoke to Daniels and told him that I was planning to run the story and he asked me not to. He hadn't raised the funds yet and it would possibly hurt his efforts to start this firm. I agreed," Kandel remembers.[9] A year later, after Daniels had secured Bell as a partner but still faced seemingly insurmountable obstacles, he reached out to Kandel to express his troubles. "A few months later," Kandel recalls, "he came to me despondently. He said the money had fallen apart." As a result of the conversation, Kandel wrote a piece in his newsletter called "The Shattered Dream," a title inspired by Martin Luther King's most famous speech. The article detailed the failed aspirations of the two men. Although it was a simple one-page story, history would turn with Kandel's printed words.

The *Wall Street Letter* reached the offices and homes of the most powerful players on Wall Street. One subscriber was William J. Casey, who had just been named chairman of the SEC by Richard Nixon. The brawny, blunt-speaking New Yorker, whose career would later be shadowed by his involvement in the Iran-contra scandal, read the article and decided to do something about it. The SEC gave Daniels & Bell an exemption from the laws that encumbered their SBIC financing. Under the original interpretation of Rule 12D3, brokerages were not considered small businesses. The SEC exempted them from that rule, reasoning that the "intent of the law had been to encourage business that could create capital for other business,"[10] Bell would later explain. With that, Daniels and Bell received money but not the $1.85 million they had originally agreed on in the summer of 1969. In the end, they obtained only about $500,000. The solution to this shortfall would also come from the Kandel article.

"Casey called some of his friends," Kandel recalls. "Among them was Dan Lufkin, who put up his own money and got some others to do the same." In many ways, Lufkin, cofounder of Donaldson, Lufkin, Jenrette (DLJ), represented the new generation of Wall Street. He was young, aggressive, and willing to buck many of the Street's oldest traditions. He cofounded DLJ immediately after graduation from Harvard Business School and, 13 years later, led his company to become the first member firm of the NYSE to go public. The move was heavily criticized because it violated an unwritten rule of the old boys' club to keep memberships private. So it was no surprise that he was ready to help Daniels and Bell. He did not listen to criticism, and as a younger member of the Street's elite, he was more accepting of change than were his older colleagues.

One day while walking across Chase Manhattan Plaza, he bumped into Daniels. Intrigued by the Kandel article, Lufkin asked Daniels to come up to his office to discuss their business plan. Bell then ran over to join them and convinced Lufkin to put up some money from his venture capital group, the Noel Fund. The business plan made a lot of sense.

In the meeting, the two men outlined their business plan to Lufkin. They laid out their dreams and ambitions to create opportunities for themselves by using all the advantages of being the first black investment bank. Although their plan was unconventional, it did make sense and was so full of ambition that it promoted the prominent Wall Street financier to say that "I was great admirer of Travers Bell and Willie Daniels for what they were trying to do."[11]

In Lufkin, Daniels and Bell found an influential friend who would become a source of advice for years to come. As a member of the NYSE Board of Governors, which set the policy of the Exchange and approved all membership applications, he would prove to be an invaluable insider. He was able to help the two black men move forward as they set their sights on becoming the first black-owned member firm in the Big Board's history.

There is no greater symbol of Wall Street's exclusionary nature than the New York Stock Exchange. Founded in 1792, its grand stature, well-crafted halls, and large market systems remain foreign to most. For decades, membership approvals were based on relationships, rather than qualifications. It wasn't until 1967 that the Big Board let its first woman, Muriel Siebert, buy a seat. "I learned that you can't break a tradition that was 175 years old and have everybody love you," Siebert later recalled. "It's got nothing to do with me as a person. People just like things status quo. One governor of the exchange said to me, 'And how many more are there behind you?' Like I was going to lead a parade onto the floor."[12] Although it was not coming easily, change was happening on the floor, and three years later an African American finally broke its barriers. In February 1970, Joseph L. Searles created great media publicity when he became the first black member of the New York Stock Exchange.

Despite the media fuss, Joe Searles actually was not the first black on the Exchange. Clarence B. Jones became an allied member when he was named a partner at Carter, Berlind, Weill & Levitt (CBWL). An allied member is a person who has voting stock in a New York Stock Exchange member firm, but has no access to the floor. Like DLJ, CBWL was a fairly new firm made up of young, ambitious people like Arthur Levitt and Sanford Weill. "We were much less bound by the traditions and cultures of the past," says Levitt. When it was suggested that Jones become a full partner, Levitt "was very enthusiastic about it because I felt the symbolism was significant, plus it made good business sense."[13] But Jones's tenure was short-lived, and Levitt would only say, "It didn't really work out." Years later after leaving CBWL, in 1982, Jones would be convicted of defrauding clients, but his NYSE membership will forever mark the beginning of a significant part of history that was furthered by the entrance of Joe Searles.

Searles's road to Wall Street was not long planned, but was a product of luck and opportunity. The son of a military man, Searles spent most of his youth moving from base to base throughout the world eventually settling in Texas. At Kansas State University, Searles majored in political science and excelled as a football player. He then went to law school at George Washington University, eventually leaving four credits shy of graduation to try his hand at professional football. After a brief, unsuccessful stint as a professional, he decided to capitalize on his political background. He had met a politician, John Lindsay, while in Washington, D.C., and joined him when Lindsay began his two-term administration as mayor of New York City.

In the late 1960s, declining resources and increasing racial tension plagued New York City. A growing Black Nationalist movement often faced off against groups like SPONGE, the acronym for the Society for the Prevention of Negroes Getting Everything. In an attempt to build unity within his city, the New York mayor extended his hand to the black community. When Martin Luther King Jr. was assassinated, Lindsay traveled to Harlem and walked along its streets without bodyguards to talk with the thousands of grieving people who lined the sidewalks. Such outreach was not limited to extreme incidents, but embodied his larger effort. Involved in that initiative was Searles who served as the deputy commissioner of local business development in the New York City Development Administration.

The department's goal was to promote minority businesses. Searles helped to organize the city's first franchise fair, which invited national franchises, banks, and the Small Business Administration to try to make matches with entrepreneurs and take black businesses beyond the Mom-and Pop-stores. His work earned him praise from his boss, Mayor Lindsay, who once described Searles as "an invaluable aide."[14] It also was the origin of bigger goals. "I think that is when the first clue of this whole business thing started with me," Searles recalls. "I thought about going to Wall Street to try to make this whole movement have a greater impact. I was really naïve! I always thought to go where everybody looks–'The Club,'–the Stock Exchange and thought I would try that."[15] As luck would have it, his friend and colleague on the Lindsay team, Jerome Becker, served on the Board of Directors at Daughters of Israel. Becker, who would later become a judge and chairman of the New York State Housing Authority got to talking with a fellow board member named Charles Gross, managing partner of the securities firm, Newburger, Loeb. The firm held a membership to the NYSE, and he indicated to Becker that he wanted to give the seat to a minority. "I think he [Gross] had high social responsibility. I never got the sense that they were doing it for publicity," Becker says.[16] In response, Becker suggested two names. The first was Simeon Golar, who was then New York City Commissioner of Housing. The second person was Joe Searles, whom Becker liked and thought was charismatic. "In the end they chose me probably because if it didn't work out, it would not create as much of a stir as someone with the exposure Simeon had," explains Searles, who had never bought a stock or bond. "They probably thought we should stick this neophyte in there because I was young and more easily led or directed because I was about to break barriers and they didn't want a clash."[17]

After four months of discussions, the management at Newberger, Loeb decided that Searles was their man. Gross, who had not worked on the floor for a number of years, agreed to transfer his seat to Searles in what is called an ABC agreement. Under this deal, Newberger, Loeb agreed to finance a major part of the cost of the seat, and Searles promised to repay the firm. On February 13, 1970, Searles became the first black member of the New York Stock Exchange (NYSE).

The historic moment was celebrated in its headquarters at 5 Hanover Square, a dozen reporters from both print and television peppered the newest member of the NYSE with questions. Yet many wondered what reaction Searles would receive once he set foot on arguably the most famous floor in the world.

While his accomplishment made many African Americans proud, there was some concern about the reception he would receive from the financial community. "My biggest fear and Bobby Newberger's biggest fear was where would I sit in the luncheon club?" Searles recalls. "We didn't want to upset or offend members of the NYSE luncheon club."[18] To resolve the situation, the NYSE gave him his own table. So, in the middle of this exclusive dining area, where many of Wall Street's most powerful ate and discussed business sat Searles, a lone black man at a table. As soon as he formed some friendships, fellow members started inviting him over to their tables, but his experiences in the dining room in many ways resembled his progress on the floor.

The floor of the New York Stock Exchange is a unique culture where securities are traded for both clients and the trader's own accounts with the hope of making money. It is often described as a cutthroat, fast-paced, tough environment, and it was unclear how the first black member was going to be treated. "Some members were very helpful, and then others, I could see beneath their smiles that they wanted to cut my guts," Searles says. "There was one crowd that I used to go into and ask for the market and the size and this guy would give me this awful look and he would always screw it up for me." Others, mostly the younger members of the Big Board, accepted Searles into their circles. "It was a time of change in America and most of the younger generation were accepting change more gracefully than their fathers."[19]

Unfortunately for Searles and all of Wall Street, the market took a serious downturn during this period. Many brokerages were in trouble, and Newburger, Loeb was no exception. A majority of their retail clients took their business out of the company leaving the firm with insufficient funds to cover overhead costs. Perhaps a broker with years of experience and deep pockets to support him could have made it, but Searles had neither. He gave up his seat in November 1970, less than a year after he broke ground, saying at the time, "The exchange is not a welfare club."[20] Searles went on to work in public finance at Manufacturers Hanover Trust and other positions before he left Wall Street for good. He eventually became chairman of the 125th Street Business Improvement District in Harlem and was an important part of the Harlem USA project. Looking back at his brief stint on the floor, Searles has mixed feelings. "It was painful to get that blaze of glory and have it snuffed but I learned to be strong, to push and fulfill your dreams," he says. "At the time I said being the first black on the Exchange was a comma in history because there are larger things like Harlem USA that have a greater economic impact than my time on the floor."[21]

While Searles's membership in the New York Stock Exchange was short, it proved that times were changing at the highest levels of Wall Street, and other African Americans took notice. When Searles joined the Big Board in 1970, Daniels threw a party in his honor with many of the blacks in the industry in attendance—about a dozen people in all. Shortly after Searles made his exit, Daniels and Bell were on the verge of making their own history.

With the SEC exemption and the financing coming together, the dream that was such a comforting companion to the two men during their period of turmoil was becoming a reality. By the summer of 1971, Daniels & Bell had secured $1.1 million in financing, half of it from the SBIC. In addition, there were the contributions of the Noel Fund, a Minority Enterprise Small Business Investment Company (MESBIC) called Pioneer Capital Corporation, and a consortium of nine banks. Daniels & Bell also brought in Raymond C. Forbes and Milton Aeder as partners. Both white, they gave the firm credibility in the businesses they sought, mainly institutional accounts. Forbes, a NYSE member who began in 1946 with Merrill Lynch, had developed a sound reputation and added value to their execution. Aeder served as the firm's accountant and was an invaluable source the first few years. With the team and money in place, Daniels & Bell, Inc., the first black-member firm of the NYSE was born on June 24, 1971. It was the subject of great publicity, and to celebrate they held a party at the Bankers Club. With news cameras present, Daniels was the star of the show. After all the struggle, he planned to enjoy the moment and to make sure that he received the proper attention. When he saw a reporter interviewing a black broker from the Street, Daniels sent his friend over to buy the broker drinks. The recipient later learned that Daniels had bought him the beverages to keep him occupied and away from the rest of the press. The party lasted all night, and when daylight came, Daniels and Bell walked over to their new offices at 64 Wall Street and began their new adventure.

Daniels & Bell, Inc. was not the only black-owned member firm of the New York Stock Exchange for long. On September 30, 1971, First Harlem Securities became the second black-owned NYSE member firm. The firm originally had been approved for membership in the summer of 1970 under the name Crispus Attucks Securities but declined to purchase the seat because of unstable industry conditions. Unlike Daniels & Bell, First Harlem had a track record as a branch of Shearson Hammill, one of the largest securities companies at the time. Even more unusual was the branch's location. While most brokerages operated downtown in the financial district, the officers decided to open the business uptown in Harlem.

The brainchild behind the whole concept of First Harlem Securities, Russell L. Goings Jr., was born in Stamford, Connecticut, at the height of the Depression in the 1930s. The Goings family had little money, so as a youngster he took a job shining shoes. One day, a customer sat down before him and asked for a shine. This customer, a stockbroker, forever changed Goings's life. "He interrupted me to take an order on the phone," Goings would later recall. The well-dressed man got up out of his chair to make his call and when he returned he had a small piece of paper in the palm of his hand. The paper detailed an order he had just taken for his customer, netting the broker a commission of a few thousand dollars. "There I was on my knees and in the time it took to shine his shoes that broker earned $2,500 and I earned 25 cents. From then on I knew what I wanted."[22]

After graduating from Xavier University in Cincinnati, Ohio, and a brief professional career with the Buffalo Bills, Goings set his sights on Wall Street. His decision did not sit well with friends and family who thought that his opportunities would be limited because of his race. "When I graduated, everybody—my family, my counselors, friends—discouraged me from going into finance. I refused to believe I would have to wind up in civil service or social work,"[23] Goings would later say. After answering a classified ad in a newspaper, he applied for and landed a job with an over-the-counter firm called Van Alstyne, Noel. Eighteen months later, the young broker moved to Bruns, Nordeman & Company and began dreaming of spreading his experience to his Harlem neighbors. At the same time, Steve Fields, the then head of Shearson Hammill's New York retail branches, had heard about Goings's work and sought to recruit him. The meeting of the two minds would bring Wall Street and 125th Street together.

Fields opened offices, developed business, and recruited talent to strengthen Shearson's presence in the New York area. So when Goings was suggested to him, Fields approached his meeting with the broker hoping to sign him with Shearson as an institutional salesman. Goings had other ideas. "I met with Russ in 1966 and in the process of interviewing him, he told me what his desires were," Fields recalls. "He wanted to open an operation in Harlem. I thought it was an intriguing idea . . . and we set about it. After hearing his story and business plan, we went to the executive committee with it."[24] Two years of discussions ensued to resolve such questions as: Could the branch make money? How would it be staffed? Where would they set up? Revenue projections were made to estimate its potential. While Shearson did not expect to break the bank with their venture, they certainly were not planning—or willing—to lose money either. Goings went around to prospective accounts to prove that he could bring business into the branch. Once these doubts were erased, Goings and Shearson chairman, Robert C. Van Tuyl held the press conference described earlier to announce their grand plans.

Although Shearson Hammill was one of the five biggest securities firms, it was second tier in status. Spurred by Charles Merrill's mantra decades before to bring Main Street to Wall Street, Merrill Lynch had developed into the premier brokerage house, far and away in a class of its own. Behind it rested a handful of firms including Bache, Paine Webber, and Shearson. Fields's firm had the clout to support what many considered to be a risk, but the requisite courage was unusual for the company.

"Shearson was not a groundbreaking firm. What excited us was that this was a bold move that Merrill might have made," Fields says. "It was a step that was uncharacteristic for us at the time." It was risky in part because few were sure how a branch would operate in Harlem.[25]

Some residents and professionals remembered the failed attempts of F. L. Salomon and Eisele & King, Libaire, Stout & Company. On the surface there were similarities between these companies and the Shearson venture. All were uptown and run by ambitious black brokers. Each were branches of New York Stock Exchange member firms. However, the similarities were external. By 1968, F. L. Salomon was on the verge of closing, and Eisele & King, Libaire, Stout & Company had been absorbed by Harris Upham. Yet, Shearson Hammill endured as one of the larger firms on the Street, and its name carried great credibility. Also, the context of the time had altered as the Civil Rights movement entered its final stages. Although Civil Rights remained center stage in the fight for equality, the quiet initiative to improve the economic conditions for black Americans was growing louder.

But, by the late 1960s, attitudes were changing, and the times called for Wall Street to give Harlem another chance. When judged in the national context of the times, a Shearson move into Harlem was far more symbolic than F. L. Salomon's former office. "We felt it was important to do something other than just talk about black entrepreneurship and see if we could help get something started that made sense," says Duke Chapman, then president of Shearson.[26] While excitement brewed downtown, the reaction uptown was decidedly less favorable.

Just a few days after Shearson announced that it had signed a 10-year lease on 125h Street, the Saturday, July 27, 1968, headline in the *New York Times* read "Broker's Plan for a Harlem Office Is Criticized by CORE Leader." Victor

Solomon, chairman of the Harlem Branch of the Congress of Racial Equality, had held a press conference of his own. "Wall Street is coming to Harlem and it's not in the interests of Harlem," Solomon began. He labeled Shearson Hammill's latest addition "a conspiracy by state, municipal, and Wall Street high finance interests to take over Harlem. They see Harlem as too valuable to remain in black hands. White high finance once in would move quickly to the rapid and total control of operations."[27] Soon CORE members were protesting the branch's proposed opening in the summer of 1969. While their point is debatable, their argument was extreme. As Goings put it at the time, "We are renting from black owners, the architect is black, we are letting bids to black contractors and we will be hiring a large number of black brokers."[28] Other black leaders like Manhattan Borough President Percy Sutton and Freedom National Bank President William Hudgins were optimistic about the move. Still, CORE's rhetoric was not unanticipated. "We assumed we would be accused of Wall Street profiting at the expense of taking dollars out of the black community," Duke Chapman says. "We guessed right on that but that did not take a brilliant guess."[29]

To resolve the conflict, a meeting was scheduled at CORE headquarters in Harlem with Roy Innis, its national chairman, as its representative. Initially, the meeting was confrontational, with both sides passionately stating their case. At one point, Innis got up and told the Shearson executives, "You're on my turf now. The troops are at the border and they are ready to go."[30] In hindsight, one must judge Innis's rhetoric in the context of those turbulent times. This confrontation took place in 1968, the height of turmoil and the black power movement. "At that time, if you didn't make waves of some sort, nothing would happen," says Mel Eubanks, one of the first black brokers to join the initiative. "Roy made waves, Russ made waves, and things got done."[31] After things calmed down, a mutual agreement came in the form of the nonprofit Crispus Attucks Foundation. The foundation was originally Goings's idea, but in 1968, it was nothing more than a concept. Named after a black soldier, the first man killed in the Revolutionary War in the late eighteenth century, its purpose was to provide and open up job opportunities for the Harlem community. The Shearson Hammill group informed CORE that the average return in the securities retail business was 7.5 percent of all gross revenues and agreed to give such a percentage to the Foundation to fund its activities. The creation of this organization had two purposes. The first and most obvious was that it quieted CORE's criticism of the Harlem branch. Second, it gave them a vehicle to do the community work. To ensure that the Foundation did not itself become the subject of controversy, both sides agreed to keep its operation in diverse hands. The board comprised Shearson Hammill and CORE representatives, along with the NAACP and Urban League. In addition, Shearson agreed to sell the branch to "responsible members of the community" at the depreciated value of its fixed assets. In other words, no matter how successful the branch became, the large company would not receive the profits.

As the executives left the heated meeting, they stood along the sidewalk waiting to hail a taxi when approached from behind by a young black man. The man identified himself as one of their new brokers, and for the next few minutes the group talked about business. As they disbanded, the Shearson executives departed with their doubts erased. If in the middle of their meeting with Innis, they had wondered why they were enduring this grief to back Goings's dream, the appearance of the African American broker reaffirmed their commitment to expose finance to the larger community. With that hurdle gone, Goings and employees could concentrate on their new business.

All attention turned to setting up the office. The most obvious need was bodies, people to perform and execute the business for the branch. To carry out the purpose of a Harlem office, the majority of employees needed to be black. The problem was that there were few experienced black account executives in the business, and it would be nearly impossible to get all of them to join at the entry-level salaries required for a profit. So the decision was made to bring in a few experienced black brokers from the Street to help manage the office, and then recruit ambitious, smart, hard-working men and women from other professions. The first person Goings hired, as mentioned earlier, was Daniels, the same man who three years later would found Daniels & Bell. The second man he hired was Jim Greene, who had worked on Wall Street for more than a decade. The three men were the only registered representatives for some time. The remaining 12 to 15 people were attracted by the lure of good commissions and unlimited opportunity.

Many African Americans who were approached with the proposition turned it down, refusing to give up their set salary for a commission-based job. Yet, a few were willing to risk beginning again with this exciting venture. One man who took the bait was Earl Andrews Jr., who was a salesman at IBM when approached by Goings to consider joining the branch. "I met with Russ and he interviewed me and offered me a job," Andrews says. "He told me that I could make more money being a broker, learn a lot more and I thought to myself this could be interesting. The come-on from Russ and others was that Shearson would eventually let us buy the office and go into business for ourselves."[32] Mel Eubanks had been about to go into a life of academia. A graduate of Colgate University, he encountered Van Tuyl, who served on Colgate's board in addition to being chairman of Shearson Hammill. He told

Eubanks about the Harlem operation and soon he joined the staff. Others who accepted positions included Martin Everette, William C. Day, and Raymond Huelen. With the necessary count on board, they went through Shearson's five-month training program to get licenses. While operations and staff were coming together, the need for actual office space became the main concern.

As Goings and Greene walked up 125th Street in early 1968, they saw what became known as *Tent City*. A group of protesters had set up tents on the proposed site of a new 23-story state building. The structure, which would later become the Adam Clayton Powell State Office Building, was a source of great controversy, similar to the reaction to plans for a Shearson branch. The community demanded that more of its own be involved in its creation, not just workers who came in from outside the community and fled to their suburban homes at the end of the day. The unstable Harlem real estate market symbolized by this dispute left Goings and Greene struggling to find a suitable place for their operation.

"When Russ and I came up there looking to rent office space, it was just after the riots," Greene explains. "All of the owners wanted to sell! None of the landlords wanted to rent to us except Al Hudgins."[33] Hudgins, son of William Hudgins, owned 5,500 square feet of space at 144 West 125th Street that at the time was occupied by Kenwood Reters. Within a matter of months, the site was transformed from a furniture store to a wonderfully furnished, well-equipped brokerage office. Goings, who had an astute eye for art, decorated the office with beautiful paintings and magnificent carpeting. His love for the arts was so great that 144 West 125th Street would later become the location for the Studio Museum of Harlem and he was its first chairman. It was unlike anything else on the block of small shops. No other Harlem store on the block owned a Dow Jones ticker or had the words "Member New York Stock

Exchange" on their space on 125th Street—and now they were ready to do business.

With the staff trained and resources in place, the office opened in 1969. After a year of working as a Shearson Hammill branch, Goings and his employees made the move to buy the firm. The employees felt that it was time to take their operation solo and become partners in what they saw as a promising concern. Meanwhile, Shearson was receiving negative feedback from some institutional clients about the practices of employees. Word got back to headquarters that many clients felt tactics of intimidation were being used to get business. Was that true or did these clients feel uncomfortable because they had never worked with black men? It is an unanswerable question, but what became clear was that a separation was the only answer. Buying the firm would allow the brokers to escape Shearson's unwritten codes and determine the manner in which they would do business for themselves.

The price to buy the branch was set at $600,000. The First National Bank guaranteed personal loans to each of the firm's employees, allowing them to buy stock at $10 per share; this raised $150,000. The balance came in the form of debentures from institutions such as the Ford Foundation, the Coalition Venture Corporation, and the Riverside Church. Initially, the new securities concern was going to be named Crispus Attucks Securities like the Foundation, but after discovering that a company was already using that name, the branch became First Harlem Securities. In about a year, First Harlem became the second black-owned firm of the New York Stock Exchange.

Their purchase of a seat did not receive the attention that Daniels & Bell had garnered, nor did it get as much press as the initial announcement of the plans to open a Shearson branch in Harlem. But it confirmed that the presence of African Americans in the executive suites and lunchrooms did not represent a fleeting fad, but a lasting presence.

Unlike Daniels & Bell and First Harlem Securities, the nation's third black investment banking firm did not come out of New York. Its seeds were planted in the deep South, the birthplace of Harold E. Doley Jr. Born in 1947, Doley's childhood was marked by memories of "white only" signs and other segregationist policies, but New Orleans was different from other divided American cities. Places like Atlanta and Chicago had easily defined white and black sections. As slavery ended in New Orleans, African Americans who remained as butlers and maids were set up in housing near their employers, which stunted black economic growth. "I grew up wishing that segregation was more severe. By having mixed neighborhoods, it kept certain African American businesses from developing," Doley explains. "For example, instead of having an African American neighborhood restaurant, the white restaurant would serve us at the side window, we weren't allowed to go in and eat. This was defeating because it prevented the full development of black restaurants."[34]

Doley's own interest in business came from his family. Experiences with his loved ones provided lifelong lessons that would serve him well. The youngster's first business exposure was at his family's grocery store adjacent to their home. While it was nothing more than a typical neighborhood shop, it soon became the scene for his first lesson about big business. One Sunday morning, Harold Senior read an announcement in the local paper of plans to build a Winn Dixie five blocks from the family store. The proposed supermarket was part of a growing chain in the South. After a few seconds of reflection, Doley's father put down his newspaper and proclaimed, "The neighborhood business is over." This harsh reality was driven home when his father moved to a new job and received his first paycheck as a teacher. "I used to make more than this on a Saturday," he lamented.

Although Doley's dad was a mentor to him, his main source of knowledge and encouragement was his maternal grandmother. In the context of southern small towns and dirt roads, she was a Texas real estate mogul. Her securities and successful investments enabled her to acquire several properties. Young Harold would visit her beautiful, lavish home on weekends, where he witnessed the benefits of having money work for you instead of having to work for the money. On these days, people would line up, with money in hand, as his grandmother rocked back and forth in her seat. "The most fascinating thing to me was watching people give my grandmother rent money as she sat in a chair in her backyard. This was cash money and I thought, 'damn this is incredible!'" His grandmother's teachings continued as Doley matured and went out on his own. She visited him at his first bachelor residence in an apartment near Dillard University and was gravely disappointed by what she saw. "This is embarrassing. You live in a project," she said. Doley tried to convince her that it was a nice place because he really thought he was living large, but she was having none of it.

"You have to stop renting. You have to move to a good neighborhood and make sure that your children live with the right people," she explained.

"How did you, in a small town in Texas, choose who your children played with?" Doley asked, thinking he had gotten the best of her argument.

"I bought the block," she calmly replied.

With that advice, Doley purchased his first property, a two-family house. He lived in one side for free while renting the other side for the full amount of the monthly mortgage. By now, he had already graduated from Xavier University with a degree in accounting. There he had formed an investment club with a few of his peers resulting in good returns and confirming that Wall Street was where he wanted to be. He'd graduated on a Friday and he began as a stockbroker at Bache & Company the next Monday morning. He went after accounts that the industry had ignored such as black insurance companies, black banks, and other black institutions. One of his first accounts came from Adam C. Haydel, owner of Majestic Life Insurance Company and the richest African American in New Orleans. By chance one day, the two bumped into each other on the street, their first encounter since Doley had become a young adult. Through casual conversation, Haydel learned that Doley had become a stockbroker and was curious why he had not been solicited. "I had heard that he did not buy stocks," Doley remembers. "He then said, 'I own an insurance company so come to my house on Thursday night and I'll show you what stocks I can buy.'" Thus Doley had another client. Such production led Doley to New York where his life would turn after a meeting with Bache's top brass.

During the early 1970s, Bache was a top securities firm with branches throughout the country. To measure the performance of each office, Bache would often fly top performers from each region to New York to talk about profits and losses. Doley was the selected representative in response to one such request, and when he arrived at Bache headquarters, he saw Harry Jacobs, then president of the firm. "I approached him and told him that there were no African Americans on the floor as two-dollar brokers and that Bache should take the lead in making it happen. He liked that idea and said he would talk to his people," Doley says. Soon, he was called back to New York to take Bache personality exams. The results said that Doley would not like the floor because its fast-paced, barbaric action would confine his entrepreneurial, freethinking manner. He found that analysis disheartening because he had been fascinated with the New

York Stock Exchange since childhood. When he was 11 years old, the Doley family spent their vacation in New York City and took a sightseeing tour. One of the stops was the Big Board and young Doley fell in love with the idea of eventually being a part of its activities. "I was so determined to be a member of the Exchange, on that floor and part of the action. J. P. Morgan and the Rothschilds were members and it represented wealth and power." Because of the test results, however, Bache was not going to let him go on the floor. Nevertheless, Jacobs saw the determination in Doley and suggested that he buy a seat for himself.

In 1973, at the age of 26, Doley became the first black individual to buy his own seat on the New York Stock Exchange. (Doley emphasizes the word *individual* acknowledging prior black participation on the NYSE. Searles was the first member but did so under an ABC agreement. Daniels & Bell and First Harlem Securities were firms.) He bought the seat for $90,000 with the help of two New Orleans banks. For collateral, he used the property he had acquired after the talk with his grandmother. His purchase was another signal of the new era of black entrepreneurship on Wall Street. Within a few short years, the increase of African American partnership in the Mecca of Wall Street, the Exchange, had soared to previously unbelievable heights. But, as is typical of so many stories throughout black history, just as African Americans reached the pinnacle of finance, the rules under which the Exchange had operated for centuries were changed.

The early 1970s brought chaos to the New York Stock Exchange, threatening brokerages that had existed for decades. The NYSE was plagued by infighting that threatened the industry as a whole. In the middle of this whirlwind, the newly formed black investment banks operated with membership in an institution whose future was in many respects more uncertain than ever before.

4

A DRY HUSK

AFTER WILLIE DANIELS RETURNED TO NEW YORK from a business trip in June 1972, he walked into the Daniels & Bell office at 64 Wall Street to prepare for an interview with a *Washington Post* reporter. The paper wanted to update its readers about the firm's first year in business. In the paranoid, often esoteric, world of finance where the slightest bit of news can affect the capital markets and the awesome power of money makes perception *the* reality, the firm had remained quiet in financial circles. When judged by financial standards, it had not participated in any historic deals, a common plight for young firms. Moreover, as the novelty of their social significance wore off, Daniels & Bell, once a front-page subject, soon retreated to the back of newspaper sections, and then eventually out of the paper altogether.

In one of the first questions, Daniels was asked to describe the year. His response was almost an oxymoron, a sad optimism. "There have been many rewards, although not all of them financial," he said. As he answered these inquiries, he sat at his desk, slumped in his chair after another long day of selling. His posture was an appropriate image to illustrate the mood of Wall Street in the 1970s: a slump. The industry was bitter from events ranging from soaring inflation to corruption in the White House. That mood was reflected on the brokerage's bottom line in those first 12 months as the article's headline would later articulate: "Despite Setbacks in First Year, Black Brokers Confident."[1] The ambitions that they had dreamed one year earlier had been reduced to the cold realization that the immediate reward for all their labor and determination was not wealth, but survival.

Like Wall Street, America in the 1970s was drab. While many expected the country to express a collective exhale after the enormous unrest that occurred in the 1960s, Americans were forced to confront new challenges both domestically and abroad. Its citizens experienced a thinning confidence in the country's actions and leaders. Events like Vietnam, Watergate, the OPEC oil embargo, and the hostage crisis all contributed to a perception of a powerless America spiraling out of control. This pessimism was visible in the despondency of Americans sitting at home, unemployed, and shaking their heads at the developing crisis' depicted on their televisions. It was seen in the worried eyes of family members who awaited word from their loved ones fighting in Vietnam. It could be seen on Capitol Hill, in 1974, as congressional members gathered to discuss the possible impeachment of President Nixon. This pessimism was represented in rising unemployment and rampant inflation, as well as a declining stock market. However, the moribund attitudes on Wall Street were propelled not just by the recession, but also by its outdated practices. Powerful institutions such as the New York Stock Exchange (NYSE) and the industry's established firms confronted obstacles that resulted from not adapting to a changing securities business. The new black investment banking firms were caught in this hurricane of financial loss.

In 1971, Wall Street betrayed the hopes of Daniels & Bell and First Harlem Securities. Membership in the New York

Stock Exchange represented the pinnacle of finance, yet once they arrived, they found an institution in a precarious state. This was not the same industry that had made so many millionaires in the previous two decades. At the end of the 1960s, the Street still gave the appearance of prosperity to all outsiders. The Go-Go Years of the 1950s and 1960s had resulted in a great expansion and now branches of brokerage firms were in cities across the United States. However, a developing crisis in the back offices of brokerages throughout the nation began a slide that would cause great monetary pain in the years to come. The rising influence of institutional investors and rival exchanges would cause the greatest turmoil in the history of the New York Stock Exchange. At the nadir, a seat on the prestigious floor cost roughly the same amount as a New York City taxi medallion. It was in this deteriorating economic environment that the first two black-owned member firms would try to establish themselves as viable concerns.

To understand the plight that faced all NYSE member firms, it is necessary to comprehend the origins of the blossoming crisis. The go-go years of Wall Street brought not only an increasing presence of institutions like pension funds, trusts, and mutual funds but a change in the attitude of its managers. Traditionally, the investment philosophy of these managers had been to protect money. These professionals executed caution by placing their funds into low-risk securities like high-grade bonds and blue chip stocks to hold for the long term. This changed during the bull market of the mid-twentieth century when hubris and excess produced a new breed of aggressive managers who sought to achieve the best results possible. After years of being content with 5 percent returns, such results were now rendered as subpar. It soon became fashionable for managers to end a year with completely different holdings from the ones with which they started, a turnover rate of 100 percent. To achieve these new expectations, professionals began to buy speculative investments that they labeled as "growth stocks," younger companies with grander possibilities. Because these stocks brought higher risk, managers were quick to dump an entire position in a company if there were any signs of trouble ahead. The result was a drastic increase in volume. In the 1960s, block trading became common, and 100,000 shares of xyz stock in a growing business would often come across the ticker executed by firms like Salomon Brothers and Goldman Sachs. While most NYSE member firms cheered the dramatic increase in volume because the commissions generated by this trading were good for their pockets, it created two major problems that would drag Wall Street into decline.

The first crisis began with the failure of the securities industry to acknowledge that their trading infrastructure was antiquated and unable to deal with the sudden growth. Unlike today's electronic trading, completing a trade required processing vast amounts of paperwork. Once a trade had been made on the floor, clerks in the back offices of brokerage houses began organizing the physical documents—stock certificates, checks, stubs, receipts, and other papers—needed to keep accurate records of the stocks traded and the parties involved in the transaction. It was a familiar sight to see men pushing carts of paper up and down Wall Street to get them to these offices. Although this setup had been adequate for hundreds of years, the explosion in volume exposed its inefficiency to a point where the industry's most basic operation was bleeding with errors.

To appreciate how off guard the industry was before this surge in activity, one need look no further than the misguided predictions of its central marketplace. A 1965 report commissioned by the NYSE predicted that its average volume would reach 10 million shares in 1975; it did so in 1967. Soon, Wall Street was drowning in a sea of paperwork; clerks were unable to process the incoming documents before more arrived at their desks. Part of the blame rested on the shoulders of brokerage management whose priority to make money overshadowed their responsibility to complete the most basic tasks. During the great bull market, firms were so consumed with expansion and other account-seeking maneuvers that they neglected to put the proper resources into their back-office operations. The adjective *back* is an indication of management's prevailing attitude about this less than glamorous area of the securities business. Back-office employees were often overlooked, deemed inferior, and received little training relative to brokers and investment bankers. So, when papers started flooding the clerks' desks, they were unable to cope with the great overflow. At one point, workload ceased to be judged by the individual trades to be processed but by the number of feet the papers stood off the floor.

As the piles grew, errors increased. Numbers that buyers and sellers had agreed to on the floor did not match those in subsequent documents. Overwhelmed by the task of sorting out the mess, some broker/dealers closed, leaving billions of securities unaccounted for. To stop the hemorrhaging, NYSE officials decided to close on Wednesdays so that firms could catch up on paperwork. To outside observers, the move was the first sign of trouble for the New York Stock Exchange. Meanwhile, inside the institution, another crisis was growing: The debate between officials and members about fixed commission rates would divide the Street.

When the New York Stock Exchange was established in 1792 the Buttonwood Tree Agreement detailed the rules of operation. A staple of this agreement was that all commissions received from trade executions were to be fixed and free from competition. Despite all the changes on Wall Street in the many years that followed, that rule was always strictly enforced. However, objections began to arise from the client side as institutions started to account for the majority of trading; the Big Board's unwillingness to adjust rates left firms open to threats from rival exchanges, also known as the *third market*. Funds were unhappy about the excessive costs of trading through a NYSE member firm. A trade for 100,000 shares of xyz stock cost 100 times more than a trade for 1,000 shares even though the difference in processing costs was relatively slight. To cut expenses, institutions began to execute their orders on other exchanges, and the NYSE began to lose market share. Despite these warning signs, member brokerages wanted to hold on to fixed commissions because they supported a financial Camelot. It was nearly impossible not to get rich with these rules. The fat fees helped to absorb mistakes and provided a safe haven in a declining market. Furthermore, it was simply tradition, a practice that had been in place for nearly two centuries. When NYSE President Robert Haack first mentioned the words "negotiated commissions" in a 1970 speech, many on the Street were outraged. These opposing views caused uneasiness in the industry and set the stage for a battle that was to continue for years. It was in this awkward, unstable climate that the first two black firms took their seats in 1971.

If stripped of social significance, the Street's first NYSE black firms barely registered on the map. All were extremely small businesses, with 20 or fewer employees and a few hundred thousand dollars in capital. Conversely, a top firm like Morgan Stanley had about $8 million. Other firms like Merrill Lynch were following Donaldson, Lufkin & Jenrette's lead into the capital markets and becoming publicly owned corporations. The differences between these thoroughbreds of capitalism and the nascent black firms extended beyond dollars and cents into the backrooms where cigars were smoked, handshakes were exchanged, and deals were made. The most obvious reason for this exclusion was race. There were virtually no African Americans in high positions in corporations or investment banks.

They had no presence in the world of prestigious and exclusive schools, clubs, and societies, all of which were woven together by a web of personal connections. Such contacts were instrumental in the way business was conducted and it was an area where African Americans did not participate. These connections did not extend to the South Side of Chicago where Bell grew up or 125th Street where First Harlem Securities sat.

But beyond the lack of ties, it is also important to remember that these black entrepreneurs were very young. At the time they purchased NYSE seats, Goings was 39, Daniels and Bell were in their early 30s, and Doley was only 26. Their inexperience left them without the connections to fill their Rolodexes. That would take time, making their present tasks even more daunting.

Daniels & Bell, Inc. and First Harlem Securities began their existence essentially doing the same business, executing buy and sell orders on the Exchange floor. As each struggled to get a foothold, like any business in its first year, the NYSE's fixed commissions system served as an umbrella to offset losses accrued while building other incoming revenue. "Fixed commissions allowed a lot of people to stay in business," says Earl Andrews, a vice president of First Harlem. "None of us at the time really understood what the Street was all about in financing sources and revenue streams. All we knew was that we received commissions for a trade. The actual nuances of the business we started to learn."[2] The firms' delayed entrance into the Exchange illustrated their dependence on these lucrative commissions and the uncertainty that surrounded the issue. Their membership was approved in the summer of 1970, but they became a part of the Exchange more than a year later. One of the developments that contributed to this delay was the Securities and Exchange Commission's proposal to institute some negotiated commissions. In an effort to end the controversy about this issue, the Securities and Exchange Commission (SEC) proposed a compromise in early 1971 that would allow negotiation for a portion of executed trades. Originally, the SEC proposed that orders as small as $100,000 be open to negotiation. If this initial judgment had come to fruition, First Harlem would have been just another unfulfilled business plan because they wouldn't have been able to compete. Rather than the approximately 40 cents a share they could receive under the existing structure, their returns would have been cut in half or worse making it impossible for the firm to survive. But by May of that year, the SEC decided to up the amount to $500,000, which hardly affected the Harlem office because few of their orders were that large.

First Harlem's early years were stamped with Goings's tough, demanding, often difficult personality. Although he had retired from professional football, his body still exuded the tough exterior of the profession. His broad shoulders and thick torso filled his business suits. Yet, he also wore black-rimmed eyeglasses that were an indication of his philosophical side. "Russell was, and still is, a very intellectual guy," says Clarence O. Smith, co-founder of *Essence* magazine. "He was extremely well read and grounded in history and philosophy."[3] In fact, an excerpt from a book called *Nature of Man* about the potential of man to push the boundaries of what is possible, beyond what is expected of him, served as a foundation for Goings. It was with these two different personas the he operated First Harlem.

"Russell had a football player's mentality," says Jim Greene. "Everybody he encountered was treated as if they were the opposing quarterback."[4] With the markets that surrounded Wall Street dwindling, it was a necessary attitude. For a black broker to fulfill the ambitions that Goings maintained, an almost irrational personality was essential because any rational businessperson would have concluded that a First Harlem could not be successful. Goings's hard-edged demeanor produced results. "A lot of the things that people say about Jesse Jackson breaking into the Fortune 500 accounts in the late 1990s Russ was doing 30 years earlier," Greene says.[5] However, the personal relationships between him and the rest of the firm were the casualties of this attitude. Often in those early years, employees would hide in the bathroom to escape a verbal lashing, warranted or not, only to hear the sound of a pounding fist banging the wall in the adjacent room—Goings's office. Because he had the most experience and brought in the majority of the business in those early years, people tolerated his style. That would not always be the case.

In the context of a rotten securities market, First Harlem Securities did well in those first few years. Their years as a Shearson Hammill branch served as a good foundation for their independent operation. Initially in 1968, the plan was for the branch to focus on the retail market. The original concept was two-sided: (1) to bring more African Americans into the securities industry and involve them in a business where monetary opportunities are limitless; (2) to get the broader community of Harlem invested in the stock market and in investments to improve their wealth and financial sophistication. Within days of the firm's opening, however, Goings scratched the idea and decided to concentrate on institutional business. In some part, it indicated the larger trend, especially with the fixed commissions system. The decision was also influenced by the mood of Harlem at the time. After the assassinations and riots, most people in Harlem did not put investing in the stock market high on their priority list.

While Goings was often out traveling on business, the body of the firm stayed behind to seek out a broader client base. Most of the salesmen had only been in the business for three years or less, and suddenly they were partners in a NYSE-member firm. While this fast track is remarkable, the majority of the employees were still raw in many aspects. The experiences at Shearson aided the group in their transition from employees to entrepreneurs. They spent this infancy stage working on smaller accounts while building their securities experience. "We were all given territories and accounts and we went out and made calls," says Andrews.[6] They acquired much of their business by approaching entities that had been ignored by Wall Street, unattractive mainstream funds, and black institutions. While a branch of Shearson Hammill, "we started calling a lot of the accounts that had fallen through the cracks," says Martin Everette. "We made many of their salesmen angry but that helped propel us."[7] They also had success with black accounts like Chicago's Supreme Life Insurance. So within a few years, First Harlem bolstered a wide range of diverse clients. They had secured business with most of the major funds and state pension funds, generally a small percentage of a few million dollars. With this mid- to lower-tier of clients, they were able to acquire larger shares of their overall funds. "We were rolling along pretty well," says Andrews.

The majority of their business was transaction oriented. While they also offered advice to their clients about market trends and securities that looked promising, they received most revenue from the execution of orders. All trades were called down to the floor of the Exchange where the firm's broker, Irvin W. Hanks, received the call and completed the order. Hanks, a Stanford Business School graduate, was the second black on the floor and the only minority at the time because Searles had left the year before (Daniels & Bell's broker, Raymond Forbes, was of Irish descent). He was First Harlem's second choice. The company had originally recruited Mitchell Johnson, a former football player. The group was ready to go with him on the floor until he received a call from legendary coach George Allen. Soon he was off playing for the Washington Redskins, and Hanks was on the floor only months after graduation. His early experience on the floor is representative of the group's first few years.

Those beginnings on the floor were educational as Hanks worked to learn the culture and language of the floor. While many have a general sense of the action that occurs on the Big Board, it cannot be fully appreciated until you are thrown into the mob firsthand. Traders talk at a codifying speed, using jargon that sounds foolish to most. It was the language and terms of his job that Hanks struggled with at first.

This feeling was widespread during those early years as the majority of partners struggled to polish their understanding of the business. This education could be costly, at the client's expense. In those first months on the floor, Hanks had trouble obtaining the best price for stocks, a problem for all rookies. "Usually when you're in a crowd, you ask how the market is," Hanks explained. "The guy tells you what's bid and what the offer is—a quarter or a half, or whatever, and the size, say five by ten [500 shares bid for at a price; 1,000 shares offered for sale slightly higher] then you make your bid or offer. In one instance I just hollered out the name of the stock and said 'buy three' and it turns out I bought it up $3/8$ of a point. But the commitment was made and that turns out to be the high for the day. It proceeded to drop a point and a half and I was a little disturbed."[8]

Soon, as he became more familiar with the institution and unwritten codes, those mistakes occurred less frequently. Once he completed the trades, First Harlem did not have to worry about the back-office crunch because it did not directly affect them. The brokerage cleared their trades through Shearson Hammill, agreeing to pay 22 percent of all commissions for this service. The practice was not uncommon among small firms because they did not have the capital or desire to set up the costly infrastructure. So the back-office crisis did not affect their backrooms, only the market in which they operated.

To diversify their business, First Harlem Securities also developed research products for institutional clients. Richard Simon learned and wrote reports about photography; Gwendolyn Luster specialized in the airline industry. These analyses were helpful in securing business, but there were occurrences when being black affected the weight that clients attached to the reports. William Day, now deceased, was then a vice president of First Harlem Securities and later recounted an experience some analysts had during a presentation to a major bank. "Our analyst, who really knew his stuff forward and backward, was stating our case. Suddenly, this vice president disappeared under his desk, tying his shoe or something, while our analyst was making his presentation—and we were taking about big bucks."[9]

On another occasion, the top brass of First Harlem traveled to a West Coast institution to pitch the firm's research capabilities. After reading the photography report written by Richard Simon, the executives were so impressed by its conclusions that they refused to believe that it was a First Harlem product. They accused the firm of copying it from another company in order to win business.

It was in these instances that the experience of black firms differed from other young firms trying to gather business. The treatment, or tone of the "no" they received was unlike rejections offered to other firms. Goings explained these obstacles as a "credibility gap with the institutions. They don't think good research ideas can be created at the corner of 125th Street and Seventh Avenue."[10] His conclusion was that "the assumption you have to draw from the institutions is that work from a black-controlled firm is inferior. Just how many times do you have to hit a home run to have people listen to what you have to say?"

Despite the frustration that he and his employees developed as a result of these instances, the early 1970s brought with it some success as a number of influential black-owned companies began sprouting, partly as a result of the work Goings had initiated while at Shearson Hammill. In 1968, Goings and A. Michael Victory, a top member of the large brokerage's management, began to hold meetings at its headquarters at 14 Wall Street. The purpose of these gatherings was to encourage, and possibly help, ambitious black businesspeople to form their own companies.

Around the same time that these meetings began forming, a young insurance salesman named Clarence Smith was sitting at his desk at Prudential Life Insurance Company. He was one of three black employees at the firm and doing fairly well. One of his black colleagues came over to him and asked Smith if he had heard about these meetings taking place on Wall Street. "They were inviting black middle management executives and entrepreneur types to come down and talk about ways to get blacks into business," says Smith. "As mundane as that sounds now, at that time, that was incredible news because one of the things that was keeping blacks from starting their own businesses was a lack of access to venture capital resources."[11] Banks, venture capitalists, or other lending financial institutions did not give adequate funding to black businessmen and women. In fact, there was a feeling that they would give less than what was required, or just enough to fail. Intrigued by the idea, Smith decided to attend and satisfy his curiosity.

Upon entering the designated room at 14 Wall Street, Smith stepped into history. Among those who would also come through this room at one point or another were Byron Lewis, founder of the UniWorld Group, and Earl G. Graves, founder of *Black Enterprise* magazine. The meeting was comprised of all men, no women were present. The proposition put forth to the young men was that if they could present both a viable idea and business plan, Shearson would examine the strategy and assemble venture capital groups for them. Under no circumstances would the large brokerage participate as an investor, only act as a middleman to find the necessary capital. Once the terms had been laid out, the meeting turned into an interactive session where the men were allowed to share their ideas. Through the course of the discussion, a young man named Jonathon Blount stood up and shared that his mother often complained that there was no magazine catering to the interest and needs of black women. Both Smith and another attendee named Cecil Hollingsworth agreed. After another Shearson meeting some time later, Edward Lewis joined the group and *Essence* magazine was born in May 1970. Although, Shearson did not put money into the venture, Smith believes that Goings was a co-founder of the magazine, although not literally but "in a paternalistic sort of way. He did do a remarkable job leveraging Shearson Hammill's wide reputation and credibility to the service of black entrepreneurs who were getting started in those days," Smith says. "He felt that there was an opportunity for huge institutions like Shearson to help cure the traditional and historic obstacles. It wasn't going to cost them anything because they were not putting any money in. He simply said 'let's use our office to showcase these guys' and that is his great contribution."[12]

Despite such setbacks, First Harlem Securities was off to a nice start, especially when compared with its fellow black member firm.

Daniels & Bell began its journey down Wall Street disoriented and soon rethinking its business. They were quickly given a lesson about the impact, or lack of it, that their race would have on winning business. Within the firm's first few months, they had awakened from a foolish utopianism about the Street's social conscience and were soon scrambling to save themselves. Not too far into its life, Daniels & Bell faced the sobering reality that the firm did not resemble anything close to what they wanted it to be.

Some of the problems Daniels & Bell encountered in its first year were typical of any start-up, especially in the context of the 1971 economic atmosphere. "The first years of business are very similar to the early stages of a child's development," recalled Daniels. "When you're in the development stages, you have no credibility."[13] Often, a salesman would call a potential client, and state the firm he was representing–"Daniels & Bell"–only to be asked, "Who?"

Because the firm had no track record, their sales pitch had as much to do with their position as the first black member firm, as it did with strategy and potential performance. While many prospective clients were sympathetic and occasionally admired Daniels & Bell's efforts, few were willing to do business solely because of their conscience. "One woman actually cried and said she'd really like to do business with us, but she couldn't because she needed research and we didn't have it," remembered Daniels.[14]

The partners overestimated the impact of their social significance. In the firm's first few months, they believed that being a historic firm would attract accounts immediately, but that assumption was soon exposed as false. "At the beginning we did come in thinking we'd get some help the first year or two but that ended after two months,"[15] Bell said. Many of these accounts withdrew for financial reasons. The rotten economics of the Street had eaten away the profits of investment banks, leaving them with no business to spare. Other accounts that had thrown themselves at the firm after its well-publicized entrance into the NYSE, left as the spotlight dimmed. Within the first two months, 75 percent of those specific accounts had withdrawn. "Everybody was sympathetic except the landlord. He wanted his rent every month. If we had time, we would have been ahead of where we are today but we wouldn't be as smart."[16]

While having the title "first black-owned member firm of the New York Stock Exchange" did not secure business, it was helpful in getting access. "Being black gets you in but it won't keep you in," Daniels said. "In an initial presentation we can almost always get to the president." In these early days, it was usually Daniels who made the presentations utilizing the experience he had perfected over his career as an institutional salesman. "Willie was the best pure salesman I have ever seen," says Harold Doley.[17] Many describe him as the type of person who could walk into a room full of strangers and leave it with a hundred friends. He was a smooth, tactful, good-humored man who could seem relaxed but he always kept an eye on what he wanted. Baunita Greer, who worked for both Daniels and Bell later in their careers, says, "Willie was just a natural salesman. He could sit you down and sell you the Brooklyn Bridge if he had you long enough."[18]

In those early years, Bell spent much of his time in the office using the lessons he learned in operations end at Dempsey Tegeler to run the office and deal with the regulators. As their respective roles began to take shape so, too, did their new strategy. After they had awakened from the dream of immediate prosperity, they raced to refocus and shift Daniels & Bell's structure. "We had to decide to be a business instead of a brokerage firm," Bell said. "We thought we were in the give-me stage but we weren't. We had to give up merchandise that customers would want."[19] The firm developed research products to lure new institutional clients and add value to existing relationships.

They also decided to improve the execution of trades in terms of speed and price. In early 1973, the firm purchased another New York Stock Exchange seat for $170,000. They hired Frank Quintana, a former Salomon Brothers trader, to work on the floor making him the first Puerto Rican member of the Big Board. In the overall picture, it did not put the firm into Herculean status (Merrill Lynch owned 18 seats), but it did increase transaction-oriented revenue. By dividing the area on the floor, the two traders could more quickly execute a client's order with a particular specialist. It also enabled the firm to take on more orders from other firms, the role of a two-dollar broker. Brown Brothers Harriman was the most helpful in steering business their way. But, that wasn't much comfort as volume dried up and the biggest investment of the brokerage, their seats, plummeted in value. To put the gloom in perspective, the seat that Doley bought, which was sponsored by Bell and Quintana, was worth slightly more than half the purchase price Daniels & Bell paid for their second membership five months earlier.

The drop in volume in the securities markets was the principal reason for Doley's decision to create a brokerage firm. After working on the floor for about a year as a two-dollar broker, he decided to retreat back to New Orleans and create what would eventually become Doley Securities. To put it simply, being a two-dollar broker limited one's opportunities, and Doley sought room to operate. Such a broker can only do business with other members, essentially executing their orders if they are overburdened with tasks. If activity is slow, the chances of getting business drop as well, making it difficult to survive. "It was a frustrating time," he recalled. "Spiro Agnew resigned and Watergate was in motion. The Arab oil crisis and inflation really dried up volume." The turmoil on the floor left a void in many of its traders, who lived hard, fast lives that often depended on the thrill of making money. "There were these guys who used to bet each day what time this really attractive woman came out of the subway. Other times they would hold competitions to see who could hit the ceiling with a piece of paper. They turned this into a sophisticated operation."[20] Despite the entertainment value from these activities, the proverbial writing was on the wall. The bottom line was all too obvious: Business was bad.

Doley's decision to build a brokerage was based on two essential factors. The first was the financial circumstances. Two-dollar brokers can only do business with other members or member firms of the New York Stock Exchange. With a brokerage firm, Doley would be able to do business with the public as he did while a stockbroker with Bache. Second, the Bache personality test that had goaded him into buying the seat was correct in its assessment. He did not like the commotion on the floor, preferring to watch the action from afar. So he set up shop, renting office space in the Bache regional branch of New Orleans. When he began this operation, he was working as a sole proprietorship named Harold E. Doley, Member of the New York Stock Exchange. In 1975, Doley Securities was born and soon incorporated and a year later became the third black-owned NYSE member firm. He spent that year fulfilling the necessary requirements to become a member firm such as upholding a high level of professionalism and meeting certain financial standards (all capital must be unencumbered—assets without any claims against them).

When it began, Doley Securities was probably the smallest member brokerage of the New York Stock Exchange. It began essentially as a two-man operation, with Doley stationed in New Orleans and James Kelly executing the orders on the floor in New York. From these small beginnings, Doley planned to grow his operation into other major cities like

Chicago and Atlanta by renting office space in the Bache offices in those cities, as he had done in his hometown. But when the regional manager with whom he had negotiated his deal left for employment elsewhere, Doley scratched those plans. From then on, his securities firm would take on a compact model, seeking only selective opportunities. Instead, Doley expanded into other businesses such as commercial real estate. He purchased an office building and moved his headquarters there. As for his securities business, he handled black institutional accounts like North Carolina Mutual and Golden State Mutual, as well as mainstream accounts including a handful of New York City banks.

All three black firms had basically the same client base makeup of small portions of big funds combined with smaller, less recognized institutions. Surprisingly, although they often had trouble convincing potential white clients about the value of doing business with their firms, they had similar troubles with black institutions. Daniels & Bell approached these accounts with cautious optimism in their first year. "Early in the century, there were actually more black banks than there are now," Bell said. "But a lot of them went broke and black people just didn't want to trust anybody with their money. That's gone on now for a long time, but we're beginning to break it down."[21] A few years later, they had not made much progress, and their cautious optimism had been replaced with sadness. "We've stood on our heads, we've offered services," Bell said in 1976. "We've done about as much as we can do. It (the money) cannot be wrestled away. The attitude of blacks in this country has been 'don't encourage the investment dollars of blacks.' "[22]

An institutional salesman working at a white-owned firm at the time says, "at that time, because there were so few minorities in business, some of our institutions were the toughest business to get. Being black and trying to do business with a black institution was harder than working with a majority-owned firm. There was a lot of distrust."[23]

As the firms struggled with these problems, larger economic issues were still threatening the industry's vitality. The changing economics forced all brokerages to make decisions that soured many relationships and created conflicts that were not drawn along class or race lines, but were based simply in business. Morgan Stanley suffered a shakeup, and so did these black investment banks. By the end of 1976, they emerged different in structure, strategy, and personnel.

The end of fixed commissions on May 1, 1975, caused panic and uncertainty throughout Wall Street. The event drew so much anticipation of impending doom that Bob Baldwin of Morgan Stanley gave it the nickname Mayday. The signal of a crew in distress, it signified his prediction that 150 to 200 brokerages would go out of business as a result of the rule. Rumors spread throughout the Street that Merrill Lynch, the top investment bank, would give up its membership of nearly 20 seats. As the date approached, many were exhausting their contacts to try to gauge what rates their competitors were going to charge. However, for all the preparation that some labored through, nobody had any real idea what was going to happen.

When May 1 arrived, as the clock ticked down toward the opening bell, Wall Street sweated with nervousness. Minutes after the open, brokerages began to hear that competitors were lowering rates, and in response, they lowered rates as well. Many less familiar firms were offering discounts to clients to lure their orders and increase market share. One company that did this was Charles Schwab, now an international powerhouse. They created the term *discount brokerage*. Rates fell from about 40 cents to 2 to 4 cents a share by the turn of the twenty-first century. The impact of this drastic drop was significant. Member firms had lost a solid revenue stream that brought in substantial money. Executing the same trades now brought in 10 percent of the cash that it had in the past. Firms that had depended on revenues from these trade commissions needed to operate with fewer dollars flowing in. Unprofitable businesses and excess employees were no longer tolerable, and firms everywhere were seeking new direction. The large securities companies such as Merrill Lynch and Lehman Brothers could diversify and build many other revenue streams (for example, asset management and mergers and acquisitions).

Smaller brokerages faced bigger obstacles. Because they only maintained a few hundred thousand dollars or less in capital, they had to make selective decisions about how to use their resources. They were forced to focus on a few areas and could not make the mistakes that larger firms could absorb. Imagine the pressure that these tiny NYSE member companies were feeling. The returns received from their main business were cut by 90 percent. Their biggest investments, seats on the New York Stock Exchange, had plunged hundreds of thousands of dollars in value in just a few years. The American economy was infested with uncertainty produced by Watergate, the Arab oil crisis, and soaring 12 percent interest rates. The unemployment rate was 10 percent as well. With all the commotion came inevitable disagreement between partners throughout Wall Street about where to take their respective firms and how to dig out of existing holes. The severity of these differences undermined the upper management of the Street's first two black firms.

At Daniels & Bell, the two main partners began to butt heads more and more, day by day, as the challenges grew. While Daniels was out selling the firm's capabilities to all who would listen, Bell's hard-edged, tough-minded, difficult personality began to dominate the office. Many describe him as a man who was smart and had a great work ethic, but who also was set in his ways with a need to control. "Travers was a down-to-earth person, but when it came to business he would just sit back, observe you, and give you a look that would scare you to death," says Baunita Greer.[24] Bell's Chicago-bred style, watch-your-back attitude was causing trouble at headquarters. When asked in a 1984 interview about his background, Bell acknowledged that his attitude caused some friction with those he dealt with, but he made no apologies. "You have to literally be willing to bite somebody's ear and chew it up to survive and I think I've done that from time to time."[25] But a casualty of this attitude was his partnership with Daniels. It was increasingly apparent that Bell's business activities were veering from Daniels's vision, an unhealthy development. "Travers had a reputation for being a pretty tough guy," says Howard Mackey, who in 1974 was president of Equico, the largest Minority Enterprise Small Business Investment Company (MESBIC) at the time. "A lot of people did not like Travers because he was such a tough guy. He was extremely shrewd as a businessman and unfortunately that has to happen to survive."[26]

In 1974, with impending doom paralyzing the securities industry, Bell made a move to diversify his business beyond Wall Street to help guard against the declining cyclical nature of stocks and bonds. The action would not only ensure the survival of Daniels & Bell but would allow it to grow. It would also serve as the ax in the business relationship between Daniels and Bell. Bell had formed a holding company named the DanBell Group that was run by Tom Bourelly, a University of Chicago graduate. Bourelly had worked under Ben Heinsman, who built Northwest Industries into one of the forerunners of the conglomerate genre. Conglomerates were becoming increasingly popular companies built on the acquisitions of unrelated business. A prime example today is General Electric, which is involved in everything from light-bulbs to the NBC Network.

The DanBell Group had heard about a company in Brooklyn named Cocoline Chocolate. The company took in $4.5 million in revenue, earning $680,000 in pretax profit. After much negotiation, the two parties agreed on a price of $1.3 million for Cocoline. DanBell got $150,000 from two MESBICs, Mackey's Equico and Pioneer Capital Corporation, the same firm that helped Daniels & Bell finance their NYSE seat. The remaining balance was supplied by Citibank in $1 million of senior debt. The respective loans were guaranteed using Cocoline itself as collateral, and the plan was to meet each payment using the company's cash. This setup later became widely known as a *leveraged buyout* and was one of the first ever pulled off by African Americans. Not only were the buyers and investors black but the legal work was done by a young, ambitious, little-known black lawyer named Reginald F. Lewis. The company itself was an integral part of Bell's plan as Cocoline debuted on the 1976 Black Enterprise 100 list as the twenty-second largest black-owned company in America. "It helped to finance a somewhat fledging investment banking firm because Wall Street was extremely difficult at that time," says Mackey. "Cocoline represented a good strategy."

Another beneficial strategy was giving Len Halpert, the previous owner of the company, 10 percent of the equity to keep him involved and running the business. After the deal was completed and the future suddenly brighter, the DanBell Group raised their arms in euphoria. However, one obvious element was missing from the transaction—Daniels. Having an asset as valuable as Cocoline in the hands of one partner gave Bell a tremendous edge. Beyond business, Daniels felt left out, and to some degree cheated out of the opportunity to own the company. In 1974, only three years after co-founding the firm,

Daniels left Daniels & Bell, leaving Bell as majority owner. He went on to form Daniels & Cartwright with former Bache salesman Jim Cartwright. Later he went solo in another small brokerage called United Daniels Securities that specialized in trading and research.

Shakeups were also occurring at First Harlem Securities. The factions in the uptown office developed because of several problems. The first originated in the tension between the head and body of the firm, a relationship that became fraught with personal and financial displeasure. Employees began to take exception to Goings's domineering personality. "People were really starting to have problems with him," says Earl Andrews. "A number of people had left and I personally felt like I was being held back so I left."[27] Because Goings was the most experienced and the firm's greatest producer in First Harlem's early years, his style was readily accepted when many of the firm's brokers were in the learning stages. Their feelings changed as they grew more comfortable with the business and their own talents. They were no longer willing to accept what many felt was unfair treatment. What deepened the wounds were the increasing opportunities for African Americans in the Street's major firms by the mid-1970s. "As the people got opportunities, they took advantage of them because there was a real demand for young accomplished black professionals because they were so few and far between in those days," says Duke Chapman. "When it frayed, I thought it was a sad event."[28]

The first real blow to the firm was the defection of several of its brokers to other firms. Jim Greene, the firm's original number two man, left in 1970 before it became First Harlem Securities, returned and left again, and landed a job at PaineWebber. Gwendolyn Luster, an analyst, left to join New York's Chemical Bank. Richard Simon, another research analyst, left and eventually settled at Goldman Sachs where he became a partner in the late 1990s. Andrews left to go to Bear

Stearns where he became its first African American on the trading floor. "At Bear Stearns I got a chance to see how major firms worked and what a big trading room was like," he says. "There were a couple of hundred people, open phone lines, big blocks of stock traded. You saw what a minority firm, which was real small, was trying to achieve. But, that would take time and capital."[29]

Time and capital were two things that First Harlem did not have. "1975, Mayday, was a revolution in the industry and I think that had a lot to do with our business disagreements. We had a disagreement and Russ lost," says Eubanks.[30] Goings held 40 percent of the voting stock with the balance distributed between employees and outside investors. Embittered by the experience, Goings left the business for good in 1978. His exit was sad and ungraceful; one can't help but admire him and weep at what happened. Goings's talent and drive had created quite an institution, yet he did not have the chance to see it to the end. Goings was one of the greatest financiers that never was.

As First Harlem drowned in its inner turmoil and loss of talent, its business suffered. In contrast to Daniels & Bell, which made a relatively smooth transition of power and turned in a very small profit for the rest of the decade, First Harlem lost approximately $320,000 in the two years after the departure of Goings. As people departed, not only did the firm lose the business they brought in, but it took time and money just to get replacements up to the same level. So rather than risk resources that the bleeding bottom line made even more precious in 1978, the top executives of the firm, Mel Eubanks and William C. Day, decided to keep the operation very small. They focused on advising and trading for their accounts, almost all of which were institutional. They also came up with research products for their clients about broad issues such as studies for Lesotho, an African nation, as well as traditional industry reports. Probably the most symbolic gesture of this new attitude was the decision in 1978 to move the company out of Harlem to 32 Broadway, in the downtown area. Because most securities firms operated in the vicinity at the time, the move made sense, and its presence in Harlem did not have the social impact that had existed in 1969. By the 1980s, First Harlem Securities had paid off all its financial obligations except for its biggest loan, $390,000 borrowed from Chemical Bank in 1974. With the deficit looming over their heads, they decided to sell the seat and use the proceeds to pay off the debt. In March 1983, First Harlem Securities ceased to be a member of the New York Stock Exchange.

The end of First Harlem's participation on the New York Stock Exchange, the shakeup at Daniels & Bell, and general industry turmoil rocked these firms to their very foundations. With such despair, they were looking for any business area that would provide opportunities and profits. Just as they were battling the recession, a dramatic change in the politics of America would change the client side, and consequently, the business overall.

5

RISING IN THE RANKS

COMPARING THE NOMINEES FOR MAYOR OF THE city of Atlanta in 1973 allowed the observer to predict the coming change. The incumbent was Sam Massell who had served in office for one term before this showdown. His height was 5 feet 6 inches, and he weighed 150 pounds. His opponent, Maynard Jackson, stood 6 feet 5 inches and weighed 300 pounds. And as the votes were counted that October night, it was official—the city would forever be different.

Maynard Jackson's election was historic: He became the first black mayor of a major southern city. His election signaled an aggregate black political movement in the city; its council was in the power of African Americans as was its congressional seat, which was held by civil rights legend Andrew Young.

Changes came to the government not only in colors, but in policy. The new mayor who sought to improve the conditions that minorities faced in his city led this drive. This initiative centered around a few key principles that Jackson would use as a foundation for his entire political life. "[African Americans] have the tools by which we can extricate ourselves from the dungeon of deprivation" says Jackson. "The three Bs. The ballot being our vote. The buck being our money. And the book being our education. So if the blacks in power who move money simply practiced equal opportunity, billion-dollar black-owned firms would no longer be news."[1] While those economic initiatives would eventually face great resistance, Jackson's background proved that he was more than capable of winning such fights.

He entered Morehouse College at the age of 14 thanks to a Ford Foundation Early Admissions Scholarship. After majoring in political science, he graduated in 1956 at an age when his peers were just entering college. Uncertain about what he wanted to do during these postcollege years, Jackson held several jobs including a position as an encyclopedia salesman. Although he would soon leave these humble beginnings for law school, the job provided experience that would help African Americans on Wall Street—a decade later he would need to use all his selling skills, not for books, but for social change. He graduated from North Carolina Central University in 1964 and then worked as a lawyer in Atlanta for three years. Then came 1968.

That year changed Maynard Jackson's life. However, unlike many who were crippled by sadness, he was able to draw inspiration from the tragedies. The death of Martin Luther King Jr., coupled with the birth of his first child on April 8, the day of King's funeral, inspired him to go into public service. The loss of the leader exposed the extremes of injustice in those troubled times; the birth of his daughter led him to wonder about the uncertain future of America. If things were going to change, he wanted not only to be a part of it, but to help lead it.

If Dr. King's death inspired him to plan an entrance into politics, the assassination of Senator Robert Kennedy a few months later propelled him into the profession. Within days, Jackson left private life behind and announced his candidacy for the United States Senate. His decision was bold but unsuccessful. The incumbent senator, Herman Talmadge, had steadfast political power. Previously, he had served as governor of Georgia like his father before him and, up until that point, had never had any serious challenge. While the race was not close (Jackson lost by a 3 to 1 margin), the young campaign showed great promise. He won thousands more white votes than the pundits had anticipated, fueling him to launch a campaign for city government in 1969.

After he was elected to vice mayor that year, the general feeling in Atlanta was that this was merely a stepping-stone to greater aspirations. On March 23, 1973, Maynard Jackson announced that he was officially seeking to become Atlanta's first black mayor.

It was a crowded field. More than 10 people set their sights on the office, but two leaders soon emerged: Sam Massell, the incumbent (who in 1969 had been elected the city's first Jewish mayor), and Maynard Jackson. Those feelings would be confirmed on election day when they emerged as the top two vote getters, sparking a runoff election.

This special contest inevitably generated questions and issues revolving around race. How could it not, with all the tension and mistrust that permeated those times? As words like *racist, white,* and *black* were thrown about in the campaign discourse, and adjectives like *bitter* were used by newspapers to describe the contest, issues soon emerged. And after each stated their case for the last time, the voters went to the polls and issued their final judgment. The results: 74,404 votes to 51,237, with Maynard Jackson as the winner.

The realization of this historic moment for the city was accompanied by extreme feelings coming from both sides of the political fence. With the anticipation building up to this historic breakthrough came unrealistic ambitions from blacks and trepidation from whites. "When I became mayor, I had to deal with exaggerated black expectations and exaggerated white anxiety," says Jackson. "Therefore, everything took a great deal of effort, strategizing, and shoring up because I was the first black mayor [of Atlanta]."[2]

This was not the first time that an African American captured a mayoral office. Carl Stokes in Cleveland, Ohio, and Richard Hatcher of Gary, Indiana, were both elected in 1969. The post–Civil Rights movement expanded in 1973 with the election of Jackson and others including Tom Bradley in Los Angeles. Marion Barry was elected in Washington, D.C., in 1979. Within this large shift, Maynard Jackson was the architect in the maximization of political influence for economic equality. It was he who initiated far-reaching policies that would affect not only his constituency, but Wall Street as well.

In the securities industry, there are always at least two sides to a deal. For someone to buy something, another party must sell it and vice versa. Up until this point, the fight for economic equality on Wall Street came through the business side. What Jackson did was push from the client side to close the economic disparity. His policies and work set a precedent for municipalities in how to orchestrate the financial affairs of their respective governments.

As the new black power structure in Atlanta took their seats in early 1974, the task before them was difficult. Although they had the momentum and support of the majority of the people for their issues, instituting the changes they wanted would face great resistance. Their opponents in this crusade were embedded in the roots and relationships that had driven the city's strength for decades.

At the forefront of the new mayor's agenda was economic equality. Quickly into his first term, Jackson set out an ambitious plan to provide more opportunities to those qualified African Americans. The result of these desires was a Minority Business Enterprise program (MBE) which set a goal that 25 percent of all city contracts were to include minorities. "We did not have any preferences or set any quotas," says Jackson. "Our whole thing was that involvement should be 'not less than,' those were the key words. The goal was a floor not a ceiling."[3] The program was a model that would soon be followed throughout the country. However, at the time of its initiation, it was such a bold move, some even called it radical, that resistance was inevitable. Those who had dominated the various businesses for so long were not happy that others were about to intrude on the profits they were used to garnering. With these polarizing agendas, a fight was to come. The showdown took place at Atlanta's Hartsfield Airport.

To travelers, the airport represented nothing more than the place to begin, continue, or end an adventure. But to Jackson and his followers and the business establishment that was forming against him, it represented the future of business in the city. Hauntingly symbolic, in some ways it represented a grand ideal for the growth of African American economic power. If minorities were to compete with equal opportunity, if the sky indeed was to be the limit, significant changes were needed at the foundation, where the impediments were rooted.

The showdown came as a result of a planned expansion for the airport. For years, the city had been wrangling over economic issues and just how to address the overwhelming need to update the airport infrastructure. The debate was between those who wanted to expand the current facility and those who sought to build a separate and completely new airport. After it was decided to finance construction to expand the existing structure, the city's businesspeople lined up in their usual spots to get ready to work and cash in as they always had.

But, Maynard Jackson put a stop to such assumptions. No longer would generations of businesspeople receive such rewards without first having to answer for their practices.

Jackson had been inspired by Robert Kennedy and Martin Luther King Jr., to run for office and make a difference; he did not intend to sit back now that he held power and let things continue as they had for years. So Jackson halted the construction on the airport until the participating white firms, the contractors, architects, and engineers were ready to abide by the rules of his new minority enterprise program.

This policy was not received well. Opponents leveled charges of blackmail, extortion, and so on to describe the new mayor's insistence. They were the qualified firms and viewed the hiring of African Americans as beneath them because they were unqualified; some even argued that such inclusion would force losses on their companies. The airlines themselves were upset because they were to pay a portion of the financing costs. The 1970s were years of economic inconsistency, when inflation would skyrocket up and down, taking with it consumer confidence and just about every other important economic factor. Airlines were worried that the longer the delay, the greater the chance of more costs.

Jackson shrugged off all criticism in the name of the greater good. He insisted that this was not a charity, that African Americans would not be guaranteed business simply because of their color. Instead, he emphasized that these measures were to provide opportunities to qualified and talented individuals who because of social factors had never been given a chance. "Just to be black will not cut it," he said to *Business Week* at the time. "A firm must be qualified to compete for business. We're just going to make sure the door is open to that competition."[4] Although many of the people he was asking to give African Americans a chance could not care less, the mayor believed such feelings would pass. Whatever problems or economic implications came as a result of his decision would be negated in the long term by an inclusive and economically equal environment.

Gradually the barriers of disagreement began to break down, and the idea of white and black firms working together became less taboo. Both sides agreed to go forward. Then, with the issuing of municipal bonds, the government had to account for another area of competition, not in Atlanta, but New York. It was in this offering that Jackson set the tone and demonstrated the power that African Americans could use to push for change on Wall Street from the client side.

A story that has traveled around the African American financial circle illustrates the impact that black political power had on the industry years after Hartsfield:

As the legend goes, a group of three men representing an investment bank showed up at a city official's office to pitch their capabilities. Word had gotten out that like other municipal governments, this one sought to include minorities in all matters relating to its business.

When the men arrived, the treasurer sitting at his desk was shocked. The group was diverse, two were white and one black. In all the years the two sides had done business, the investment bank had never been known as a proponent for diversity. Yet all of a sudden, here they were, a splendid mix of racial harmony.

As the parties sat down to discuss the particulars of the deal, the black man sat quietly. The only indication of his existence came from an occasional sip from his glass of water.

Once the presentation was over, the treasurer was compelled to satisfy his curiosity.

He turned to the black man and asked:

"How long have you worked with the firm?"

"Over 30 years," he replied.

Stunned because he had never heard or seen him, the treasurer probed for further information.

"How come I have never heard of you before?"

"I don't know. I turned up for work and my boss just told me to put on this suit."

It was later learned that the man was a janitor.

123

This whimsical tale highlights a serious turning point for African Americans on Wall Street. Black political power had a profound impact on the way many deals were done. For the first time, pigmentation was not an obstacle to getting business; rather, it added value. Opportunities opened in the banking area that had never been there before, even for the most qualified African Americans. When the promise of high finance began to take hold among the educated, participation grew as did the numbers.

The post–Civil Rights era was the next phase for African Americans working in the Street's major firms. Two groups were always at odds with each other, the bankers and the brokers. Stockbrokers were often deemed as streetwise and second class, whereas investment bankers were the elite highbrows of the workforce. The bankers maintained a rarified air; after all, theirs was the profession of J.P. Morgan. Traditionally, African Americans had been excluded.

That would change in the 1970s. "There were two waves," explains Mel Eubanks. "The first wave wanted to be brokers and we came from all walks of life. The second wave came from the b-schools and wanted to be bankers."[5] For several reasons, that initial move would primarily be in the area of public finance.

The most obvious was the growing number of black officials who demanded equal participation in their city's business. One of the most dependable and instrumental homes for social equality has been the state of Connecticut, which would not be the first place to come to mind in terms of diversity. Yet since the 1970s, it has consistently demonstrated a commitment to diversity regarding fiscal policy thanks to four black state treasurers, Henry E. Parker, Francisco Borges, Joseph Suggs, and Denise Nappier. Without question, Parker was the pioneer becoming Connecticut's first black statewide elected official in 1974. His decision to run for state treasurer came after two close, but unsuccessful runs for mayor of New Haven. After such a showing, the state's Democratic Party approached Hank Parker with a proposition. "The Chairman of the party asked if I had ever thought of running for State Treasurer," he says. "The population at that time of African Americans was 8 percent. If I had tried to run for it, I would not have gotten it. I was promised that if I could get the African Americans' vote supporting me, I would be running with the support of the state Democratic Party. All of that happened and we won the nomination."[6] As part of the Ella Grasso ticket, the first woman to govern the state, Parker won and became the Connecticut State Treasurer.

The responsibilities he inherited were heavy, but held potential for more power to make social as well as fiscal changes. So great was this promise, and Parker's ability to fulfill it, that 1975 would be the first year in a run of more than a decade that he would be named to *Ebony*'s annual 100 Most Important Blacks list. To earn that reward, Parker worked hard to strengthen his financial acumen. His background somewhat prepared him for the job at hand. He and his wife operated a nursing school and handled its financial matters. He also served on the board of the Connecticut Savings Bank and as a member of the New Haven Chamber of Commerce. Yet, he felt the need to learn more because he "was without the necessary training to be Treasurer." Every day until his inauguration, Parker made an effort to go to the office so that he could orient himself.

Upon entering office, Parker knew that he was in a special position where the proper exercising of influence would garner tremendous results. In addition, almost fittingly, most African Americans who aspired to work on Wall Street grew up in the Civil Rights era with a reservoir of political sophistication and experience. "Each elected official has to use their influence to make things happen," he said. "The State Treasurer of Connecticut is the most powerful person with statutory responsibilities other than the Governor!" Parker was in charge of a $800 million pension fund and all the cash management. He was now a member of the Connecticut Developmental Authority, which was the business arm of the state for all corporations that wanted to do business within the perimeters. That plus the bond commission, the bank commission, and other Authorities gave Parker access to a wide range of financial responsibilities.

Such power allowed Parker to alter the way business was done in his state. Just as he allowed minority-owned firms to do business, he also helped to persuade bigger firms to create a seat at the table. "I got involved with investment banking firms when we were interviewing 20 to 30. I told them that I want everybody to understand, and word got around, if you are going to Connecticut and I see you have a lot of staff, how come I see no minorities on your staff? I asked that tough question. Finally, nobody came to see me without an African American on their staff. Whether they said anything was a different story but the firms soon got the message that if you are doing business with Connecticut, you have to be fair."

The importance of people like Hank Parker, Maynard Jackson, Marion Barry, Coleman Young, Harold Washington, Willie Brown, and others is more than their procurement of power. What made these political pioneers so significant was their ability to understand the creative use of power. Unfortunately, there have been African Americans in positions of authority who did not use their reach to force change. Public servants like Maynard Jackson and Coleman Young understood that although politics can be a defensive game, in the sense that one tries to avoid making public mistakes, one must also find balance and take chances to correct existing inequalities, despite whatever risk that may entail. These men understood that the correct application of political power can institute substantive reform. Among the many who were forced to adjust to these calls for change were Wall Street's municipal departments.

"Towards the end of the seventies, concurrently with the rise of African Americans on the political side, it became the right thing to do as well as make good business sense," says Gedale Horowitz, then head of Salomon Brothers' municipal department.[7] "In certain parts of the country, there was a push and it soon became standard operating procedure that African Americans were to be a part of these deals, particularly at the management level," remembers David Clapp, who led Goldman Sachs' muni-department.[8] As a result, investment banking opportunities opened up.

In addition to political power, the perception of public finance opened up opportunities for African Americans. It was not as if all investment bankers were viewed the same. Within the context of the industry as a whole, public finance was perceived as unattractive and a second choice. After all, corporate bankers got to work with American icons like IBM and Ford Motor. Municipal bankers were relegated to working with politicians and at times lowly city public servants. "The industry was pretty much the backwater of the securities business," says Horowitz, who led his department for more than a decade. "Corporate equities were the big thing. It [municipal finance] did not necessarily get the most interest and it was the least profitable business."[9]

The barriers to entry were lower, but that did not mean it was easy. This movement was no tidal wave; it was more like a ripple in the ocean. An informal survey produced a count of no more than 10 African American investment bankers before 1980.

∞

One of the first on the scene was Theodore Martin Alexander Jr. who, like his father, had the nickname "T. M." His father was a pioneering businessman and an Atlanta legend. In 1931, he created Alexander & Company, an Atlanta insurance firm that eventually became the oldest black firm in the city and one of the most successful. So synonymous with the industry would he become that he was often referred to as "Mr. Insurance."

T. M. graduated from Morehouse with a degree in economics and New York University with an MBA, and then began a career that would be a mix of real estate, finance, and banking. After a stint in commercial banking with Chase Manhattan Bank and Dun & Bradstreet in the 1950s, Alexander packed up and moved back to his hometown.

In these familiar surroundings, Alexander withdrew from the commercial banking of New York City and established himself in areas with greater promise. After leading Alexander & Associates Real Estate for eight years, Alexander became the first investment banker for a small firm called Courts & Company.

In 1974, T. M. entered public service after being appointed by the president of the United States as the regional administrator for the U.S. Department of Housing and Urban Development. He also headed the Atlanta Development Corporation when the racial policies of Maynard Jackson were changing the economic dynamic of the city and the country. Alexander went back to investment banking in 1979 as a first vice president of public finance national accounts with E. F. Hutton.

Alexander's presence on Wall Street was important not only because he was one of the first African Americans but also because he took time out to teach and influence younger, budding black financiers. "T. M. Alexander was my mentor," says Napoleon Brandford, a banker who would later achieve fame with Grigsby Brandford. "I consider him the number one business development investment banker in the history of public finance. He knew everyone, black and white. His whole life was geared around making the proper introduction for his firm."[10] So great was his reach, that he soon acquired the nickname "The Black Tornado," if T. M. Alexander came to town, he would leave with the business.

A great deal of Alexander's success resulted from his ability to network. He had ties to people ranging from his old chums in the Nixon administration to childhood classmates like David Rockefeller. The black book he carried everywhere contained more information than the traditional names and phone numbers. It also included hobbies, birthdays, and other information that he thought might come in handy.

Never was this more evident than in a deal he orchestrated with the support of a new player at the firm, Bernard B. Beal, who joined E. F. Hutton in 1980. Alexander had his eye on business in Atlantic City, New Jersey.

"I have arranged a meeting in Kansas City, Missouri, with people from Detroit, Chicago, Washington, D.C., and Alabama there," Alexander said to his young associate.

"Nobody from Atlantic City?" Beal asked in disbelief.

"No, we don't need anybody from there," Alexander replied.

The pair traveled to Missouri to attend the dinner. It was a simple gathering, full of pleasant chit chat, but not much substance. A week later, Alexander told Beal to get ready for a short trip to Trenton, New Jersey.

"Well, when are we going to Atlantic City?" Beal asked again.

"We don't have to go there. This deal is done!" he exclaimed as he winked at Beal. Sure enough, E. F. Hutton got the business. "To this day, I still don't know how he pulled it together," says Beal. "He taught me that you have to look not just for the decision maker, but also the people who influence the decision maker. He knew people everywhere and what was most amazing was that he had both a black and a white network."[11] Alexander's power of persuasion allowed him to escape stereotypes that might have hindered other black bankers.

On another occasion, Alexander set up a meeting with the top fiscal officers of a key client. E. F. Hutton had just gotten the deal to work on a joint parking facility. They sat at the designated conference room table with Bernard Beal, all looking at their watches, waiting for a late T. M. Alexander. As the minutes ticked by, Beal used the time to build up the investment banker who was coming to execute this big deal for them. "This guy is great," he said. "He is the first black vice president at the firm and he is wonderful at structuring deals and executes every time." Of all of sudden, Beal looked up and his jaw dropped at the sight. Alexander had walked in with two enormous watermelons under each arm. Embarrassed, Beal got up and pulled Alexander over to a corner for a quiet chat.

"Dammit, T. M., we got all these white folks here and you brought these watermelons in here. You might as well have brought the fried chicken," Beal said sarcastically.

"I'm sorry I'm late. I saw this guy by the side of the road and figured I'd make amends for being tardy," he replied.

Alexander brought the fruit over to the conference table where the corporate officers sat and pulled out a knife, to start cutting them at the table. With no plates, fork, or napkins, he started handing out the fruit to these important clients. The sight of this forced Beal to put his head in his hands, uncertain what reaction this would draw. When he looked up, he saw each person eating the fruit. "This is great!" one exclaimed. The feast soon turned into an exchange about people that they knew in common and experiences they shared. During the conversation, Alexander smiled at Beal. He had done it again.

Tragically in 1983, Alexander's life was cut short in a boating accident. Many blacks who later gained significant recognition like Beal and Brandford credit him for helping to open up opportunities in the field.

Another prominent banker during this period was William H. Hayden, who entered the business with First Boston in 1974. Like so many others, he had never expected that Wall Street would be his destination. His background had set him up for a career in public service.

A graduate of New England Law School, Hayden spent his early 20s working for then Massachusetts Attorney General, Edward Brooke. His labor there inspired an unsuccessful run for the Massachusetts House of Representatives. "I was very young, barely old enough to run, and my only qualification was that I had worked for Brooke," Hayden explains.[12]

He returned to work for Brooke shortly after Brooke's historic election to the United States Senate. However, a talk with his boss, along with a caring nudge out the door, sent Hayden down the path to finance. "He said, 'You're not going to work for me here because you have better things to do with your career than writing letters for my signature,'" he recalls. Brooke helped land his protégé a job with the Treasury Department, specializing in tax policy during the Lyndon Johnson presidency. He went on to work for Hubert Humphrey's presidential campaign in 1968, and then joined New York Governor Nelson Rockefeller's Urban Development Corporation (UDC). He stayed there until Rockefeller was appointed vice president of the United States after Spiro Agnew's resignation in 1974. At that point, Hayden turned his attention to Wall Street.

When Bill Hayden decided to pursue an investment banking position, he was quickly confronted with the homogeneity of the business. "At the time, I had no access to an investment banking firm on my own. There were no African Americans in major positions that I could go talk to," he says. Luckily, he found a mentor and connection to guide him along the way.

While he was working at UDC, the organization's chairman was George Woods. A well-connected man, he was also in charge of the World Bank under President John F. Kennedy, and more importantly for Hayden, Woods was a founding partner at First Boston. In a flash without an interview, Bill Hayden had a job in its public finance department. "I was just told to show up one Monday morning."

Hayden freely admits that life inside a major Wall Street firm was difficult in those early years. "I didn't understand what I was getting into. It took me five or six years to get my feet on the ground and fully understand what I was doing." He was extremely fortunate to have found two mentors early in his career. A common complaint from those days was that African Americans had few role models to emulate, an essential part of the learning process. For Hayden, that was never a problem because Woods looked out for him while maintaining a behind-the-scenes role in the firm. That knowledge allowed him to grow, eventually producing some key deals including the landmark Hartsfield Airport deal in 1977.

As well as demanding that black contractors help build the airport, Maynard Jackson insisted that black bankers be part of the bond offerings. He hired Daniels & Bell and First Harlem Securities to serve in the underwriting syndicate. Doley Securities was in the selling group, but he was also looking for a black banker to help lead the deal with the major firm.

"The smartest company around was First Boston," says Jackson. "Into Atlanta came this New Englander, this lawyer, this brother, and nobody had ever seen an African American investment banker. It was almost like we were touching him to see if he was real and he was smooth as silk. He won us over and the company had a great proposal, so our decision was pretty easy and that deal helped to make Bill."[13]

"There is no question that I was able to secure the deal because of his influence," says Hayden. "I was the only African American pursuing the deal at the time." He was named senior banker of the $305-million offering. Because Jackson and Atlanta were so happy with his worth, Hayden was also named the senior partner for the $100 million Metropolitan Atlanta Rapid Transit Authority a year later.[14]

In addition, Hayden was also securing business where African American influence was no factor at all. Places like Wyoming, Utah, and Iowa, where the clear majority of people were white, also signed on with Hayden as their banker.

As the profits grew, so did his status within the firm. Even if things were improving on the outside, however, attitudes within First Boston were still lagging behind. "They made me managing director of the firm and one guy actually tore up his office because I became one before he did," recalls Hayden. A serious man who maintains a slight Boston accent, he deflected such incidents with little rancor and went about his business. "There were individuals who used the 'N-Word' and told jokes. It was a very difficult time but I had seen a lot and done a lot so I just decided to let it roll off my back."[15]

Bill Hayden's story was like many others developing during this period. Smart, well educated, and capable black investment bankers were demonstrating that they could perform when given a chance. Goldman Sachs set the stage for a rising banker named Garland E. Wood. Along with T. M. Alexander, E. F. Hutton also employed Bernard Beal. James Haddon began his career at PaineWebber in 1982. Salomon Brothers hired Wardell Lazard and Marianne C. Spraggins; Lazard Freres, Franklin Raines; Drexel Burnham Lambert, Kenneth E. Glover and Patricia Corbin; First Boston, Ron Gualt, Frederick Terrell, and Jeffrey Humber at Merrill Lynch.

Modern articles that attempted to summarize this history have directly correlated the progress African Americans made through the 1980s with political power. Unlike the minority-owned firms who are traditionally more open and willing to be publicized, minorities in the major firms have been a harder group to interview and understand. It is always easier to understand those who are running their own firms, especially if it is a small securities company (which all-black ventures usually are). The credit or blame is easily attributable to certain people in the firm. They are willing to share their experiences with the press because it is always useful to publicize the firm, as long as it's in the right context. African American professionals in the major firms have received less attention and that is a development that many are content with. Firms like Goldman Sachs and Morgan Stanley have historically preached the practice of teamwork and discouraged making stars. "The pressure is on you, whether it is said or not, if you are in a majority firm to be more careful," says Maynard Jackson, who himself would later own a minority firm.[16] Usually, the only public spokesmen for a major investment bank's activities are its corporate leaders or public relations people, and this has been an area where few African Americans were. Furthermore, a banker is just one cog in a huge, diverse business that employs thousands of people. As a result, it has been harder to attribute the success of certain deals and profits compared to the minority-owned firms, which early on was essential based on the work of just a few people.

As a result all these factors, information sources had focused on minority-owned firms. When black bankers in major firms began reeling in these large, public deals in municipal finance, the press took noticed and attributed all the progress made in the industry to politics. That was not the case. Pioneers like Milton Irvin and Myron Taylor were making significant inroads into the trading business, however, each day's gains and losses were not posted in the *Wall Street Journal,* like the tombstone of the Hartsfield deal was. The impact of political power was huge not only because of the tangible business it brought to capable black investment bankers, but also because it was the most public.

Did African American mayors create an opportunity for black investment bankers in the late 1970s and 1980s? Absolutely. "It was all about demand from clients," says Jeffrey Humber, who joined Merrill Lynch in 1984, after a stint in the Marion Barry administration. "Wall Street wasn't looking to diversify itself. Wall Street went kicking and screaming into a world where clients wanted to see African Americans. All of us who came in through the public finance window did so because that avenue was made available to us because Marion Barry, Maynard Jackson, Coleman Young, and others were saying, Where are your black people? Before you knew it, we owned those accounts and you survive because of your account base."[17]

Without question, politicians used their muscle to influence the financial ways of their cities. In many respects, African Americans through politics established an "F. Scott Fitzgerald" world of their own. After years of exclusion from the traditional networks, blacks had now staked out their own space in Wall Street. One of the first to recognize this growing network was the master networker, T. M. Alexander Jr. "Of course, it's important to have credentials and a good track record, " he said in 1979. "But it's also true that more and more blacks have been coming into public office and on boards and commissions handling public finance, and it's just good business to have blacks in front-line positions. We can frequently get in the door when others can't."[18] This network was not just comprised of mayors, bankers, and treasurers, but also of other notable black politicians who acted as intermediaries but have often been overlooked.

Ernest G. Green was thinking of entering the investment banking business in the mid-1980s. One of the "Little Rock Nine," the group of students who integrated the city's school system, Green was successful as a consultant and moved into Lehman Brothers' public finance department in 1987. One of the first people he talked to was Harlem congressman, Charles B. Rangel, who was enormously helpful. "There are many players like Charlie who get overlooked that have really contributed a great deal and are helpful to our success," says Green.[19] Another person instrumental in this network was Rangel's close ally, Harlem businessman and former Manhattan Borough President, Percy Sutton. "He raised the awareness of investment banking to people who have carried the banner since . . ." says Kenneth E. Glover. "He also introduced most of us to elected officials who he knew—which was almost all of them. Most importantly, he did everything without public attention or asking for anything in return."[20]

Although this network took on a "clubby feel," it was not unlike other clubs present throughout Wall Street's history and it certainly did not come at the expense of the quality of financial services received. "Many of the black mayors were taking over these big cities with huge budgets," says Franklin Raines. "It was a must for political survival that they showed sound fiscal management."[21] While political power helped give people like Ken Glover the opportunity to perform, both Drexel and Chicago benefited from Glover as well. It certainly was helpful to them to employ a man who had started his career as an aide to his local government's executive, and went on to serve as campaign manager for Mayor Harold Washington of Chicago and as treasurer for the reelection campaign of David Dinkins. These ties, plus his banking skills, put Glover in an extremely powerful position in the middle years of the decade. "Through his relationship with Harold Washington, he became the most power brother on Wall Street!" says

Napoleon Brandford.[22] So large was Glover's importance, that Drexel took out a full page add in the *Wall Street Journal,* the *Los Angeles Times,* and other national publications. Frederick Terrell began working at First Boston Corporation in the early 1980s and was able to bring in business within his first few weeks because of his background working in the Los Angeles City Council.

A misconception had developed among some that political power propped up all African Americans in public finance. What political power did was help give opportunities to succeed that were not there before. It did not guarantee success. Those who were not qualified, like the janitor who was used to portray diversity, quickly disappeared. Those who stayed did so because they brought in business. "Wardell was a damn good banker," says Dale Horowitz. "The work he did in Washington, D.C. alone made him more than worth everything he got. The fact that he was black was just an added bonus."[23] Bill Hayden distinguished himself with the Atlanta Hartsfield deal, which was a watershed event, but his work in states like Wyoming and Iowa that had little black political presence showed his ability, which was proven when he later became a senior managing director in charge of public finance at Bear Stearns.

Many major cities would soon follow Maynard Jackson's lead. They instituted their own versions of his program, but he was the architect of this movement. Some set exact percentages; others were less committed and simply spread the word about the new policies. Who did the most is open to debate. Bankers name the people they were closest to. But, a few names are mentioned by everyone. "The three mayors who did the most were Maynard, Marion Barry, and Harold Washington," says Kenneth Glover. "I think that from the client side, two names are obvious, Maynard Jackson and Marion Barry," says Bernard Beal. "There is no question that Harold

Washington was an outstanding mayor in terms of breaking open the Chicago markets to minorities in investment banking," says Hayden.

The political machine founded by the late Richard Daley controlled Chicago, its policies, and businesses for decades. Although its hold had been in decline since the death of Mayor Daley, the organization still exuded power and intimidation. In 1983, it still appeared unbeatable. Few believed that a black man would be the one to beat it.

Washington at the time was a Democratic congressman from the south side of Chicago. He grew up on the same tough streets as the Jones brothers, early black speculators. Washington represented much of Chicago, he was no outsider. Over 40 percent of the city was black, yet until 1983, they had never been able to pull together an unbreakable political presence that would force "the machine" to take them seriously. If Washington were to get elected, he would have to reverse that trend. He did.

A record number of African Americans registered to vote and helped elect the long shot, first as the Democratic nominee, and then as the first black mayor of Chicago. Washington defeated the Republican nominee, Bernard Epton, with 51 percent of the vote. Despite its historic quality, the moment did not come without some reservations and uncertainty. Many citizens and onlookers were unsure how the city would recover after what was an extremely bitter and divisive campaign. Like Maynard Jackson's win, the road to victory was littered with racial overtones. Politicians of "the machine" crossed party lines to support the Republican candidate to keep Washington from office. Their desire to keep him from power did not stop once he reached city hall. This conflict was labeled the "council wars."

Despite the importance of Harold Washington's magical victory, it did not upstage the inevitable oncoming collision with the city council. Although, the new mayor had broken through the barriers, some of the political winds did not shift as "the machine" held the city council in a tight grip with a majority of seats in the 50-member council. It was going to be a showdown. Chicago's system of government restricted the powers of a mayor who had to have a majority of the council approve his actions. Because of this division, the early months of the Washington administration was plagued by arguments and accusations. The machine aldermen demanded all but 3 of the 29-committee chairmanships, 5 of which were then held by African Americans. With all the jostling and bickering, many of the city's initiatives were left dangling. Projects like the completion of a transit line to O'Hare Airport, dealing with the school system's monetary woes, and the city's budget problems remained untouched. Compromises were soon reached with the help of a mild-mannered, articulate, Wall Street professional named Frank Raines. "During the council wars, Frank was pivotal in helping people understand, both in the city council and within the administration, that at the end of the day, they needed to protect the financial viability of the city," says former Washington Chief of Staff, Ernest G. Barefield.[24] "As the council tried to take Harold down, Frank helped them see that as a practical matter, there were some things they couldn't avoid working with the mayor on."

The term "Wall Street professional" does Raines an injustice. His career in the securities industry was just one part of an extraordinary record of accomplishment that would include director of the Office of Budget and Management in the Clinton administration and Chairman of Fannie Mae. However, when Raines first stepped onto Wall Street in 1979, he had a pristine educational background and experience in Jimmy Carter's White House. Born in Seattle, Washington, he was a honors graduate of Harvard University, a Rhodes scholar, and a graduate of Harvard Law School. His commitments exemplified a larger theme of the municipal bankers of his era who have successfully based their financial sophistication on their life in public service and government.

After law school, Raines went to work in Washington during the Carter presidency as an assistant director to the White House domestic policy staff. Shortly before Ronald Reagan defeated Carter's bid for reelection in 1980, Raines engaged in a number of conversations with contacts about possible career routes. "I had a legal background and had just finished with Carter and was looking at my options," says Raines. "Then someone suggested investment banking and I said what is that?"[25] The conversation landed Raines on Wall Street with one of the most prestigious firms in the business, Lazard Freres. The house was built by Wall Street legends like Andre Meyer, Felix Rohatyn, and Michel David-Weill, and in addition to Goldman Sachs and others, was one of the last remaining private partnerships. Its private persona gave Lazard an exclusive, serious image that fit Raines well. In a land of bravado and chest thumping, a person with his qualifications could have worn his background like a badge, Raines did not. "Frank came in with great energy and had the ability to sell a dead man a grave and have him wake up long enough to pay him," says Ken Glover. "He never tried to overwhelm you with how smart he was. There was not one person who could ever say that he did not get the job done."[26]

Being a part of a firm with an impeccable reputation, coupled with his own abilities, helped to cement his appearance to both his peers and clients. "Frank was the most elegant of the bankers," says Napoleon Brandford. "Frank has a tremendous gift of gab. He was very meticulous in conveying legal and financing documents to clients. I didn't know anybody who had more connections with powerful elected officials."[27] Raines' work also extended into places like Cleveland and

Iowa, yet it was his work in Washington, D.C., that would get the most attention.

The fiscal predicament of Washington, D.C., was dire. The city had never issued a bond. It hadn't been audited for more than a century. In addition, the new home rule charter separated the district from the federal government even further, which left more responsibility in its hands. Into this mess, was the charismatic, energetic, Marion Barry who was elected in 1979.

Despite events that occurred later in his political life, particularly a 1990 arrest in a motel room for drug use, Barry was an incredible mayor, especially in the very early years. "Marion Barry was a stalwart," says Frank Raines. "It was only later into his tenure, when he began to have personal problems, that he lost his focus."[28] The Barry background is familiar to many. The Mississippi born son of a sharecropper, he overcame poverty to attend LeMoyne College, where he graduated with a degree in chemistry. However, the Civil Rights movement consumed his attention. As a member for the Student Nonviolent Coordinating Committee (SNCC), he became engulfed in its activities, especially the protests and other peaceful demonstrations.

As the decade wore on and the Civil Rights movement became increasingly violent, Barry became interested in government work. He soon began wearing pinstriped business suits. He began to meet with politicians, asking them to address the nation's inequalities through their powers. Among his successful efforts was procurement of $300,000 for a program called "Youth Pride" that employed black youngsters for city work such as cleaning streets. He also won grants for Pride Economic Enterprises, an organization involving small businesses. Meanwhile, he continued to show an interest in financial aspects of business and the potential impact he could have.

He was elected to the city council in Washington, D.C., in 1974 and soon became chair of the city's finance committee. Once in office, he learned skills that helped him better understand what was needed when he was elected mayor in 1978. Throughout his tenure, he committed himself to opening up opportunities for African Americans.

Marion Barry in his first years as mayor was a star. Few have ever matched his political skills. He entered office with full concentration and ambition. What made Barry especially good during this period was his staff, a team of advisors who provided discipline to the new mayor as well as ensuring that all necessary tasks were completed. On the political side, there was Ivanhoe Donaldson and Elijah Rogers. On the finance side, there was Alphonse G. Hill, Jeffrey Humber, among others. Once the administration took office, they discovered that the fiscal challenges before them were much greater than they had anticipated. "It was dire in the sense that as a business school graduate, I had a basis of comparison for how bad things were run, how bad things were set up," says Humber. "The district was lacking in basic systems to make things work. It was about as ugly as anything you could imagine. It was like the Titanic after it hit the iceberg and we were trying to keep it afloat."[29] On the verge of insolvency, the team, led by Barry, worked to strengthen the district's finances. They also enlisted the help of Wall Street advisors such as Frank Raines and Wardell Lazard. After a few years of work, the city was able to do an audit and demonstrate an ability to tap into the capital markets. The turnaround was so extraordinary that Raines considers it his finest work on Wall Street. "I was proud of the work I did in D.C.," he says. "They had never done an issue before we got there. We didn't get paid the first three years because our compensation was based on results and that took time with the financial condition Barry inherited."[30]

Sadly, Barry's personal fortune dwindled as the 1980s progressed. Both Donaldson and Hill were convicted of felonies. Humber went to Merrill Lynch. Rogers left for Grant Thorton LLP. As his closest advisors left, an undisciplined Barry was left to manage the city, eventually resulting in the infamous FBI bust in a motel room. Despite his political comeback just a few years later, this incident will forever shadow the gains made during his administration.

When Raines was named a partner at Lazard Freres in 1985, the first African American to make partner in a major investment bank, followed by Wood a year later at Goldman Sachs, another glass ceiling was broken. "I felt it was significant because for years, people would be wowed by the fact that you were black and a vice president, now partner or managing director became the new standard"[31] says Raines.

Garland Wood, the first black partner at Goldman Sachs, was also a standout. An even-tempered man who sought little attention for his accomplishments, he began at the firm after graduating from Columbia University in 1972 with an MBA. degree. He became a vice president in 1976 and at the time concentrated on clients in the U.S. territories of Guam and the Virgin Islands. He also did work in Texas, Kentucky, and California, all of which earned him a spot in the revered Goldman Sach's private partnership. It was the last of the top investment banks to remain private so a partnership was especially prestigious for anybody, and a proud moment for African Americans. However, his entrance caused a few waves says his boss, David Clapp, "Some people were upset that he became a partner but he earned it. He was a good banker."[32]

Marianne Spraggins, arguably the most accomplished black woman in the history of Wall Street, was the first to become a managing director at Smith Barney. She got her start at Salomon Brothers in the mortgage-backed securities market, a profession she chose because it was the opposite of the trend toward public finance. It wasn't until 1986 that she made the decision to enter public finance, with Prudential Securities. Eventually the business she brought landed her on the top floors of Smith Barney. Before her entrance into securities, she appeared to be destined for a career in law. Once on Wall Street, she managed a meteoric rise to the top. What does it take when you are both black and a woman to orchestrate such an achievement? By all accounts, she is an extremely tough woman, who is financially savvy. "Marianne is a wonderful woman," says Horowitz, who was the first to hire her. "She is a terrific business getter but Marianne is unique! That's the only way I can describe her."[33]

Not all prominent African Americans to enter Wall Street during the 1970s did so in the field of finance. One such person was Milton Irvin, a trader who eventually became the first black managing director of Salomon Brothers. When Irvin arrived at Salomon Brothers in 1977, it had established itself as one of the most powerful investment banks, largely because of the strength of its trading desk. Some of Wall Street's most recognized names–John Gutfreund, Michael Bloomberg, and John Merriwheater–drove the business. Salomon Brothers was one of the firms that profited the most from the surge in volume and could translate that prowess into other areas such as banking.

Although its strength was notable, Salomon Brothers also was known for a unique culture: Its traders were edgy, swaggering, high-flying risk takers, who had little regard for political awareness or sensitivity to social or human values. To not just survive in such an environment but succeed as well took a special personality. Irvin describes himself as "a person with thick skin, not taking no for an answer, with just a bit of cockiness."[34] A graduate of the Wharton School, Irvin chose a career in commercial banking because the action was too good to pass up. Irvin made his mark in money market instruments. When institutional funds from foreign corporations and banks wanted liquidity for securities such as money markets and treasuries, it was Irvin's responsibility to get the trade done. He executed with great success and was sent to turn around the struggling Chicago office. After two years and great progress, he was brought back to be the product's national manager. After declining margins forced Salomon out of the trading business, Irvin went to PaineWebber in 1988, only to return two years later. In 1995, Irvin, who admittedly is suited to the Salomon Brothers style was rewarded for his dedication and service by being named the first black managing director.

While public finance received the most attention, inroads were being made in the most cherished and lucrative of investment banking fields, corporate finance. Generally, the two who get the most credit for their pioneering work in the field are William Lewis and Raymond McGuire. Although these men were not the first African Americans in the area, they did remain there throughout their career to achieve positions where blacks had never been.

African American corporate finance bankers entered in the 1970s as well, and although had successful records on the Street, are best remembered for other business accomplishments, thus often ignored for their contributions. One such person is W. Don Cornwell who joined the corporate finance department of Goldman Sachs in 1971. A Harvard MBA, he rose to vice president within a few short years and eventually served as chief operating officer of the department for his last seven years at the firm. During this period, he worked with companies ranging from Bristol-Myers to Essence Communications. But, despite his success, Cornwell left the Street in 1988 to found Granite Broadcasting Co. which eventually went public in 1992.

Another early pioneer who left Wall Street for other business endeavors is Ira D. Hall, a former senior vice president at then L. F. Rothschild, Unterberg, Towbin, Inc. A Stanford business school graduate, Hall left Wall Street and went on to have distinguished tenures at IBM and Texaco.

Lewis and McGuire are linked, both for their similar education and commitment to investment banking, as well as the employer they shared when McGuire joined Morgan Stanley in 2000.

McGuire's interview with the First Boston Corporation out of college has become legendary on Wall Street. Sitting across from the young Harvard graduate, the interviewer said, "You have five minutes to convince me to hire you."

"Could you clarify or give me some direction as to what to say?" a stunned McGuire asked.

"No, You have 4 minutes and 45 seconds left," the interview replied.

Without further hesitation, the young man said, "Harvard College, Harvard Law School, and Harvard Business School pride themselves on taking the cream of the crop. I pride myself on being the film off the top of that cream."

"Half of your Harvard Business School class is interviewing for two positions in our firm," the interviewer. "Why should we pick you?"

"In the heat of battle, it is better to have me with you than against you because I'll figure out a way to win." McGuire got the job.

The firm's high M&A department was driven to prominence by Bruce Wasserstein and Joe Perella, two luminaries who left in a high-profile exodus to found their own firm, taking only the best bankers of the department with them. One of them was McGuire. It was significant that he became a managing director there in his early thirties and later at Merrill Lynch he helped lead the division to the top of the rankings.

William M. Lewis went to Harvard, where he graduated cum laude with a degree in economics, and Harvard Business School. He almost never made it to Wall Street because an offer from Morgan Stanley was rivaled by another offer from Procter & Gamble who offered more money, but placement in Cincinnati. He decided to go to Morgan Stanley in New York and has worked at the firm all of his professional life. In 1989, he made managing director. A decade later, he was co-head of the firm's worldwide corporate finance department. A year later, McGuire joined the firm.

Lewis and McGuire are important figures in this history. The corporate area has long been the most prestigious Wall Street business to be in—dominated by some of the most famous names in the financial industry: Kravis, Wasserstein, Perella, Meyer, Rohatyn, Greenhill, among others. Not only did the pair penetrate the highest levels of the business, they excelled in those areas.

6

THE BUILDING

My father, Travers J. Bell, co-founded Daniels & Bell, Inc., with Willie L. Daniels in 1971. Bell was described by the *Investment Dealers Digest* as "the father of the modern minority-owned investment bank."

Russell L. Goings Jr. standing in front of his Harlem office in September 1971, the day his First Harlem Securities became the second black-owned member firm of the New York Stock Exchange.

As mayor of Washington, D.C., Marion Barry balanced the city's budget and executed the city's first bond offering; these feats have been overshadowed by his notorious personal problems.

The late Harold Washington was elected mayor of Chicago in 1983. He is best remembered for his political savvy, which he used to open doors for black securities professionals.

Maynard Jackson, former mayor of Atlanta and architect of affirmative action programs, included African Americans in all aspects of the city's business.

Harold E. Doley Jr. purchased a seat on the New York Stock Exchange in 1973; two years later, he founded Doley Securities, the third black-owned firm on the Big Board.

John W. Rogers founded Ariel Capital Management, Inc., in 1983 at the age of 24. It was the first of the modern money management firms.

First Boston's William H. Hayden was the senior banker of the 1977 Hartsfield Airport offering. He later became one of the highest-ranking African Americans on Wall Street, at Bear Stearns.

Franklin D. Raines (seated next to former Secretary of the Treasury Robert Rubin) was the first black partner at a major investment bank. He eventually became director of the Office of Management and Budget and later chairman of Fannie Mae.

Garland Wood became the first black partner at Goldman Sachs in 1986. Once described as "the hardest working man in the business," Wood covered municipal accounts.

In 1985, the charismatic and energetic Wardell Lazard formed W. R. Lazard & Company, which became a top black investment bank and asset management firm, managing more than $2 billion at its peak.

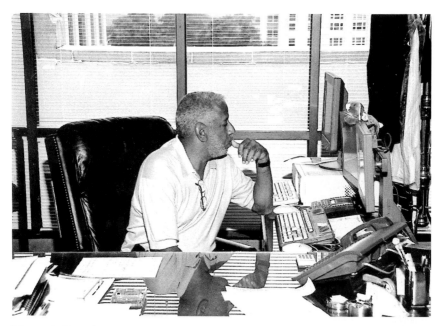

Maceo K. Sloan founded NCM Capital Management Group in 1986; it would eventually become the largest black-owned asset management firm in the nation.

William M. Lewis Jr. (left) and Raymond McGuire (right), both graduates of Harvard, are credited with being pioneers in the corporate finance field, once thought to be a nearly impossible area to penetrate.

Malcolmn Pryor (left), Raymond McClendon (center), and Allen Counts (seated) were the principals of Pryor McClendon Counts, the leading black investment firm of the early 1990s.

Calvin Grigsby co-founded Grigsby Brand-ford, pioneer of a financing instrument called certificates of participation. In 1993, his firm led a historic offering for the Los Angeles Convention Center.

John O. Utendahl founded Utendahl Capital Partners, heralding a new generation of black investment banks. It has earned spots in top deals for companies such as Goldman Sachs and PepsiCo Bottling.

Bernard B. Beal formed M. R. Beal & Company in 1988. He is widely heralded as a survivor. After an unsuccessful investigation into his firm he rebounded, leading his company back to a top-ranking position among black investment banks.

The Reverend Jesse Jackson, talking with C. Michael Armstrong, AT&T Chairman, and Sanford I. Weill, chairman of Citigroup, in 1998, established the Rainbow/PUSH Wall Street project in 1997.

In July 2001, E. Stanley O'Neal was named as the heir apparent to the CEO of Merrill Lynch and is due to take over in 2004. The appointment will make him the first African American to lead a major investment bank.

Philip M. Jenkins (above), in front of the New York Stock Exchange in 1955, the year he co-founded Special Markets, Inc., on nearby Liberty Street; landlords refused to rent him a space on Wall Street proper.

Norman L. McGhee founded the first black brokerage licensed to deal in securities in 1952; he later founded (in 1967) what is believed to be the first black mutual fund, the Everyman Fund.

AS THE INDUSTRY BEGAN TO RECOGNIZE BOTH the political benefits of including African Americans in deals and the talent that existed within this pool, a market began to develop for minority-owned firms. As more municipalities set policy to include these firms in each deal, minorities from varied personal and professional backgrounds went out on their own to compete for this business. This budding opportunity was the catalyst for the creation of more than 20 black investment banks by the end of the 1980s. Almost all of these new securities firms would place tremendous emphasis on municipal finance to cash in on the growing market. This movement would be led by what was informally known as the Big Five: Daniels & Bell; Pryor, McClendon, Counts; W.R. Lazard; Grigsby Brandford; and M.R. Beal & Company. These firms more than any others received publicity in newspapers and other publications as examples of progress on the economic front. Most of this group spent the remaining years of the Cold War era building their companies for the great success that was to come in the early 1990s. One of them cashed in on the work it had already put in.

The initial leader in the field was Daniels & Bell. Contrary to the majority of firms, which were just babies when Harold Washington and Wilson Goode took office, Daniels & Bell began in 1971. It had planted the seed for municipal business in the early 1970s as the Street rotted in the weeds of recession. Its investment banking operation was small, beginning in the proverbial corner with no formal division. Those who operated in the syndicate process were multitasked employees who also maintained roles as traders and salesmen. The firm's performance in corporate finance was meager, an indication of the few resources put toward the area. In its first year or two, Daniels & Bell was included in more than 10 selling groups to the primary market, but participated with limited success because of both financial and social pressures. The aggregate corporate market was suffocating under the weight of a bleak economic climate leaving few companies healthy enough to go public. Even if one did, the pessimism of the market would probably not treat that stock well.

This picture was so dark that the corporate finance business practically shut down for a brief period. In 1974, there were just three initial public offerings (IPOs). With the shrinking pie, competition increased, shutting out small players like Daniels & Bell. Being black was not what hurt them, so much as being small and young. In an industry where deals are based on relationships and tradition, the firm was terribly lacking in all departments. They simply did not have many strong relationships with corporate treasurers and executives. It was not all due to race. In general, people tend to do business with those they are comfortable with, and few of them knew the African Americans in the business. The CEOs and CFOs who came from Ivy League backgrounds were used to dealing with Ivy Leaguers, and Daniels & Bell were not of this ilk. Faced with this problem, the firm pursued opportunities where their thesis that black business can be good business would be received and considered: public finance.

Daniels & Bell's argument was simple. Because a substantial portion of government employees were minorities, some government securities related business should be handled by a minority-owned firm. The big city officials disagreed. "I do think that there was prejudice from municipal administrations, which were all white at the time," said Bell. "As a municipal firm, we would go to people who did business in the city of New York or the city of Chicago, and they would say, 'You've got to be kidding. This is not an arena you can play in.'"[1] Those in charge of the city's money had the same reservations that corporate America did. Some were more blatant than others.

In the early 1970s, a team of the firm's officials including Bell and another early partner, Herbert N. Britton, went to a meeting with a city's municipal administrators. The group of four laughed when the Daniels & Bell team walked into the room. As the firm made its presentation, one of the officials pulled out a ham and cheese sandwich and started munching, another used the time to take a nap, and the remaining two stood up without any word and left the room. Daniels & Bell did not get the business.

That experience failed to deter the firm; their choices did not include stopping because the bills would continue to roll in. It was not the first time they were mocked, nor would it be the last; and if the trend continued, public finance would be the area with the most potential. However, these large accounts in major cities would come to them kicking and screaming, a struggle that would continue for years.

Daniels & Bell were unwilling to wait for these governments to come around and decided to pursue more receptive alternatives. They sought municipal clients who had fallen through the cracks. They had to be small and within the young firm's limited capabilities. "There were small, regional firms doing business with various cities across the country," Bell said. "We thought our best hope would be to try to find some black mayors. The only place we could find them was down in rural towns in the South. Mound Bayou, Mississippi, was a classic because it was the oldest black municipality in the U.S."[2]

In 1973, Mound Bayou, Mississippi, was a town rich with history, but little else. Its residents depended solely on the local health clinic for jobs. No other meaningful, long-term employment was to be found in the vicinity. Those who sought work had to find it in other areas, causing a great migration away from the town. It was poor, knee-deep in the recession, and in need of a drastic improvement of its infrastructure. The insufficiency hung like a dark cloud over the town but made it an attractive proposition for Daniels & Bell. Wall Street had never serviced the town or even acknowledged its existence, so the Daniels & Bell team went south to introduce themselves, as well as the capital markets, to Mound Bayou.

Daniels & Bell hammered out an agreement with the town in January 1973. The firm became the first black investment bank to complete a municipal bond deal when Herbert Britton, an investment banker for the firm, led the $780,000 housing issue into the market. (Britton also made *Black Enterprise*'s Annual Achievement Awards list in the late 1970s.) The transaction did little for the bottom line but was a success in terms of significance. Citizens Trust, a black bank in Atlanta, was the cotrustee for the transaction. They also used black bond counsel. Both were firsts on the Street. Within a year after that deal, Daniels & Bell completed a $5 million housing issue for Prichard, Alabama, another small black town. These deals were the first ever completed by a black investment bank.

Aided by hindsight, it is easy to see that this was the foundation for the municipal market to come.

As the 1970s came to a close, there were now African Americans in charge of large amounts of money in the big cities. Maynard Jackson was the leader in providing opportunities for minorities to participate in city business. Other notable black political pioneers like Marion Barry were also beginning to open the doors to equality in all areas of their municipalities' business. At the time, Daniels & Bell was the only black investment bank aggressively pursuing municipal bond business. "Travers Bell was building a real franchise for himself," says Earl Andrews. "He understood the investment banking business. He went out and developed political relationships and started underwriting municipal bonds. He was also doing transaction related business that politicians and governments could do."[3] Despite the changing tide in public finance, Bell remained upset at his failure to underwrite larger investments. Many black mayors had said, "Yes we're going to put you in deals. But we're getting feedback from the financial community that its okay if we give you a deal for, say 15 or 20 million bucks, Travers, but when you're talking about $300 million or $400 million it's hard for us." The municipalities had logic behind their reasons for withholding substantial roles from small investment banks.

"The older firms could not do a difficult deal in their first few years," says Kenneth E. Glover. "They might not admit it, but they couldn't."[4] The inherent early difficulties that all firms experience prevent them from meaningful participation in the underwriting process. Investment banking is essentially buying securities from an entity such as a corporation or municipality and selling them to clients and other buyers. The hope is that the selling price is higher than the buying price, enabling the firm to make a profit in addition to the management fee earned just for being selected by the syndicate.

Because of this structure, large allotments put more pressure on small firms relative to the larger investment banks. Major firms maintain a reservoir of capital and large salesforces that can unload securities with ease. Small companies like Daniels & Bell, with four or five bodies on the trading desk, found it impossible to sell the same amount in the same period. In addition, much of their clientele were second-tier; small institutions did not demand large groups of securities. If unable to sell bonds, a brokerage theoretically would have to keep the securities and eat the loss, a predicament that would have wiped out small firms with only hundreds of thousands in capital. Therefore, the advice municipalities received (and that Travers Bell lamented) was somewhat justifiable.

It was at this turning point that black elected officials, who were sympathetic to the cause, helped nurture black securities companies past the seemingly impenetrable wall, and gave them the time, space, and chance to grow. Predictably, the two sides soon fostered a relationship with each other. The outcry against such friendships between black politicians and bankers was ironic because similar relationships had tied Wall Street together for decades. Before black elected officials slammed their fist on the bargaining table to make their presence known, municipal treasurers had no incentive to help black firms get the necessary experience to procure greater shares of underwriting deals. Despite the numbers, there was evidence that these smaller firms could compete in the upper echelons of finance if experienced and connected. In the late 1970s, an effort developed to allow black firms to move higher.

The state of Connecticut thus became a key client for Daniels & Bell. When the state treasurer, Henry E. Parker, referred to by friends and associates as Hank, took office in 1974, he set out immediately to change the way business was done in his state. "My view was that there were other firms that were smaller and just getting started," he says. "I believed that there had to be what one calls a 'Corporate Social Responsibility.' Their responsibility in my view was to make sure that since they (bulge bracket firms) did business for the state of Connecticut, they were to be certain that doors were open so that African American firms could participate, not at the same level as they were, but on a smaller scale."[5] The leading municipal firms at the time, such as Salomon Brothers and Goldman Sachs, did not necessarily agree with these new rules but jumped in anyway because they were not going to turn down the money they earned in the state. "I think that most of the Wall Street firms, if it's not unethical, will participate. They may not like it because it changes the way they do business. But the truth is if they are taking on a $250 million underwriting, and we say '$30 or $40 million goes to minority firms,' then they are not going to find fault with that. They are making a hell of a lot of money!"

With Parker's declaration that minority-owned firms would be allocated a portion of each bond offering, issues of capital and accountability still had to be resolved. For years, the argument was that black investment banks lacked the capital to take on the risk of underwriting hundreds of millions in securities. Parker decided to work out an arrangement with the majority firms that would hedge the inherent risks of the market. He demanded that these established firms take back the bonds originally designated for the black firms if a drastic change in the market or other sundry factors made them unable to unload securities. When a big firm won the lead position in an offering, it agreed to distribute the bonds among others in the syndicate including black firms, and take them back if they did not sell. "I was saying that you guys have got to help these minority firms strengthen themselves," Parker says. "You have got to, so that they can move up; and then they begin to do that and say, 'We think we can handle a little larger piece of the action.' They then got the comanager experience and the pressure of selling bonds."[6]

Such setups helped minority firms gain access and gave them the chance to succeed that they had never had, but did not make them immune from wrongdoing or incompetence. Hank Parker made sure that he was informed if a black firm conducted itself in a less than satisfactory level, so that it could be weeded out. Such measures ensured that whether a minority-investment bank failed or succeeded, its participation was judged by performance and not race.

Without question, Daniels & Bell was the high riser in the state in the early 1980s. It was still the only black firm aggressively pursuing the business. Doley Securities was focused on the corporate side of the industry and was actively building a base in Africa. They chose to pursue opportunities in public finance only in selective situations. Others had to be contacted, like Daniels & Cartwright, for them to enter the field. "I had been hearing about this firm Daniels & Cartwright so one day when I was in New York I decided to go check them out," says Parker. "I walked in and asked to see the two of them. They asked, 'Who is here?' and the receptionist said, 'The Treasurer of Connecticut.' They couldn't believe it! They didn't know I was black."[7]

What put Daniels & Bell over the top in Connecticut was its now solid experience, a file full of the phone numbers necessary people, and the development of relationships with the main bankers in the major firms. A key to Bell's success was his involvement in the Securities Industry Association (SIA), Wall Street's chief lobbying group. Here he was able to establish a repertoire with top municipal bankers like Gedale Horowitz, who led Salomon Brothers' municipal department. This plus his persistence led to the Daniels & Bell's landmark deal: being appointed an equal co-manager with Shearson Lehman, American Express, Goldman Sachs, Merrill Lynch, and other prominent firms, to a $5.5 billion Connecticut transportation infrastructure renewal program.

Parker explained, "They worked their way up. He [Travers Bell] was always in the state and wherever we were going, he was there, meeting the people," says Parker. "Some of the other major investment bankers began to recommend that they be given an opportunity. He had more initiative then anybody else. He would fly from California to Chicago, then somewhere else within a 24-hour period."[8]

"This was a significant arrival point for us," said Bell. "Then anybody saying they couldn't put us on a $300 million deal had no argument. There was no longer any reason to say that we couldn't do it because it had been done."

The Connecticut deal gave Travers Bell more confidence, but better yet, more credibility. He then set out to get more involved with the political side of the business, not only with black officeholders, but with those who sought to be elected. "Travers was the architect in dealing with black elected officials, getting them elected and raising money for them," says Harold Doley.[9] He began organizing fundraisers for politicians like Tom Bradley, Harold Washington, Wilson Goode, Julian Bond, Doug Wilder, and others. Bell served as National Finance Chairman to Bradley's 1986 run for Governor of California. One night at a dinner in Bell's Park Avenue building, with the CEOs of 10 investment banks in attendance, Bell netted the campaign $100,000 in one night. That relationship translated into business for the firm. "Travers Bell was the one who brought Bradley along and convinced him to give more business to African Americans," says Bill Hayden.[10] Another older investment banker noted that Travers went all around the country raising money while getting Tom to say, "This is my investment banker."[11] His other connections led to significant municipal contracts including $350 million in Chicago O'Hare Airport bonds and $230 million in Philadelphia notes. By 1986, the firm stood as one of the top 20 investment banks in municipal financing with participation worth $9 billion.

This success was truly wonderful, but in many ways misleading. Despite success in municipal finance, stylish new offices at 99 Wall Street, and expansion into other cities such as Washington, D.C., Chicago, and Pittsburgh, the firm was not making huge profits. Even though the investment bank ranked in the top 20 of the muni field, it barely ranked in the top half of SIA organizations in terms of capital position. What really led this great expansion was Bell's other significant holding, Cocoline Chocolate. The company was a cash cow. At one point in the early 1980s, it returned 40 percent of its equity, thanks in large part to a partnership with Nabisco. Its success allowed Daniels & Bell to grow and weather the storms of Wall Street. "Daniels & Bell is what we call a 'loss leader,'" says Harold Doley. "It took losses to break into business that would help all other firms. It was the flagship"[12]—so much so that other black bankers saw an opportunity to follow in its footsteps.

"I look at Travers as the Jackie Robinson. He created the allure of Wall Street" says Napoleon Brandford, co-founder of Grigsby Brandford. "So many times we would go meet a potential client and there would be a picture of him with Travers on the wall. He was a legend."[13]

"I think that all of us looked up to Travers," says Bernard Beal. "He was the first one to think outside of the box. Here was a man with great integrity and style who was doing things with this tiny firm and it made a lot of us think we can do this."[14]

As the public finance market grew, and opportunities opened for minority-owned firms, some African Americans decided to pursue the municipal bond business independently. Some set out to focus on other areas but quickly moved into munis as they became the shining light. For example, Pryor, Govan, Counts began 1981 as a business focused on trading and arbitrage and decided to start an investment banking arm two years later. W. R. Lazard began in 1985 as a financial advisory firm, and then expanded into underwriting a year later. In many ways, the firm and its founder, Wardell Lazard, symbolized a new breed of aggressive black investment banks. Whereas the older firms such as Doley, First Harlem Securities, and Daniels & Bell grew slowly (Bell once said, "We chose to grow by design rather than for the sake of volume alone"), Lazard wanted to build and expand fast!

Wardell Lazard's desire to attack the business is not surprising considering his meteoric rise through life. He grew up in California where he was raised on Edwards Air Force Base. Education was not immediately an endeavor that he took on with full effort finishing 62nd out of his high school class of 67. This performance was in no way indicative of a limited capacity; it was the starting point of a growth that would lead him to great success at one of the Street's biggest firms. After finishing California State University, Lazard took a job at the California Public Employees Retirement System (CalPERS), as an investment officer. Here he learned about asset management, knowledge that would serve him well years later and differentiate him from other black firms. He also expanded his abilities into other areas such as law, obtaining a degree at night school. In 1980, he moved to Salomon Brothers where he did notable work, especially in Washington, D.C., and quickly rose to prominence in the municipal department. Soon he was on the verge of becoming a managing director but shunned the opportunity for more dangerous waters.

Despite his rise at Salomon Brothers, Lazard wanted to test the waters on his own, without a life preserver. In 1985, he visited his boss to discuss an arrangement that would help him realize his desires. "He wasn't a managing director yet, but he would have been," reflects Gedale Horowitz. "He said, 'I don't want that. I don't want to be a managing director. I am going to leave no matter what happens.'"[15] Horowitz then went to Salomon Brothers Chairman John Gutfreund who that same year was featured on the cover of *Business Week* as the "King of Wall Street," to discuss those dreams. After the three men discussed the plan, all parties agreed that Salomon Brothers would loan Wardell Lazard $250,000 to create W. R. Lazard & Company.

The firm began as an investment advisory business, serving as a sounding board to municipalities. It began with only two employees, Wardell and his wife Betty, who was officially the treasurer but in reality served in several capacities. A combination of factors allowed it to expand from these humble beginnings faster than its predecessors. In direct contrast to the early 1970s, the pursuit of money and profits soared to new heights in the 1980s. All firms were executing greater volumes of business as the market recovered from the wretched conditions that had characterized the previous decade. This climate was helpful, but what really enabled Lazard to weather the treacherous first year, was his experience at Salomon Brothers. There he established a network and clientele that would help him set his feet firmly on the ground.

When Wardell Lazard was a Salomon banker, he secured and procured business from Marion Barry and his city. They developed a good relationship that translated into great profits for Salomon. The connection carried over to W. R. Lazard, where the Washington, D.C., business set the foundation for his building. "Marion Barry helped to make W. R. Lazard," says Bernard Beal.[16]

Earl Andrews, one of W. R. Lazard's first securities professionals, says, "Wardell had one client back in those days, the city of Washington, D.C."[17] Lazard Freres (no relation to

Wardell) served as the main advisor to the city and here was little W. R. Lazard serving as a co-adviser. "That year the city of Washington sold about a billion dollars worth of bonds and we earned a pretty substantial fee for being their co-financial adviser." From 1985 to 1987, it earned $2.8 million in fees according to the *Washington Post*.[18]

This was a good starting point for the firm as W. R. Lazard built staff and business. However, Lazard was not satisfied with slow growth and sought to expand his business into municipal bond underwriting. "He always said that he wanted to be like Salomon Brothers," says Gedale Horowitz.[19] That grand ambition was perfectly fitting for a man who stood 6 feet 6 inches tall, often towering above the people he was talking to. These characteristics fell in line with his attitude and demeanor. People close to the firm describe Lazard as Salomonesque. He was a self-assured man who exuded confidence. Although he could be moody and had some personal problems, he was always fair to his employees. The compensation system at the firm was generous. Those who worked to bring in a deal were always paid for it. While this policy helped bring great spirit to the company, it did not help keep expenditures within reason. The lack of control over money spent started a pattern that would haunt the firm in the years to come.

Wardell Lazard's appetite to move quickly began with a hitch that prevented the firm from jumping into the municipal underwriting, sales, and trading business. What stopped them wasn't racism or incompetence, but the absence of a license. Investment advisory companies are required to be registered with the SEC but not the NASD, which is needed to underwrite, sell, and trade securities. There are two ways that a company can obtain a license: They can file for one, going through the process with the NASD, or they can acquire a firm that already maintains one. Sitting there was the small but historic First Harlem Securities. It had given up its seat on the New York Stock Exchange but still operated in businesses like municipal financing on a small scale. Most importantly, the NASD had approved it for more than 15 years. "I said First Harlem was probably for sale and it's a member of the NASD," Andrews recalled. "Why don't we buy it out, see if we could combine the two firms because we could probably get it real cheap."[20] The stock was languishing. The same people all still owned it because nobody wanted to buy it. Although its price was in the gutter, its widely recognized name carried some weight in the financial community. It had been around for 15 years, doing work in the equity markets, dealing with businesses like Ford Motor and many other leading corporations. The name recognition looked attractive enough to warrant Lazard's interest.

From the other side, the management from First Harlem Securities saw the partnership as a means to get bigger and finally bounce back from the capital woes of the late 1970s. "The reason it became part of W. R. Lazard was because it infused about a million dollars in capital," says its CEO, Mel Eubanks. "It allowed the firm to do all kinds of things it couldn't do because of this minimal capital beginning in 1978."[21] Because there were relationships between the two firms, and stockholders in one company worked for the other, an outside advisor was brought in to remove any conflict of interest. The deal was done in 1986 and, when it was acquired, it operated as a separate arm of W. R. Lazard. According to Eubanks, the new partnership was set "to expand the franchise, to get into more equity underwriting, equity securities, debt securities, Treasury securities, and to get into the municipal business." Those ambitions would nearly choke the firm to death before it had a chance to gain strength.

Lazard's aggressive nature needed a fine balance. On one hand, aggression and persistence were needed to grab business on Wall Street, especially when confronting the impediment of prejudice. At times, however, that desire turned into desperation and his reluctance to be satisfied blinded him to acknowledging what was feasible and what was not. The event that pushed him past this balancing line was the stock market crash of 1987. To many, Black Monday was a day of panic, but to Wardell it was an opportunity.

In October 1987, the stock market crashed. The Dow Jones Industrial average dropped 504 points, a fall of more that 20 percent, on what has become known as *Black Monday*. With hindsight, historians and financiers look back at that remarkable day as a blip in the longest bull market in history, but the immediate reaction was not as forgiving. For good reason, many were shaken by the sudden disappearance of prosperity and confidence was low, resulting in lower prices all around. In theory, it was a good time to buy other securities firms, but Wardell went on a binge, buying several companies and taking on too much debt.

Initially, they built on the First Harlem branch of the firm. In contrast to the commissions earned in the advisory business, where deals may occur weeks or months apart, the broker/dealer business from the purchase of First Harlem Securities supplied daily revenues that established a cash flow. It proved to many clients and others in the financial community that the firm had potential. Lazard saw the stock market crash as an opportunity to bolster this success and sought additional resources to build a viable concern. Lazard soon focused on a company called Kuhns Brothers & Laidlaw, Inc., which was willing to listen to offers for some of their businesses. In particular, its broker/dealer had an established presence in institutional equity sales, over-the-counter stock transactions, and syndicate formation, areas that Lazard thought would fit well with the First Harlem unit. Also available was its asset management arm, Laidlaw Capital Management, which oversaw approximately $690 million of pension funds. The price tag surpassed $2 million, even in the depressed post-Black Monday market. So, Lazard approached his old bosses, Gedale Horowitz and John Gutfreund at Salomon Brothers, for another loan to cover the costs of his target. Much to his dismay, however, he came away with nothing; they refused to loan him the money. "John told him that he shouldn't buy Laidlaw," says Horowitz. "He should have listened to John but he was bound and determined so he then went to Drexel."[22]

Drexel Burnham Lambert rose to prominence in the 1980s on the coattails of its powerhouse high-yield debt department, which dealt in securities known as *junk bonds*. It became a premier source for financing, most notably the record-breaking $25 billion leveraged buyout of RJR Nabisco by Kravis Kohlberg Roberts. It also had been making a concerted effort to work with minorities in the business. It supplied the bulk of the money for black financier, Reginald F. Lewis's historic leveraged buyout of TLC Beatrice International Holdings. They had developed a larger-than-life reputation, and as the Street took precautions after the shakeup of the Crash, Drexel was the only firm bold enough to loan money to Wardell, but with a catch. They received warrants that could be converted into a 40 percent stake in W. R. Lazard. They also charged the prime lending rate plus three percentage points on a majority of the debt. These were less than favorable terms, but Lazard in his quest to be big agreed, a decision he would later regret.

Not only were the terms of the loan wretched but the target for the borrowed money was not what it appeared to be. On one hand, Laidlaw Capital Management was a complete success. It put W. R. Lazard over the billion-dollar mark in assets managed, a significant milestone for any firm, and a first for a black company. *Billion* is an almost magical word on Wall Street and a word that resonated well when pitching to potential clients. Laidlaw had been managing assets since the 1960s and held a reputation, history, and experienced portfolio managers to produce returns. But, "the broker/dealer was a complete bust," says Eubanks. "We never made a dime off that."[23]

The problem with the expansion was that the payments for the Drexel loan swelled the overhead costs of taking on this new company. The buy increased the number of employees from about 20 to more than 100, many of whom were under contracts requiring specific tenure and pay. They also inherited enormous real estate liabilities that deepened the already self-inflicted wounds they had opened at 14 Wall Street, where W. R. Lazard had set up headquarters. This building stood directly across from the New York Stock Exchange, and like the securities market, the price of that space was relatively low because of rumors that its owner was deep in the red. Still, renting the huge, lavish space cost approximately $1 million a year, according to Eubanks. Half of the space was unused, left empty except for boxes and the occasional piece of spare furniture. The Laidlaw acquisition brought an additional 12,000 square feet at 275 Madison Avenue, leaving the firm strapped with too much office space, a swollen workforce, and extraordinary debt. Then, the Drexel debacle hit.

In 1989, Junk Bond King Michael Milken, head of Drexel's high-yield department was caught engaging in an insider trading scheme with trader Ivan Boesky. As the allegations surfaced, Drexel Lambert Burnham imploded and eventually filed for bankruptcy in 1990. This could not have come at a worse time for W. R. Lazard, which had lost hundreds of thousands of dollars since taking its loan two years earlier. If Drexel needed money to pay off debts, it could demand that Lazard repay the aggregate amount of the loan within 30 days, a proposition that would have closed the shop. Advisory work and the growth of the asset management business were the only reasons the firm survived. The advisory area had been beefed up by the purchase of James J. Lowrey &

Co., a municipal advisory company, for $100,000, which by ost accounts was a steal. Nevertheless, Drexel's trouble spread to W. R. Lazard, causing many to wonder if it would survive. Drexel was their biggest creditor and, under the terms of the agreement, could demand instant payments. Luckily, Drexel escaped the situation in relatively good shape, and after much negotiation, both sides agreed to more favorable terms for the small black firm. Also, Lazard restructured a number of its leases, ending some, such as the Madison Avenue office, and paying a lower price for others, such as 14 Wall Street. Last, it cut its workforce to about 50 people, and by 1991 was relatively healthy. Although most employees who now look back remember its impressive successes, most wonder what could have been if they been more careful during the early years. One employee expressed deep regret saying that Wardell Lazard's biggest mistake was expanding too fast. This source feels that if they had kept the firm small and did not have to spend those years digging themselves out, they would have all been millionaires. Even Lazard himself expressed some unfulfilled promise and uncertainty in a 1991 *Wall Street Journal* article saying, "We got caught up in the expansion euphoria. We weren't sure what the hell we were going to do. We were running for cover."[24] In that same article, however, he declared with great optimism that the firm's future would be bright. It was a proclamation that would come true. "The shift from a ma-and-pa operation to a professionally run operation has been made." Now out of the quagmire of debt, the firm would rise to prominence in the years to come.

The early 1990s were a period of unprecedented success for African American firms. Like W. R. Lazard, many of these investment banks spent the 1980s building businesses that would thrive in the decade. Perhaps the most intriguing of these firms was Grigsby Brandford. Unlike most of the major players on Wall Street, who operated in the Northeast, usually New York, the firm opened in San Francisco in 1985. As superficial as it seems, being located in the historically free-loving town presented the firm with additional challenges; they were not taken seriously. That would not last for long.

Grigsby Brandford was built on the vision and experiences of one man, Calvin Grigsby. His background and story had all the elements of a fairytale. In his 1992 Democratic nomination acceptance speech, Bill Clinton said, "I still believe in a place called Hope," referring to his hometown of Hope, Arkansas. It was also the birthplace of Calvin Grigsby in 1946, and this connection was a symbol of the political network he would so successfully plug into later in his life. He graduated from the Boalt Hall School of Law at the University of California-Berkeley, and began a career in securities law.

By all accounts, Grigsby was a complex man, whose personality was full of contradictions. He was charming, sweet, well-mannered, and cultured; but he was also relentless, overbearing, ruthless, and uncaring if anybody stood in the way of his goal. Although that attitude of indifference would serve him well as he aimed for the big leagues, it rubbed people the wrong way and as a result, he made enemies who sought any chance to take him out.

In 1979, Calvin started Fiscal Funding, a firm that leased equipment such as fire engines and police cars to public agencies. A request from Florida's Dade County for proposals to finance a 40-ton crane would bring him business and his future partner.

Napoleon Brandford was born in East Chicago, Indiana, a town of 35,000. After graduation from college, he became the assistant to the finance director of Dade County. There he started meeting black securities professionals and developed a love for Wall Street. "The first person I met was T. M. Alexander Jr., the first black investment banker from the South," Brandford says. "I then met Ken Spaulding and Wardell Lazard from Salomon Brothers and it was then that I knew I wanted to do what they do."[25]

When Brandford's boss put out word about the Dade County's financial needs, they received two proposals. One was from a firm called William R. Hough, with a bid of 11 percent. The other proposal came from a then unknown firm in California named Fiscal Funding, which bid 7.45 percent. Because the interest rate was significantly lower, meaning that the county would have lower payments over the life of the contract, the director chose Fiscal Funding. However, nobody in the office had ever heard it so they took references and other precautions to ensure that the firm had the capability to back up its numbers. Such measures were necessary because it is common on the Street for a couple of unknown, well-dressed, articulate men to make fantastic presentations, but careful research reveals that they maintain offices with no furniture, heat, or electricity. "In the meantime, I called three of his references in Atlanta, the state of Massachusetts, and New York and they all said he was really good," says Brandford. A meeting was then set up for the sides to finalize the deal; the night before it took place the finance director had dinner with Grigsby and later told Napoleon how well he thought he would like him. The next day the Fiscal Funding group walked into the room for the meeting. "He walked into the room with five white guys and then sat at the head of the table. It was then that I realized he was black! I thought he was just a young associate or lawyer but it turns out he was the man."

In many ways, the beginning of this relationship between the two men—and this deal—would come to symbolize their firm. The early 1990s saw Grigsby Brandford come out of nowhere to beat the competition with its technical expertise and better bids. The only difference was that the competition was not William Hough, it was Goldman Sachs and Smith Barney (but, that was still a dream in 1980). After the meeting between the two men, they created a plan to try to expand the business into municipal finance, an endeavor that could not be pursued right away. "In order to do that, Calvin needed to raise more capital than what he had and somebody needed to build up a client base because all of his were leasing clients." So Napoleon Brandford went off to Shearson American Express to work in the public finance unit beginning in 1983. Meanwhile, Grigsby went around trying to raise capital, a quest that frequently was successful, but not to their liking because, white investors often would only agree to put up money in return for equity. "That was the rage at the time," says Brandford. "Daniels & Bell, United Daniels Securities, Pryor Govan Counts were all 100 percent black and we felt we needed to be to compete."

Beginning in 1981 as Grigsby Associates, the name was changed to Grigsby Brandford Powell in 1985. Arthur Powell, another leasing business entrepreneur, was brought in to be a partner. He eventually left in 1989 to found Powell Capital Markets in New Jersey. The partnership and roles inside the firm essentially matched the partners' personalities. "I was Mr. Inside and Calvin was Mr. Outside," says Brandford.

"Napoleon is basically a very low key guy and is very good at building relationships," says Clifford Graves, who joined the firm in 1986 as a vice president. "His client skills were just outstanding. He is very even-tempered. Calvin as the creative genius was very mercurial, very aggressive. He could really work the hell out of the team but he still worked harder than anybody else."[26]

The firm focused 100 percent on municipal bonds. It was different from other firms in that it publicly shunned set-asides and went for senior managed deals right away. What enabled the firm to handle these deals was Calvin's mastery of a little-known method of financing called Certificates of Participation (COP). These are basically securities that act like municipal bonds but don't need the approval of voters. At the time, California was struggling for available funds because the passing of its Prop 13 rule cut taxes and municipalities were struggling for funds. COP filled an enormous niche and Grigsby was one of the early pioneers of the security. Years later, Grigsby Brandford was using the instrument to make its mark, beginning in little senior-managed deals, yet most of the public did not understand what was going on. In response, *USA Today* published an article about the firm using the following example:

Say that a school district needs $5 million for a school but voters have rejected a proposal for the issuance of municipal securities. The municipality or investment bank would then set up a shell corporation with the sole purpose of this one transaction, and borrow $5 million backed by a 15-year lease from the school. Investors would purchase participation certificates, an indication of ownership in a pool of assets, in the shell corporation's lease-purchase agreement. The school pays rent to the corporation which in turn makes tax-exempt payments, like municipal bonds, to the COP holders. When the lease expires and the certificates mature, the school district buys back the building for one dollar.[27]

The deft use of this method of financing allowed Grigsby Brandford to differentiate itself from other black-owned firms. "Calvin Grigsby was smarter than God. He made all minority-firms get more technical," says Ken Glover.[28] "We were virtually lead manager on all of our deals because we had an expertise," says Brandford. "Most of the other minority owned-firms were comanagers." This attitude led the firm through a fantastic period of growth as capital grew from Grigsby's initial pot of $100,000 in 1979, to $5 million 10 years later. Its workforce expanded from 3 to about 30 employees. It had also done 260 COP deals totaling $850 million. In 1989, it ranked 20th in the nation in terms of municipal volume that it lead managed. Calvin did not like the idea of being a comanager because there was no money in it.

Grigsby Brandford did not much care for the idea of set-asides, at least not in public. More than any other minority-owned firm, it emphasized that it was an investment-banking firm first and that they just happened to be black. "When I started in '79 I would always go to the meeting as the general counsel of the firm," recalled Grigsby in a 1995 interview with *The Bond Buyer*.[29] "I had a little card that said general counsel, and the last thing I would ever do was let anybody know that I was the owner of the firm because there was no way I would get business." Grigsby Brandford senior managed five deals for Dade County and three deals for BART [Bay Area Rapid Transit in California] before they knew we were a minority firm. Once they qualified for BART as a minority firm, the firm became a comanager for the first time, and when they qualified as a minority firm in Dade County, Grigsby Brandford became a comanager for the first time.

The problem the firm was experiencing was that being branded a "minority firm" immediately put them into the pool of comanagers, the secondary players of an underwriting syndicate. As a black firm, they were not judged by the merits or the creativity of their numbers and ability, but were relegated to the low levels. "The problem with set-asides is when the rule becomes the cap," says Brandford. "We had been doing deals with a number of issuers and all of sudden they said we can get only 15 percent of the deal because we were in the minority pool."[30] Despite these setbacks, Grigsby Brandford was poised for a move in the 1990s and was ready to do it.

The only other major black investment bank that would spend the decade building toward the fertile 1990s was Pryor

McClendon Counts. It began in 1981 as Pryor Govan Counts, a trading firm that originated in the city of Philadelphia. The two forces that would drive the firm over the course of the next two decades were co-founders Malcolmn Pryor and Allen Counts. The third original partner, Gregory Govan, left the firm after two years, when they decided to transform it into an investment bank.

Pryor entered the business in 1974 as a trader at Goldman Sachs. His background was representative of the coalescence of institutions of higher learning in the United States. He graduated from Howard University and received his MBA from the Wharton School. Allen Counts was also educated at those two institutions and used his knowledge to enter the commercial banking field, spending several years at Citibank before founding the firm. In addition to their venture capital ideas, they also maintained an arbitrage business to capitalize on Pryor's experience in the market. Together, their experience in public finance was nil but the firm decided to move into investment banking with a concentration on muni business because there was "a clear opportunity with some of the changing politics."[31]

It seems more than just coincidence that Pryor Govan Counts jumped into the public finance business the same year that Philadelphia elected its first black mayor, Wilson Goode. The new mayor, like so many other newly elected black officials, was committed to opening up the city's business to the broader financial community. Because of these new policies, the city maintained a roster of minority-owned firms to rotate with each deal, one of which was Pryor Govan Counts. The client was key in helping the firm establish its investment banking operations.

Although the majority of the Philadelphia contracts that helped the firm early on were municipals, they were also able to get into a few corporate deals. The year 1983 also saw the firm run a $350,000 equity offering for Comcast Cablevision of Philadelphia. From there, the business grew, mostly in their public finance unit. Like Grigsby Brandford, it sought some senior-managed business and received its first deal in 1986 when it led a $20 million bond issue into the market for the Philadelphia Hospitals and Higher Education Facilities Authority. A year later, it was included in the historic Conrail $1.7 billion government offerings. With this success, the firm wanted to build in the public finance area and in 1990 they saw an opportunity to do so by partnering with R. J. McClendon & Company a small firm in Atlanta, Georgia.

The new firm, named Pryor McClendon Counts (PMC), was stronger and ready to take on the opportunities that were to come its way. "That was unique in itself because as we've seen with a lot of the small firms, they were basically one-person shops," says Howard Mackey a vice president with the firm from 1991 to 1997. "The fact that these guys merged interests I think was fairly foresighted in terms of just building a company."[32] The force behind R. J. McClendon was its sole founder, Raymond McClendon, a graduate of Morehouse College. Before he started his company, McClendon worked at the Federal National Mortgage Association and more importantly as the City of Atlanta's chief investment officer, where he controlled its $600 million securities portfolio. The connection he maintained in the state would help propel PMC to become the largest black investment bank in the nation within a few short years. It would also ignite a cloud of suspicion that would haunt the firm as the 1990s progressed.

The 1980s were years of building that would deliver these major investment banks into viable positions. They were ready not only to capitalize on the new access African Americans had attained, but to cope with those issuers who sought their substantial financial experience. M. R. Beal, the latecomer in this group of prominent black firms, was founded in 1988 and would also stand at the foot of the door, ready to embark on a period of success that would see black investment banks rise to the top of the tombstones.

7

MONEY MANAGERS

B Y THE MID-1980S, AFRICAN AMERICANS HAD made significant strides in most areas of the business. As owners of seats on the New York Stock Exchange, some were able to profit from the exchange of ownership between two parties. A growing number of investment banks were participating in underwriting syndicates and could offer their clients products from the sell side. Some African Americans also were developing their businesses from the buy side, a movement launched in 1983 with the first black money management firm of modern times.

Traditionally, African American money management pioneers have received less attention than their peers in other businesses. In 1991, *Black Enterprise* began to include a list of top investment banks in their annual year-in-review issue. They began a similar list of top asset management firms nine years later. Perhaps the lack of recognition in money management among African Americans lies partly in the general perception of the business. Money management has become a specialized area because success is judged strictly on the numbers. One can produce good returns or not. Personality and other character traits that can be advantageous in other aspects of business have less impact in this field.

Another factor in this disparity is the effects of history. Earlier generations of black people were handcuffed by lack of opportunity and consequently accumulated little wealth. The passing down of such limitations through time manifested itself in the low percentage of minorities who made investments during this period. African Americans have traditionally had less life experience investing because they have had relatively little money to manage. Because few of them grew up thinking about the preservation and augmentation of wealth, it is hardly surprising that African Americans were slow to break into asset management. "I think people have not gone into money management because of exposure, we have not had the exposure to these firms," says Maceo Sloan, chairman of Sloan Financial, one of the first and largest of these firms. "Most of us grew up not knowing what a money management firm was so if you don't know, how can you start one?"[1]

With such limitations, it was no wonder that the securities industry did not see the creation of the first black asset management firm until 1983. Nor was it surprising that the person who founded the firm was the antithesis of all that prevented exposure to this side of the business. He came out of a family of achievers, with an Ivy League education. His even-tempered personality would suit him for managing money, and his firm for earning returns. At the age of 24, he was young and ambitious. His name was John W. Rogers Jr., and his efforts would prompt Sloan, as well as many others, to call him "the Godfather of this industry. Without John, there would be no industry."[2]

Rogers was born in Chicago, Illinois, the son of accomplished and highly educated parents. His father was born in Knoxville, Tennessee, graduated from Teachers College in Chicago, and from the University of Chicago's law school in 1948. He went on to become a judge in the Circuit Court of Cook County. Rogers's mother, Jewel Lafontant, was a pioneer in the legal world. During the course of her life, she also served on the board of directors of TWA and Revlon, earned 15 honorary degrees, and worked in high-ranking positions in the U.S. State Department.

Because of his wonderful background, John Jr. received an exposure to and education in investments and securities that would serve him well later in life. "My father felt that it was important for me to learn about stocks at an early age," recalls Rogers. "He decided when I was twelve years old that every Christmas and birthday, he was going to buy me investments rather than toys." The reasoning stemmed from a conversation his father had with a white investor about the state of African American investing. "They were both lamenting the fact that African Americans knew little about the stock market," he says. "The man said, 'African Americans know as little about the stock market as my twelve-year-old son.' So that is when my father got the idea that when I was twelve, I was going to have the same experiences that this man's son had."[3]

His father's decision was not immediately well received by his young son. As others proudly showed off the brand-new bicycle or skates they had received as presents, all Rogers could produce was an envelope with a stock certificate. "At first I wasn't too happy about looking under the tree and seeing an envelope," he jokingly admits decades later. Such resentment slowly turned into optimism and interest in the securities process because his father made a clever decision. "The smart thing he did was to let me keep the dividends. Every three months I got a check. Over time they got larger and I started to look forward to reading the reports issued by the companies."[4]

As the boy's interest and financial sophistication grew, Rogers's father decided to translate these secondhand experiences into firsthand observation. Stacey Adams, his stockbroker, was the first African American stockbroker on LaSalle

Street, in the heart of Chicago's financial district. Occasionally, the judge would take his son to look at the action. No longer were securities just an envelope under the tree, a check in the mail, or a story in the newspaper. This was real action: people on phones buying and selling, tickers rolling out the latest prices. What had before been a foreign world, suddenly became an untapped province of excitement and enrichment. In addition to finding visual inspiration in this environment, Rogers discovered that Adams was a smart, articulate broker. "It was a great place for me to be able to learn and ask a real experienced stockbroker about Wall Street."

Although he had advantages that were rare for any African American youngster in the 1960s, Rogers shared a common passion with many American boys, basketball. His love of the game was so great, that at some point he thought about becoming a basketball coach. At Princeton, Rogers went on to captain the varsity basketball team. Although he concluded he was not good enough to play in the NBA, his experiences playing his favorite sport taught him competitive leadership skills that helped him with his chosen career in the securities industry.

After college, Rogers went to work for William Blair & Company, a medium-size firm in Chicago. He believes that he was the first African American professional to work there when he began as a stockbroker in the early 1980s. "It was a great opportunity to learn an awful lot very quickly," he says. Because it was modest in size, access to the people with knowledge and experience was not as closed as is often the case in huge, bulge-bracket firms. "It was the kind of firm where everybody was available to approach and learn from."

Such access was important in Rogers's decision to take the entrepreneurial route. Often, the chief complaint from African Americans trying to work their way up in the large firms has been that they could find no mentor, no patriarchal figure to put a hand on the shoulder and give advice. Rogers found such a person in Ned Jenetta, a high-ranking member of the William Blair team. The two first met when Rogers was just a college student interviewing for the job, and from there the relationship developed into something quite special. "Ned gave me the opportunity to get started there and also he was terrific when I started Ariel. He gave me lots of ideas and put me in touch with people that were helpful in showing me how to start a money management firm."

Rogers began Ariel Capital Management at the age of 24. His decision was based on two different approaches that he used at William Blair. The first of these mismatched ideas was his philosophical approach to investing. The firm had an investing style that Rogers credits with influencing him. "When it came to investing, they focused on smaller to mid-sized growth companies. That found a niche here in the Midwest and that was important." However, Rogers also believed in approaches based on value as opposed to the growth stocks that dominated William Blair's choices. He had been developing this approach since his final year at Princeton. A self-described contrarian, he earned the title in the early 1980s because growth stocks were the strategy of choice.

Rogers's investment style also forced him to examine the limits and constraints of his job. "I felt that the brokerage business was transaction oriented, and I was more value oriented." Stockbrokers derive much of their earnings from the commissions received executing trades. The value strategy that Rogers so deeply believes in depends on patience and holding on to stocks for longer periods, the opposite strategy from the method a stockbroker uses to maximize income.

In founding Ariel Capital Management, Rogers found the freedom he had lacked. Since it was his firm and under his control, he was able to stamp its business with his own personality. He says, "The money management business allows for a person to develop a track record on their own. It just seemed more fitted to my personality, where compensation was based on the long term and how assets grow."

Ariel may have allowed him to escape the trappings of working in a company that had a history and a set philosophy, but he soon learned that such freedom has a cost. Companies with a long and well-known track record can approach potential clients with ease. The newly formed Ariel Capital Management had no track record and was not taken seriously during its early days. To set the company's foundation, Rogers sought the help of his parents, family, and friends. He was fortunate to have successful parents, who worked and developed relationships within a distinguished circle. "Both my parents were very supportive both personally and financially in terms of getting friends and contacts," says Rogers. His mother helped secure Ariel's first client, the Howard University endowment fund; she was on the school's board of trustees. They agreed to let Rogers manage $100,000.

He was also able to procure assets a little at a time from friends of the family, usually allotments in the range of $20,000. Such scraping and effort gave the firm about $400,000 in assets managed by the end of its first year. As the firm branched out beyond this circle, Rogers encountered much more skepticism: "As we called the bigger institutions, the corporate pension funds, endowment funds, people were skeptical. I was young and African American and people had never seen a pitch like this to manage these assets. But, we did have a few people who came through. If you knock on enough doors, a few people will be receptive." Many of these early clients were also friends of the Rogers family and thought highly of Rogers's ambition and abilities. One such person was Cecil Partee, then Chicago's treasurer, who gave the firm $1 million in assets to manage from the municipal employees pension fund. "It made us $10,000 in fees which wasn't a lot but it gave us confidence," says Rogers.

Clifton R. Wharton Jr., former chairman and CEO of the Teachers Insurance Annuity Association-College Retirement Equities Fund (TIAA-CREF), was also contacted in Ariel's beginning years. "I remember when John Rogers started Ariel Capital. I know him because his mother was on the Equitable board with me. John was good. And when he started , a number of us tried to see to it that he got a fair shake in terms of having access to people to talk to about his investment firm. But there was still a lot of questioning and unspoken doubt about him. Then he started performing, and you couldn't stop him because his performance was measurable."[5] It also gave the firm credibility, which was demonstrated in its growth. By 1987, its assets under management had grown from $400,000 to $217 million. It would rival W. R. Lazard's asset management arm as the top African American money management company.

Despite the growing success of his institutional business, Rogers wanted to build his fledging operations into other areas. In 1986, he partnered with Calvert Group Limited so that he could include mutual funds in his product line. The two sides brokered a deal in which Calvert would serve as a transfer agent distributing, marketing, and keeping track of the day-to-day activities. Ariel would just continue along the lines of its original strategy—pick the stocks and do the investing. The joint venture was called the Calvert Ariel Mutual Fund.

As time passed, Rogers became more confident and Ariel strengthened its reputation and businesses. The need for such a partnership then waned. "We were building our own infrastructure here and, frankly, I thought it was confusing when people saw the name and they didn't know who owned who or whether it was a partnership," explained Rogers. In 1994,

Ariel Capital Management bought out Calvert's stake in their firm for a reported $4 million. "I think it was important that people see an African American mutual funds company going head to head, toe to toe with Fidelity and T. Rowe Price."

Now named the Ariel Funds, Rogers still manages using his mantra "Slow and steady wins the race." The fund invests in companies with market capitalizations primarily under $2 billion, with an emphasis on small-cap stocks. It identifies the common stocks of undervalued companies with long-term growth potential. A stock is held until it reaches its true value—usually three to five years.

Ariel has continued to add products to its offerings. Its Ariel Appreciation Fund is managed by Eric McKissack and maintains a similar value strategy, but instead focuses on mid-cap stocks with capitalizations up to $10 billion. It also offers fixed-income and money market alternatives. By the end of the 1990s, Ariel Capital Management had more than $3.5 billion under management.

Rogers wasn't the only money manager for long. Eddie Brown founded Brown Capital Management in 1983 shortly after Ariel Capital Management began. Seventeen years later, Brown Capital would boast nearly $6 million in managed assets, the most held by any black firm. "Eddie came right after John," says Maceo Sloan. "You have got to consider them the forerunners, the pioneers of money management."[6]

Many are familiar with Brown's name or face from his guest spots on the TV show *Wall $treet Week* every Friday night. However, viewers watching him would never imagine that decades earlier, he had been heading in a totally different direction.

Brown grew up in Apopka, Florida, a small town just a few miles from Orlando, and moved to Pennsylvania when he was

13. In his new school, counselors and advisors tried to convince him to learn a trade and to take shop classes instead of college prep courses. Brown resisted and enrolled in Howard University after high school graduation. Still, his future as a money manager and investor was not yet in the picture; his concentration was in engineering. After graduation and a stint with IBM, he went Indiana University School of Business, ready to throw himself into the securities business.

He began his work for a company called Irwin Management and established himself at T. Rowe Price as its first black professional. He served as a vice president and portfolio manager. In 1983, at age 42, Brown had a decision to make. He had always wanted to be out on his own. Although he was satisfied at his position, he was at a crossroads and decided to form Brown Capital Management.

What has emerged as his investing style is described by the acronym GARP, which stands for *growth at reasonable prices*. Brown wasn't able to implement that strategy right away. After setting up shop in his Maryland home, he needed assets to manage. One of his first accounts came when a woman saw Brown on *Wall $treet Week* and contacted him to seek advice about investing money she had won from a lawsuit.

"So who should I invest this money with?" she asked.

"I think that you should let me manage the money," Brown replied.[7]

Brown Capital Management grew from there. His first institutional client came from Minnesota in the form of a Catholic religious order. Soon, he racked up significant sums from the most notable public and private funds in the nation. At first, the firm's goals were small, in the range of $5 million, but that amount grew in the early 1990s. One of their biggest clients was the California Public Employees Retirement System (CalPERS), where in 1990 he received $40 million in one account. So pleased was CalPERS with his performance that within six years, they had given him almost $200 million to manage.

By the mid-1990s, Brown had a reputation as a top performer who regularly beat industry marks. His most notable achievement was outperforming fellow *Wall $treet Week* panelists with his selections, averaging nearly a 22 percent return over a five-year period. With success, more clients followed: $80 million came from the Philadelphia Board of Pensions, $100 million from the California State Teachers Retirement System, and $250 million from the Oregon Public Employees Retirement System.

In 1992, Brown Capital also became one of the few minority-owned asset management firms to offer mutual funds, creating three to meet the appetite of its various investors: the Balanced Fund, the Equity Fund, and the Small Company Fund. In the year 2000, such innovations and performance helped position Brown Capital Management as the black-owned firm with the most managed assets.

Number two on that list was NCM Capital Management. Its founder, Maceo K. Sloan, like Rogers, emerged with the help of a wonderfully supportive family whose success in business provided lifelong lessons about finance. Sloan's NCM Capital Management originated in 1986 as a subsidiary of North Carolina Mutual Insurance; in 2000, *Black Enterprise* listed it as the number one black insurance company.[8] The firm has been a staple of the North Carolina community for more than a century, and Sloan's bloodlines run throughout its existence. He is related to its co-founders Aaron McDuffie Moore and John Merrick. His father was chief operating officer of the company, and such exposure introduced young Maceo to securities at an early age. He bought his first stocks in his junior year of high school and continued throughout his tenure at Morehouse and business school at Georgia State—the only African American in his class. Before he was 30 years old, Sloan returned to NCM and began working there, as had always been his plan. However, his young age and his experiences in investing made him feel confined in a company that had been in existence for more than 70 years.

Sloan had originally written the business plan for NCM Capital when he was just a year out of graduate school, but the powers that be sat on it. It wasn't until they saw Ariel Capital, then Brown Capital, and others that they decided the asset management business had a future. Finally, after serving as chief investment officer, Sloan received approval for NCM Capital from William Kennedy, then the president of North Carolina Mutual Insurance, and the rest of the company's advisory board.

Initially, NCM Capital operated as an arm of the insurance company in an attempt to help it become more of a financial services company. The original strategy, which Ariel Capital also used, was to point out to large endowment and pension funds that a significant percentage of the people represented with those assets are minorities. They also received some business in those early years because they were a black-owned firm, and public funds sought minority managers. "I think that when we started business in the mid-eighties that probably the first seven or eight years it was a novelty," Sloan says. "People had never seen minority-owned investment management firms. So it helped us build but it can only get you so far." For those black managers who sought to build their asset management firms into viable and growing companies, set-asides became limiting after a short period. According to Sloan, "It is one thing to come in and ask for $3 million. It is another thing to come in and ask for $300 million!"[9]

The purpose was not to live on set-asides, but to fulfill the grand ambitions of Affirmative Action. The purpose was never to give African Americans a piece of the action because they were black, it was always to give them an opportunity to show that it was good business for both sides. However, Sloan believes that race and social factors had more effect in the public funds than the corporate. Public funds were run by ordinary people with whom one could argue about equal rights and opportunities. The corporate managers were professionals and the arguments were more business oriented. "I don't think that we argued inclusion as much as we told these funds that they are not getting the best returns possible because they are not looking at all the candidates." NCM Capital's argument worked. About 50 percent of their clients were corporate including Chrysler and Coca-Cola. After they had procured some business, they were able to let their performance do the talking when approaching a potential client.

In 1991, *Pensions & Investments* ranked NCM as the fastest growing money manager in the business with $500 million to $1 billion in assets under management over a five-year period.[10] Within that period, assets under management rose from $7 million in its first year to $761 million, an increase of 10,000 percent. In second place was Schroder Real Estate with 900 percent growth. Ariel Capital Management was also on the list with a growth rate of 640 percent. While at first glance, this headline would seem to be a strong positive, Sloan freely admits that the numbers were misleading and in many ways hurt the firm's business. They were misleading because at the start of this time chart, NCM was still in the nascent stages of its business, so any rise would seem Herculean if judged by percentages. "It was still only $700 million," he says.

As for the impact of the headline, its founder believes that it shifted attention away from the firm's investment strategy to its growth. "As soon as that article came out, until 1993 or 1994, the first question that was asked of us was, 'How can a firm like yours handle growth as fast as you grow?' The assumption was that we couldn't." Although growth had slowed, Sloan and his employees bought NCM Capital from North Carolina Mutual in 1986 and then sold 40 percent of the equity to American Express. The day-to-day business did not change all that much, but the capital allowed development of the holding company—Sloan Financial Corporation.

The firm's investment style was aggressive and active. At first, they were heavily weighted in fixed-income investments because that was Sloan's background and the only track record they had to sell. During this initial period, they were equally balanced between fixed-income and equities and looked for value midcap stocks to choose from. As the 1990s moved on, and they acquired more assets, their style evolved. In 2000, they had $5 billion under management and about 75 percent committed to equities. They also shunned the midcap market and focused on large growth stocks.

What made Sloan such a visible presence in the 1990s was his evolution from a money manager into more of an entrepreneur. Sloan Financial, because of equity infusion from American Express, was able to expand. He still made his frequent trips to appear as a guest commentator on CNBC, and his dynamic mannerisms were attractive to many. His other businesses included PCS Development Corporation, which was a wireless company designed for phones, fax machines, and other communication devices. He also launched the Calvert New Africa Fund and Africa.com in an attempt to broaden his business to Africans and South Africa.

By 2000, however, those plans and ventures were courting disaster. As of the writing of this book, lawsuits are pending between Sloan and his former employees, including his protégé Justin Beckett. While the outcome of these lawsuits and the reasons behind them are yet to be revealed, NCM is still the second biggest black asset management firm in the nation; and if Sloan's talents are any indication, his companies are likely to rebound from their recent troubles.

∞

These trailblazing companies prompted the growth of about 300 minority-owned asset management firms, according to some estimates. Although most of these are niche businesses that have not approached the status of the pioneers, there are a few notables including Smith Graham & Company and Paradigm Asset Management.

Smith Graham is the largest African American firm dealing with fixed-income asset management. It was founded in 1990 by Gerald Smith and Ladell Graham, who eventually left to join the ministry. What is unique about fixed-income strategy is that most pension funds invest less in bonds than equities, meaning that fewer managers are included for those investments. Still, Smith Graham has been able to grow from its Texas roots through a global strategy and the revered marketing skills of Gerald Smith. In 1996, it sold 40 percent of the firm to the Robeco Group in the Netherlands, which maintains $45 billion under management. This allowed Smith Graham to become the only black firm with a substantial reach overseas. By 2000, it held $2.2 billion in assets.

"We could no longer focus on U.S. fiscal and monetary policy as a way to determine where the markets were moving," says Smith. "We saw a shot coming from abroad, foreign capital flows in and out were having a direct impact. We realized that we had to have a global perspective."[11]

In 2001, Smith Graham bought back its interest from Robeco, selling the equity to its employees, while maintaining a strategic alliance with the firm, to keep its international reach.

Paradigm Asset Management began as Beal Investment Company, an arm of M. R. Beal & Company. (Bernard Beal frankly admits that he got the idea from Wardell Lazard.)[12] In 1994, James E. Francis, the CEO, bought it from M. R. Beal, and renamed the company Paradigm. Its unique strategy involved assembling a portfolio based on the stocks of the most successful funds. The firm read the required quarterly reports of the best performing funds, and assembled a group of stocks reflecting their investment philosophy. The sell of this strategy was that index returns would be guaranteed, but the potential for upside was greater than that of other funds.

Because the strategy was unique, some clients were reluctant to sign on. However, *Pensions & Investments* would soon rank Paradigm as one of the best performing companies.[13] By 2000, it maintained over $3 billion in assets managed and was ready to embark on a plan to grow into a huge black-owned firm through acquisitions.

According to Sloan, such steps are necessary, "If we don't all come together and have a black-owned firm with about $25 billion under management, we are toast." Such sentiment applies to all areas of the business. A financier once said, "It is not the strongest that survive, not the smartest who survive, but those who adjust the best." As asset management firms were growing, other black financiers were about to profit from the changing markets.

8

THE BREAKTHROUGH

I T WAS JULY 1993 AND GRIGSBY BRANDFORD had done it. To the shock of all those in the municipal bond industry, from competitors to the observers who stood on the sidelines, they had pulled it off. The firm had beaten Goldman Sachs, Banc America, and more than a dozen major firms to lead the largest bond offering in the history of the city of Los Angeles. There were many, including the city's politicians, who praised the deal for being equivalent to Jackie Robinson's entrance into Major League baseball—it was the first time a black firm had broken into the big leagues. Others complained that Grigsby Brandford's selection had little to do with merit but was the result of lobbying, an example of the excessive politicking that had imbued the selection process. Without question, many saw the deal as a turning point for black-owned firms who had spent years building to break into this action.

For this first generation of black investment banks, the early 1990s were Camelot—a period of greater profits, bigger deals, and larger roles and responsibilities. In the previous decade, the underwriting process was essentially two-tier, with the major firms on top, vying for the lead positions, and all minority-owned investment banks relegated to a secondary role.

Now the two worlds began to merge. The top black firms were able to break into the top positions. This persistence and knowledge peaked in 1993, when four black firms ranked in the top 70 when judged by long-term municipal issues. As these companies were running the books, progress was also occurring in other areas such as the mortgage and asset-backed securities markets because organizations like the Resolution Trust Corporation (RTC) aggressively lobbied their participation. Major firms that used to look down on the black investment banks were now sometimes forced to acknowledge their power and abilities. Tradition was eroding, and as the market swirled with bundles of cash, the top black firms seemed to be on the verge of securing their existence for the future.

The success of any company in any industry, white or black, rich or poor, is greatly swayed and to some degree determined by the health of its overall industry. Beyond the social issues that surround any economic movement, regardless of racism and other sundry factors, the success of a company always correlates with the health of the market. The early 1990s were a terrific time for the fixed-income business: As interest rates dropped, issuers of debt were prompted to take advantage of the lower costs. Both municipal officials and corporate chief financial officers were quick to take advantage of market conditions and refinance their existing debts. Such actions were not only a sound course to follow, but also an almost impulsive maneuver considering how quickly the market had changed. Just a short time earlier, the United States was pursuing the Gulf War, unemployment was rising, and a recession was coming. However, the Federal Reserve continued to lower interest rates in attempts to spark the economy, moves praised by profit-hungry bankers of Wall Street.

After a slowing in all debt and equity offerings in the last months of 1990, the next three years each brought more activity, business, and action than the year before. In 1991, the municipal market offered $164 billion compared with $125 billion from the year before, an increase of 31 percent. The year 1992 topped that figure. At the height of it all, in 1993, municipal bond offerings worth $300 billion were recorded, largely due to the refinancing trend. An almost manic pace of deal making permeated the Street and lured the ambitions of even the most junior of underwriters. Still, the underwriting markets were dominated by the same firms like Merrill Lynch; Goldman Sachs; First Boston; and Smith Barney, Harris, Upham & Company. African Americans could not break into that group in terms of yearly performance. It just could not be done, no matter how much activity occurred, because their lack of capital restricted their ability to play in that area consistently. However, this period demonstrated that if black firms were selective about their choices, they could be the senior managers on big deals and best the major firms that were competing against each other.

The early 1990s were an important period for the Street's biggest black investment banks. The climate was perfect for those who were ready to capitalize. The opportunity to expand operations and increase revenues was there. Black politicians of this post–Civil Rights era were at the height of their power. Major cities posted African American mayors as their leaders: David Dinkins in New York and Wilson Goode in Philadelphia. Tom Bradley in Los Angeles and Maynard Jackson in Atlanta were both serving second stints. Many of the policies of the "Harold Washington Movement" were still in place three years after his untimely death of a heart attack in his City Hall office. The result of this power ranged from specific policies to unwritten codes of inclusion. More than 70 cities enacted goals and quotas for minority participation in city business. Houston officials required that 19 percent of its yearly business be executed by minorities. The laws of the state of California set the numbers at 15 percent, with an additional 5 percent for women. Exactly how each of these policies was carried out varied from city to city. Some governments stipulated that each deal or piece of city business was to include that percentage of minorities. Others looked at the bigger picture and insisted that deals could occur without minorities as long as they represented a certain percentage of the city's business by year's end. Beyond these numbers, many municipalities let it be known that minorities were to be included in all deals despite the absence of any written mandate.

While the climate was inviting, it would take more than laws for established black firms to get the positions they wanted, the leads. In reality, it was more than just leading, they wanted to be in charge of the huge deals. The big firms could not care less if a Pryor McClendon Counts or Daniels & Bell led a $5 million issue in Florida. Nor did they care if black investment banks got 5 percent, and a comanaging role in the massive offerings. Those positions were of no consequence to firms like Merrill Lynch. The fees earned were inconsequential relative to those they were receiving for being senior manager of a $300 million offering. Those were the positions that were the holy grail. Despite the progress that had been made in investment banking, senior managing in the big offerings was off limits. But with the abundance of activity came a greater chance for African Americans to break free of the comanaging shackles. More deals translate to more opportunity. Coupled with the experience that many of them now had under their belts, they felt equipped to push harder to cross that final frontier.

For this push to succeed, the black firms needed more than sympathetic city officials. Political connections for any group could get a small allotment of any business; however, when the numbers and responsibilities were titanic, such connections would not be enough. Instead, they would have to demonstrate talent and ability when orchestrating deals with a reservoir of money on the line. Many more small municipal firms were popping up to capitalize on the quotas—not just black-owned—but Hispanic-, Asian-, and woman-owned. However, those who dreamed bigger wanted more; they educated themselves and learned through experience about the nuances of the art of the deal. "In the old days minority firms focused on getting in because of political connections," Wardell Lazard commented at the time. "Now you have to have a combination of political connections and technical expertise."[1] Certainly, Lazard's success during the first half of the 1990s was emblematic of this historic period for the aggressive firms that began in the 1980s. W. R. Lazard would wrestle with Grigsby Brandford and Pryor McClendon Counts (PMC) for the symbolic title as the world's largest black investment bank.

Pryor McClendon Counts & Grigsby Brandford jockeyed back and forth for that title and the number one spot in *Black Enterprise*'s new Top Investment Banks lists. The mere fact that the list was created in 1991 was proof of progress. Such a list could not have been created just a few years earlier when only a handful of such companies existed on Wall Street. The two firms would engage in this superficial battle with two different styles. Grigsby Brandford would participate in smaller but many more senior transactions to account for its overall numbers. PMC would complete fewer but bigger deals, transactions that were a coup for the period and involved astronomical numbers.

More than anything, the goal for the major black firms in the municipal area was to lead the transactions. "Pryor McClendon Counts was the first firm to convince black mayors to let them lead the deals," says Napoleon Brandford.[2] Pryor McClendon Counts pulled off its first big lead deal in 1990—a $325 million bond offering to finance additional infrastructure for the Hartsfield Airport expansion, the largest ever managed by a minority-owned firm. It was only fitting that the deal encompassed all the historic elements of the first deal in 1977. Maynard Jackson was back as Atlanta's mayor. Because statutory limits prevented any Atlanta mayor from serving more than two consecutive terms, Jackson retreated from public life, first as a lawyer, and then as the founder of his own investment bank, Jackson Securities, in 1986. After some years, he decided to reenter the public sector and was elected again as mayor in 1989. His campaign manager for that run was Raymond McClendon who was widely reported in all publications as a close aide to Jackson. The relationship was so strong that he was often heard to say that if "I had 10 Ray McClendons I could run the world."[3] However, the downside of this friendship was the curiosity that its closeness generated. Moreover, it became an issue that caused many, mostly competitors, to question the merits of the transaction, even though PMC had substantial experience with airport issues. "That deal had a lot of controversy, a lot of very vicious fights on the part of some major firms who did not want us to senior manage,"[4] says Howard Mackey, a senior vice president at the firm. The buzz around the deal was so great that it led to an article in the city's major newspaper, the *Atlanta Journal-Constitution* entitled, "Lucrative City Bond Sale Goes to Mayor's Friends: Aides say he just has many contacts in field."[5] Jackson's people argued that all deals are in some way done with an associate: "The mayor wanted to put together a team he feels comfortable with. The process clearly doesn't lend itself to total objectivity. It's a personality-sensitive thing."[6] Despite the attempts to defuse the issue, people began watching the firm, and the scrutiny would last for some time, prompting Jackson to joke, "It brought tremendous heat. People were wishing the plague upon my children for that deal."[7] But for now, PMC was on a roll.

The significance of that deal was enormous. It was at a level that the firm had never reached before, and they received accolades for this breakthrough. Some came from the financial community, who took notice of the firm's ability to sell bonds. Pryor McClendon Counts disproved the traditional argument that little firms could not do a big deal because of a lack of capital. Keep in mind that its early business dealt in arbitrage, which often depends on the swiftness of sales and trading. The firm was built in the image of its founders, and their salesforce was near or at the top of all minority-owned firms. For its principals, the firm's trading prowess was a source of pride; in fact, it was the criterion by which it judged itself. The amount of an offering that a firm is involved in often can be misleading because each manager receives full credit, even though he might not have sold a bond, so PMC chose to calculate the growth of their firm by the amount of bonds traded through its salesforce. From 1986 to 1991, such volume grew from $186 million to $2.8 billion.

The growth of business, activity, and profits was remarkable when judged against the deals PMC had led in 1986. In contrast to the $300 million plus offered in the Hartsfield Airport deal, it led a $20 million bond issue for Philadelphia's Hospitals and Higher Education Facilities Authority. It also led a $6 million bond issue for the New York State Dormitory Authority. Such expansion was reflected in the physical appearance of Pryor McClendon Counts. The firm was swelling and occupied nearly 10 offices in cities across the nation including San Francisco, Atlanta, and Denver. The purpose of such expansion was to create a national reputation and show a commitment to the municipalities where they did business. Rather than be limited by their Philadelphia office, they sought to establish relationships with local politicians and other officials to debunk any hints of being outsiders or unfamiliar with the needs of each municipality. Such efforts helped

to break down walls as shown by its next big deal, a transaction that would better its previous standard.

In 1991 they snagged the lead position in a nearly $400
million debt offering for the Denver airport. The deal topped
their previous record, making it the largest ever managed by a
minority-owned firm. It also drew similar controversy when it
was disclosed that the firm was one of the largest contributors
to Mayor Wellington E. Webb's campaign. Initially, Goldman
Sachs had been chosen for the lead role but at Webb's request,
PMC replaced it. The deal would later receive even greater
scrutiny as the firm and all of its peers, white and black, would
later be challenged for misleading investors in the bonds. That
controversy was yet to come, but even if it had come at that period, who would have noticed with all their success?

PMC had become a cash cow. By 1993, SEC records indicate that the firm was earning over $18 million in revenues.
Relative to other periods, such cash flow and activity was
truly astonishing and a testament to their penchant and ability
to continue landing big deals. Most of these earnings came
from a frenetic period in the summer of 1993 when the firm
completed 12 senior-managed deals totaling more than $1 bil-
lion; the centerpiece was an offering for the Pennsylvania In-
tergovernmental Cooperation Authority worth more than
$800 million. Although the deal again pushed the envelope of
what was possible and again redefined the term, "the largest
offering ever led by a minority-owned firm," it was not without its complications. "There were about 22 co-managers,"
says Mackey. "I remember that the day we priced that deal,
the market dropped about a point and a half so there was a lot
of scrambling to change the structure of the deal, changing the
couponing, maturities, insurance orders to fit certain customers. It took a lot to get done but in the end it ran very
smoothly."[8] On the opposite end of the spectrum was the deal
it had done in December of the previous year for Howard

University. The completion of the $33 million offering represented the first time that an historically black college used a black investment bank to lead the way into the capital markets. Life had come full circle because Allen Counts was an alumnus of the university.

In addition to the firm's success in the investment banking field, it was also building an asset management business with its subsidiary Wedgewood Capital Management. In 1991, the goal of this affiliate was to procure $100 million under management. In 1993, it maintained approximately $330 million by using a conservative strategy of fixed-income investments. Although it was nothing near the business W. R. Lazard was generating, it provided the firm with footing outside the banking sectors and served as another example of PMC's desire to use these good times to firmly entrench itself for the future.

∞

All firms that added asset management to their business were in some way responding to a successful strategy implemented by Wardell Lazard. Although, W. R. Lazard's underwriting business traditionally fell behind Grigsby Brandford and PMC, the early 1990s were so successful that one former employee remembers, "There was so much cash flowing in at that point, it just wouldn't stop."

The most profitable period in the firm's history was from spring 1993 to early 1994. In addition to being the largest minority-owned asset management firm, peaking at about $2.8 billion, W. R. Lazard won its biggest deals. Perhaps the most significant was its largest account, the senior managing position of a $375 billion issue for New York City Municipal Water Finance Authority. It ranked equally with other senior managers such as PaineWebber. The supporting comanagers included Goldman Sachs and Bear Stearns. It marked the first time a black-owned firm had ever participated in that capacity for the biggest city in the world. It was also the centerpiece for its broker/dealer business that year accounting for most of the $490 million in debt they led to the market. Beyond the numbers, it was a sign that after years of piggybacking on the vitality of its asset management business and, to some degree, its advisory work, its broker/dealer effort was starting to pay dividends. "We started to make money from the broker/dealer business so we were making it on both sides," says Mel Eubanks.[9] The firm was earning enormous returns, $15 million to $18 million by one estimate and seemed positioned and ready to survive any turmoil the economic markets may have had coming its way.

Grigsby Brandford had not branched out into as many areas as PMC and W. R. Lazard; they chose to apply all of their resources into public finance. They did so in a very large and well-publicized fashion. Beginning in 1991, the firm began to organize and throw an annual three-day retreat for public finance professionals to network and discuss issues. Brandford says they got the idea after attending a junk bond conference thrown by Drexel Lambert Burnham. Nicknamed the Predators' Ball, the conference helped its leader Michael Milken secure his reputation as an almighty talent. In many ways, Grigsby Brandford's retreat did the same for its public face, Calvin Grigsby. Already known for his talent and creativity in constructing a deal, such public grandeur helped to propel Grigsby's aura. One publication even labeled him the "Bond King."[10] This attention was a response not only to the work they were doing or the business they were getting, but also to the style in which they got it.

Expanding the work they began using COPs, Grigsby Brandford continued on its senior binge, completing nearly four times the senior transactions that PMC accomplished in 1993, just smaller ones. Many of the deals came from the Bay

Area because that was where the firm was based. Although Brandford once indicated that in terms of national business, setting up in San Francisco hurt the firm because the city was better known for its hippies than its financiers, it helped in securing the local contracts. "On the West Coast we had an advantage," says Clifford Graves, a former vice president with the company. "We could say that we are in your neighborhood. We know the projects and your situations and that we can be at your office within an hour or two."[11]

Such tenacity and location helped them land numerous deals in California. In 1992, they led a $75 million issue for the San Diego Gas & Electric Company. They also brought in the Los Angeles County Transportation Commission for a $107 million bond issue with a syndicate of all minority-owned investment banks. The most prominent, and the one that received the most criticism, was a landmark $503 million refunding for the Los Angeles Convention Center. Articles and rumors soon arose that Grigsby Brandford won because of aggressive lobbying efforts to the Los Angeles City Council. Some highlighted this effort as the sole reason that they decided to go with the firm despite the recommendation from city financial experts that they go with Goldman Sachs. On the other hand, Grigsby Brandford attributed the success to one thing only, "hard work." The firm insisted that the contract was won based on the merits and quality of the proposal. "Calvin was a creative genius," says Graves. "He had this uncanny ability to tweak something to make it better in terms of price, in terms of structure."[12]

Also unique was the firm's salesforce, who sold their bonds to everybody, from the more common choice of institutional investors to retail investors. For the landmark deal, they were able to unload about $140 million on its first day in the market and completed the balance within a week. Such was the norm for the firm, and for most of the black investment banks of the era. Unlike major firms, which could and would often keep some of the securities when executing bond issues, these African American companies bought them and then sold them right out the door. They simply did not have the capital to maintain such a portfolio.

In return for the convention center deal, they received $1 million in fees. Such rewards obviously made them happy, but the loss of business was not taken well by those who had monopolized it for so long. In fact, some attribute all of the negative press that came after the selection of Grigsby Brandford to rumors spread by the losing firms out of spite and bitterness. "That was the home run that Calvin had wanted for so long and the firm worked its butt off to get that deal," says Graves. "It was the first time that the big firms discovered that they weren't invincible. And it is not much fun for a white vice president to go back to Wall Street to explain why he lost this huge deal to a black kid from San Francisco."[13]

Despite the rumors, that deal set up a string of big successes like a $212 million offering for New York City and $224 million for Sacramento. Even when the bond markets changed in 1994, Grigsby Branford continued to do well, hiring 20 more institutional salesmen to unload the growing amounts of bonds coming in. They also were expanding offices into cities like Detroit and Sacramento. To many, it was the firm that had the best chance of becoming something great.

In addition to success in the municipal area, barriers were falling in other businesses like the market in mortgage and asset-backed securities, which are essentially collateralized debt securities. Part of this move was the result of one particular agency that aggressively promoted a plan to include minority- or women-owned banking firms (MWOB) in all of its issues beginning in 1991. The organization that established this policy was the Resolution Trust Corporation (RTC), which was given the task of bailing out insolvent S&L institutions.

Part of these efforts resulted from the passing of a law requiring that minorities be involved in the business generated from the bailout to the maximum extent possible. No quotas or set percentages were ever established to further define it. Shortly into the process, however, word got out that minorities had participated in as little as 5 percent of the bailout work, far below even the lowest expectations. Soon such efforts were reenergized, and taking the lead were organizations like the RTC and the Veterans Administration (VA). They aggressively sought minority-owned firms to help unload the mortgage-backed securities.

Like most inclusion endeavors, the opening of this market had a two-sided effect. On the upside, it represented a new market, a way to diversify their current product base beyond municipal bonds. On the flip side, the securities that these organizations were willing to give them a chance to sell were dominated by a few big players. Minority-owned firms had few professionals trained to handle the action of the securities' attributes. Some firms hired experienced people to help them enter the market. Others were content with educating their current employees. That decision was often based on commitment to the businesses or the length of time a firm thought that the market was going to be open. Would the RTC and the VA always be giving them product and an opportunity to sell it? That was the deciding question.

Perhaps the firm of this established guard that embraced this opportunity the fastest was Pryor McClendon Counts; in 1991, it led a $200 million RTC offering. Other firms that were included in the minority pool were Doley Securities, W. R. Lazard, M. R. Beal, and a newcomer named Utendahl

Capital Partners. It was certainly a new era and area for African Americans to explore.

∞

As all this success was achieved by the top black investment banks, a company called TLC Beatrice International stood atop the annual Black Enterprise 100 list that chronicles the nation's largest companies. It consistently racked up sales of over $2 billion. The second largest company had yet to reach $500 million. The force behind TLC was Reginald F. Lewis, a Wall Street lawyer who had moved to the client side in the early 1980s. He did so by playing ball in the game of the era: corporate restructuring.

While the mergers and acquisitions (M&A) business can be traced back more than a century, it had never had the impact that it displayed in the 1980s. Like a tidal wave, its effect was so overwhelming that it captured the imagination of those outside Wall Street and reached into the homes of Middle America. Never before had astronomical figures ranging into the billions been thrown about as if they were pennies. These deals—the sale of assets and cuts in jobs—affected ordinary Americans.

The business itself gained prominence beginning in the 1960s with people like Andre Meyer and Felix Rohatyn. Its growth into a major industry began in the 1970s, when the brokerage business knew it was embroiled in the uncertainty of Mayday. This event in the mid-1970s led the major firms to begin building their M&A departments. Joseph Perella set up his department at First Boston Corporation in 1973. Lehman Brothers set up M&A operations in 1976. Also in that year, three virtually unknown people who had been doing little deals called *leveraged buyouts* for Bear Stearns left to form their own company. Their names were Jerome Kohlberg, Henry Kravis, and George Roberts.

Kohlberg Kravis Roberts (KKR), Perella, his partner Bruce Wasserstein, and others would become symbols of American capitalism a decade later. The dominant instrument of corporate restructuring was the leveraged buyout (LBO), in which a group of small investors can take control of a publicly owned company.

The growth in the industry and in deals accelerated as resources became available to take advantage of a clear opportunity. When inflation took hold in the 1970s, the price of assets in most corporations rose, which in turn increased the values of these items in the open market. Yet, the depressed times kept the market capitalization of publicly owned companies down, and an imbalance of value developed. Because individual parts of these huge corporations were worth more than the sum, buying control of these companies and then selling their assets and/or restructuring their configuration could lead to enormous gains.

As with any purchase, however, there was a price, and for these huge companies, that price often ran into the billions. The resources to finance these acquisitions in most cases did not come from the people seeking control but from outside sources. Michael Milken and his junk bonds in particular came to define that period on Wall Street. He sent shivers down the spine of CEOs because he had the power to single-handedly fund a raider or financier's efforts. His ability to raise money allowed for the explosion in LBO prices, and in effect made it the biggest business of the day.

Like so many other areas of elite business, blacks had been excluded from this high-stakes game. Traditionally, LBOs had been the most successful with the blessings and cooperation of management. Social factors such as race made it difficult for a black man to foster this relationship and convince the big operators to supply the capital to participate on the grand stage.

Reginald Lewis brought the walls crashing down. A native of Baltimore, his story has become legend and, for many, the standard against which all financiers are judged. "From age 7, he knew what he wanted to do," says his wife, Loida Lewis.[14] After graduation from college and then Harvard Law School, Lewis went to work at Paul, Weiss & Rifken. But, in the spirit of entrepreneurship, he decided to leave the prestige and comfort of a career at the revered legal powerhouse to open his own law firm.

The firm specialized in Minority Enterprise Small Business Investment Companies (MESBIC) deals, essentially venture capital companies that invested in minority-owned businesses. MESBIC were a popular industry for the black financiers of the 1970s, many of whom would later succeed in other high-profile areas. One of the largest MESBICs was a company called Equico, which was led by Frank Savage, a Howard graduate. Savage went on to become chairman of other notable institutions such as Freedom National Bank and Alliance Capital Management. Doing the negotiating in these deals was Reginald Lewis.

Although Lewis received recognition for his legal work, he felt limited by his law practice. "Because law is based on fees, the returns were limited to the amount of hours he could work," says Loida Lewis. "So he thought, 'I want to be in a business where the returns are endless, where the money can work for me.'"[15]

With this realization, Lewis decided to switch to the other side of the table and be the one acquiring companies. Still, despite his reservoir of energy, persistence, and intelligence, he did not immediately achieve that goal. Lewis first set his sights on a legendary black company called Parks Sausage. Founded by Henry Parks in 1951 with $60,000, it was one of the first black companies to go public. When it had grown to more than $9 million in revenues in the late 1960s, it offered 220,000 shares at $8 a share. Yet the company lost much of its luster and star power when the almost universally revered Parks became sick with cancer. Lewis's inexperience negated the two sides from getting anywhere close to a deal. Lewis also had interest in other companies such as Almant and Nobert Simon Inc., all of which resulted in nothing but disappointment.

The big breakthrough came years later in 1983 in the form of McCall Pattern. This company was part of a large conglomerate called Esmark Incorporated. It was viewed as a declining business mainly because women were leaving their traditional home lives and not sewing. After careful analysis, Lewis and his team thought differently, especially comforted by its strong cash flow. After arranging financing that included groups like MESBICs and $1 million of his personal capital, the newly formed TLC Group, a holding company under which Lewis would orchestrate his deals, bought McCall Pattern for $22.5 million.

What at the time was an extraordinary move, was in fact merely a prelude. Within three years, the TLC Group sold McCall Pattern for $63 million. But, in addition to other assets involved in the transaction, the return was $90 million. Because Lewis held nearly all the equity in the company, he received all of the money, or "90 to 1" returns as the *New York Times* would headline it.[16]

As soon as the McCall deal was closed, Lewis began searching for a bigger conquest and soon set his sights on Beatrice Company. In 1986, Beatrice had been taken private by Kravis Kohlberg & Roberts and its high-ranking executives. KKR was the premier name in LBOs. The price was by far the biggest ever pulled off at the time, a record $6.2 billion. In the years following the acquisition, the group was looking to sell off some of its assets, one of which was of interest to Lewis—the international division.

Beatrice International's business was mainly food distribution. It operated in 31 countries, with revenues of $2.5 billion. Lewis believed that its future lay largely in Europe, so after careful analysis by the TLC team, they decided that they would sell some assets if they could to buy the company. Months of 20-hour-plus days, poring over every detail, calculating every number, were all summarized in TLC's bid in 1987 of just over $900 million. But, competition was fierce because about 12 other parties were seeking control over various aspects of Beatrice.

Additional pressures came not from competitors, but from the inherent impediments that are associated with first-timers. Credibility soon became an issue as Salomon Brothers, Beatrice's financial advisor, the company's owners, and other officials began to question the bid from the nearly unknown Lewis or TLC. Lewis was able to overcome this anonymity with the success of the McCall deal, as well as a source of financing that had agreed to back his efforts—Michael Milken and his department at Drexel Burnham Lambert, which helped to finance the second and final stage of the LBO boom. Milken's reputation for providing groups with the billions of dollars needed to buy these corporations helped TLC's efforts immensely.

Once the bid of just above $900 million was submitted, the TLC team soon got antsy and uncertain. Had they done everything right? Had they calculated the value of all of the assets correctly? More importantly, would their bid be enough? After some thought about it in the car ride home, they decided to up their bid. Lewis got on the phone with one of the principals of KKR and said that they were going to up their bid to $985 million. They would later find out that they were bidding against themselves, basically upping their own price because they already had the best offer but that was the cost of entering the big leagues. "That was the premium he had to pay to play with the big guys," says Loida Lewis.

The symbolism of Lewis's purchase of TLC Beatrice International was extraordinary. At that time Wall Street was dominated by a few select names and personalities, all of which were involved in the deal in an almost magical fashion, as if to make the deal more historic. Salomon Brothers' swaggering and boisterous ways coupled with their enormous profits during the period was perfect for the times as was reflected when its chairman, John Gutfreund, appeared on the cover of *Business Week* as "The King of Wall Street."[17] There were none bigger at the time than Michael Milken and KKR partner Henry Kravis. To have a deal involving all these parties, with Lewis, a black financier rising to the top, was a watershed event. *Black Enterprise* publisher Earl Graves compared the TLC Beatrice acquisition to the 1954 *Brown v. Board* decision.[18]

During this exciting period for African Americans in finance, they were leading deals, beating major firms, executing leveraged buyouts, and learning new areas of business. But as history would dictate, the next years brought turmoil. These financiers learned, as had earlier generations, that great success is often followed by serious difficulties.

9

THE TURMOIL

THE YEAR 1994 WAS THE BEGINNING OF A sorrowful period for African Americans on Wall Street. People mourned the loss of business, the changing markets, and even the limits of mortality. It signaled the end of a chapter for African Americans on Wall Street because the hard-earned reputations of many of its most prominent people and businesses were dragged down in a whirlwind of decline. The black community was shaken by an astounding series of unbelievable events that would have only seemed possible in the movies or one's imagination. Even though the majority of the black financial circle maintained the highest standards, each day's newspaper seemed to bring more of an endless supply of tragic news of death, political scandal, or financial impropriety. The problems cast a shadow so large that it captured the attention of the media and financial community and left the landscape for African Americans on Wall Street forever altered.

What made the year so catastrophic for all of Wall Street was an exploding economy. After enduring the post-Gulf War recession of the early 1990s, the economy was now posting an annual growth rate of nearly 6 percent. But, with any economic growth comes the inherent worries of inflationary

219

pressures, and the Federal Reserve was watching closely. Convinced that the United States was recovering too fast, Federal Reserve Chairman Alan Greenspan decided on February 7, 1994, to raise interest rates 0.25 percent, the first increase in five years. Another five hikes would follow resulting in an aggregate increase of 2.5 percent in the federal funds rate for the year. With hindsight, these moves would prove to be correct as the decade went on to record an historic expansion leading to great profits and record unemployment. But, in the context of that time, many were unhappy. Wall Street was especially cranky.

After years of record activity that led to fat wallets and celebratory cigars, the industry hit a thud. Wall Street had traveled piggyback on its booming businesses such as trading and bond underwriting only to see those areas, like others, drop to ulcer-causing levels. Things got so bad that the Securities Industry Association, the Street's chief lobbying group, predicted that total profits would drop an amazing 80 percent. Total issuance of securities dropped more than $400 billion from the previous year as the buying market seemed unable to receive any offering with fair optimism.

In the municipal bond industry, the story was even worse. The glorious environment that had been shaped in large part by a refinancing trend, was over as the muni business reached its crescendo. Just as declining rates encouraged volume to its highest levels in 1993, rising rates choked it a year later. Issuance dropped a shattering 44 percent from $289 billion to $162.2 billion, according to Securities Data Company. In addition, profit margins continued to fall as they had since the early 1980s when munis were most rewarding. Management fees that had been about 3 percent of the total issue in that golden era dropped to as low as 0.5 percent. The situation was so dire that many of the Street's most established and well-financed investment banks were forced to reconsider their commitment to the business. Within a matter of years beginning in 1987, Salomon Brothers; E.F. Hutton; Donaldson, Lufkin & Jenrette; and CS First Boston had all shut down their departments and left the business. Others like Morgan Stanley and Lehman Brothers took less drastic measures and cut their public finance staff by 25 percent in 1994. Observers could only wonder: If the major firms are fleeing, what is happening to the African American firms?

It is misleading to say that all African American investment banks were totally dependent on municipal business. Other sectors such as government and agency business were opening their doors to minority firms and this banking was beginning to move. Companies like W. R. Lazard, Pryor McClendon Counts, and M. R. Beal were doing well with their asset management arms proving that their revenue sources were fairly diverse. However, municipal business was a substantial contributor to most African American firms at the time, especially the second- and lower-tier banks. Therefore, the current problems with munis adversely affected these bodies, eventually wiping many of them out.

There were three levels of the municipal-oriented investment banks. Prominent companies like Pryor McClendon Counts and M. R. Beal maintained a relative national presence. Smaller regional firms like Charles A. Bell Securities in San Francisco and Apex Securities in Houston were participating in lesser volumes, but had successfully developed their niches.

On the last level, many less committed, unqualified, and opportunistic minority-owned broker/dealers were created simply to profit from the minority-friendly policies of municipalities. Most of these founders had never participated in any area of public finance but the impact of their firms was twofold. First, the competition of minority-owned firms vying for a capped percentage helped drive down the economics of the business. In addition to African Americans, there were numerous Hispanic, Asian, and women-owned brokerages angling for this business—too many. One estimate counted between 150 and 300 minority-owned firms at the time, effectively making it unprofitable for those who only worked as secondary players in the offerings. "There was no money in it as a co-manager," says Harold E. Doley. His firm had never concentrated on the municipal business, focusing more on corporate and foreign activity, especially in Africa. Others like the big black investment banks could survive in the business because they were getting senior managed roles and generally had greater capital reserves. So as the volume disappeared in 1994 and Affirmative Action programs became a punching bag of choice, so, too, did any hopes that these small firms could make a profit.

The second effect of these newer firms had less to do with the numbers and more to do with general perception. A feeling was spreading within the municipal bond industry that many of these less experienced minority-owned firms had little interest in participating in the business in traditional ways. Older firms like W. R. Lazard and Hispanic-owned Guzman & Company had participated in the co-manager role, but they made it abundantly clear that they had ambitions for greater things. A few years later, as municipalities began to enact laws that gave minorities a certain percentage of city business, many of the new firms left the impression that they were simply cashing in on the current trend without any long-term aspirations. Some of these firms did not attempt to procure product to sell, choosing only to take the management fee.

Needless to say, the growing political aspects of municipal bond deals did not sit well with major firms and competitors. It did not take long for such sentiments to reach the press. To get a true feeling of the scorn heaped on the municipal bond industry, one need look no further than media headlines. *Business Week* came out with articles entitled "The Trouble with Munis"[1] and "Affirmative, Yes—But Is It Fair?"[2] Within a few months, *Forbes* came out with its own version called "The Set-Aside Charade,"[3] and so it went. The *Forbes* article made use of a company named FAIC Securities to illustrate the race-based political implications that were involved in municipal deals. The broker/dealer had little underwriting experience (its founders had come from the sugarcane business), yet it was able to secure business. One deal in particular with Dade County came after one of the firm's principals wrote a letter to the finance board stating, "FAIC is a 95 percent Hispanic-owned and controlled firm. The firm's Hispanic ownership allows for the opportunity to participate in programs available to minority-owned firms."[4] The company was later included in many of the county's deals.

Such participation struck a nerve of suspicion particularly among the major firms; they resented the neophytes who were garnering fees for doing little work. Furthermore, there was increasing politicking to distinguish companies from the hoard of beginning minority-owned firms that sought a place in each deal. The casualty of all this was the disappearance of fairness and meritocracy as donations and relationships were stressed more than ever before. But major firms that did have a gripe could not do much about it. One municipal banker at the time said, "It's like being a part of the club. If you start to complain about what minorities get for doing nothing, the city commissioners and people like them just won't give you a piece of the action."[5]

❧

While the exact number of the minority-owned firms that only took this superficial approach is unknown, it cast a pall over many of the others. This perception was aided by the context of the time because the municipal bond industry as a whole was plagued with impropriety—it was not restricted just to minorities. The muni business was now the dirtiest on Wall Street as the political aspects and money involved became intertwined within loose regulatory boundaries. But in the early 1990s, the walls that surrounded the backrooms and shielded the public from such improprieties came tumbling down and, ironically, these deals involved white bankers.

Probably the greatest reason for the widening target on municipal deals was the growing importance of money in politics. As the costs of campaigns and lobbying efforts soared to record heights, the relationship between candidates and Wall Street grew stronger and more important. Investment bankers and other securities professionals were a prime target for fund-raising efforts for one simple reason: They had money. In addition to their large bank accounts, their friends and cousins were blessed with similar luxuries, a useful network for raising money. As the numbers grew, so did the curiosity of outsiders who began to question the correlation between contributions and those hired by city officials to do business. Those who examined such relationships were soon given a high-profile case that many argue led the industry down the road to reform. An investigation began in 1993 into the sale of $2.9 billion worth of bonds by the New Jersey Turnpike Authority. Officials from both the Securities and Exchange Commission (SEC) and Manhattan's U.S. Attorney's office probed into allegations that Merrill Lynch and other firms who won roles in the offering, made illegal payments to a company that was co-owned by an aide to then New Jersey Governor Jim Florio. The investigation led to the conviction of this aide for securities fraud. However, no charges were filed against any major firm and no evidence pointed to Florio's involvement in the illegal dealings.

Another significant case was that of Mark Ferber, a partner with Lazard Freres, who failed to disclose a fee-splitting agreement with Merrill Lynch to his clients. Ferber served as an advisor to four agencies and was supposed to offer independent opinions but instead steered business to Merrill Lynch and profited from the transactions. In the end, he was convicted on 56 counts of fraud and corruption.

Perhaps the most famous episode of this period was the bankruptcy of Orange County, California. To maximize returns, the county's treasurer, Robert Citron, decided to invest in the complicated and often esoteric instruments called derivatives. However, these interest-rate-sensitive securities plummeted in value as the Federal Reserve acted to slow down the economy. The result led to billions in losses forcing the county to file for bankruptcy. In the aftermath, Citron indicated that he was pushed to invest in derivatives by his financial advisors on Wall Street, leading more people to view securities firms with a skeptical eye.

Events like these drew a call for reform from many Americans. The key opponent of all these illicit transactions would come to office just as the industry appeared to be at its most corrupt. Arthur Levitt, former chairman of the American Stock Exchange, was appointed the head of the SEC in 1993. By the end of his tenure in early 2001, he would be credited as being one of the most active chairmen in the history of the office and most recognized for his work to protect the small investor. But, all this acclamation was ahead of him as he assumed his position, and among his first priorities was reformation of the municipal bond market.

In Levitt's eyes, this industry was a prime target for reform for two main reasons. One was his concern for the small investor. The early 1980s were ruled by the institutional investor and accounted for the majority of all buying. A decade later, however, the opposite was true: Individual investors bought more than 70 percent of all municipal bonds. So the SEC initiated steps to tighten disclosure rules so that buyers would be better informed about the securities they were buying.

The other reason was the high-profile cases of scandal, and the SEC thus sought to limit the impact of contributions in the selection process. In the 1970s, the majority of deals were competitive, meaning that firms were asked to submit a proposal and selection was based on the strength of their ideas and calculations. Two decades later, the opposite was true; about 75 percent of deals were negotiated, meaning that firms were chosen and then the specifics were ironed out. Critics of the emerging trend feared that government officials could select an investment bank based on considerations unrelated to the deal and possibly hurt the municipality.

The SEC's commitment to clean up the municipal bond industry was part of a larger effort from Washington, D.C. A call to action was issued by members of Congress who wrote letters to the SEC, the National Association of Securities Dealers (NASD), and the Municipal Securities Rulemaking Board (MSRB) to look into these matters. It added to the enormous pressure for regulation. One of the letters asked these organizations to "take a comprehensive look at the present scheme of regulation in light of the current scandals involving illegal payoffs, influence peddling, conflicts of interest, and questionable practices."[6]

One of the landmark decisions to clean up the process was a rule called G-37 that became effective in April 1994. It sparked a great outcry from many, especially in the black financial community. Essentially, G-37 said that a person cannot engage in any municipal business with a official within two years of contributing money to that issuer. The purpose of the rule was to reduce conflicts of interest in awarding municipal contracts.

As soon as the rule's approval was announced, many in the industry lined up to voice their criticism. In particular, African Americans felt that it was disproportionately harmful to them; in effect, the rules of the game were being changed just as they had mastered them. Some went as far as to say that the ban was a violation of their civil rights.

The rule had its greatest impact in the political world. "There is no question in my mind that it had a greater effect on minority officeholders," says Bill Hayden. "We didn't have a lot of people in office. We didn't have a lot of people with high incomes who understood the political process and made contributions."[7] Black politicians relied heavily on minority contributions to finance their campaigns and political initiatives. "It snuffed out a significant level of contributions to minority officeholders who traditionally had trouble raising money."

The drastic results stamped 1994 with a political shift to the right. Notable black political pioneers such as Tom Bradley, Maynard Jackson, and David Dinkins either lost or decided not to seek reelection, often leaving their cities in the hands of successors who placed less emphasis on inclusionary policies. Affirmative Action was under attack, and there was no better symbol of the changing politics than the "Gingrich Revolution" that November, which won back the Republican Party's control of Congress in the landslide midterm elections.

Some bankers went even further to question the motives of those who made the rule. It was originally proposed by the MSRB, a body made up of professionals with ties to the major firms. One longtime municipal finance insider wondered aloud if it was more than a coincidence that the rule was enacted shortly after major firms started losing big deals to minority-owned firms. But David Clapp, who led Goldman Sachs's muni department to prominence for decades and served on the MSRB in 1994 says that isn't so. "1993 was as bad as I had seen it," he says, referring to the amount of lobbying and money influencing decisions.[8]

Some African Americans also believe that the ruckus made over G-37 was excessive and at times unnecessary." G-37 was not a business killer, it was a market obstacle," says Kenneth E. Glover, who joined W. R. Lazard as vice chairman in 1993. "Many of our firms did not react appropriately. Instead, we became so focused on G-37 that we left municipal-related and corporate business on the table."[9] Instead, Glover argues that G-37 helped business because it removed some of the expenses from operating in the market. "In a very weird way, G-37 helped bring the economics into the municipal business since it lowered the expenses of new business efforts." As for the political impact of the rule, he argues that it, too, was overblown. Glover served as treasurer for both the Harold Washington and David Dinkins reelection campaigns and referred to that experience when he said, "Fund raisers did not bring in that much money. All it was about was meeting people!"

Some point to the upstart firms such as Utendahl Capital Partners and Williams Capital Group, which later gained prominence without any involvement in municipal finance, as examples of the direction others could have taken. But the prominent African American firms of the day were fully occupied in a struggle to adjust not only to a changing market, but to changing rules as well.

Although the impact of G-37 may be debatable, the uproar was symbolic of the aggregate doom. Who can blame some of these professionals for their reactive paranoia? Within the context of the dismal bond market, many black firms were forced to acknowledge that consolidation or liquidation would be the best route to follow. Charles A. Bell Securities was sold to the Chapman Company, which used it to complement its retail brokerage business. Apex Securities was later sold to Rice Financial Products, an up-and-coming derivatives firm. Others all but disappeared under the weight of mounting expenses and dwindling revenue. The destruction of many of these lesser known firms is sad, but the market often determines the fate of those who work in finance. What made this period so deeply disturbing, even tragic, for the entrepreneurs is the fate that befell the Street's most recognizable African American investment banks. The adverse market conditions, of course, affected these companies, but they were done in by incidents that went far beyond the simplicity of deals and interest rates. In a few short years, the seemingly strong companies that had grown steadily for more than a decade were never the same.

After decades of firsts, Daniels & Bell had the pain of being the first of these high-profile black firms to fall. Many feel that its fate was sealed in January 1988 when Travers J. Bell Jr., its co-founder and chairman, suffered a massive heart attack and died at the age of 46. In addition to spilling tears in the halls of the New York headquarters, the employees, as well as clients around the nation, expressed doubts about the firm's prospects. Despite a history of heart problems, Bell had failed to name or groom a successor, leaving vacant the chair at the top of the firm. Even if he had developed a protégé, people doubted that anyone could have filled the shoes of the firm's fallen leader. Just days after his death, clients began calling the firm to express their concern about its viability. "We didn't hire you or Daniels & Bell, we hired Travers Bell," many said.

The vacuum left at the head of the firm was not unusual. Succession is always a question with smaller companies, especially if the firm and its founder have seemingly merged into a single image. With death comes a tendency to enlarge and revere that image leaving a daunting task for those left behind, especially if the person's legacy is impressive. Perhaps the most famous example of this phenomenon is John F. Kennedy. He became president winning less than 50 percent of the aggregate vote. Days after his assassination, a poll recorded that more than 65 percent of Americans claimed they had voted for him. A similar predicament occurred with Daniels & Bell—clients expressed their concern immediately because they all believed they had been, and in some sense were, dealing solely with Travers Bell.

To overcome this hurdle, the firm's board of directors moved quickly to reestablish stability with pomp and name recognition. Dwight L. White, who had served as a vice president for the firm for about five years was named president. White headed the firm's Pittsburgh office and was a celebrity in many circles from his earlier days as a defensive end for the Pittsburgh Steelers's renowned "Steel Curtain Defense." Although he had been in the business for a relatively short period and had no management experience, White had proven himself a capable banker, which coupled with his fame made him an attractive replacement. Another important position was filled by Travers J. Bell Sr., who came out of retirement to serve as chairman. Bell was important because he was the only person who maintained a principal's license and his name and presence were intended to calm uneasy clients. At age 75, however, he did not get too involved in day-to-day operations.

At first, the firm appeared to band together. It concentrated on essentially the same businesses that it had pursued in previous years, municipal finance, equity, and research. The business that still received the most attention was the muni department, and it appeared to be achieving the same success as before, dropping only two spots on *Institutional Investor*'s important annual public finance list summarizing 1988. The rankings are important to all investment banks because in the ego-driven world of Wall Street, they indicate who is the biggest and best. Although Daniels & Bell did not drop dramatically, the rankings suggested that a change was brewing. Relative to those minority-owned firms that followed it to the Street, it was losing ground. Grigsby Brandford gained more than 10 spots. W. R. Lazard improved 22 places.

Such results fed an ongoing disagreement between the body of the firm and its owners about the direction the company should take. Travers Bell Jr. had left his firm to his children, the majority of stock to his 24-year-old son, Darryl. A year into the firm's new era, its owners were dissatisfied with the declining municipal market. Spreads were falling, the Tax Reform Act of 1986 had changed the business, and the growing competition from other minority-owned firms led them to believe that cutting down their public finance department would be in their best interests. It was not an unusual move considering that Salomon Brothers had exited the business in 1987.

As these sentiments seeped down to the rest of the firm, many of the muni professionals began to leave. Others were fired to save costs. Those who remained focused on existing clients but declined to pursue new business. In effect, this new attitude toward public finance left no place for Dwight White, who himself was a municipal banker. He left in January 1989 to go to W. R. Lazard.

With this scaleback in its most prominent business, Daniels & Bell decided to focus on equity execution, its initial business, to provide cash flow while it attempted to enter new areas. Its prime target was asset management. Because pure money management firms such as Ariel Capital and other investment banks such as W. R. Lazard and M. R. Beal were growing their assets under control, the market seemed to be full of opportunity. The firm had limited experience in the field, maintaining only a few small institutional accounts as well as high net worth investors; to focus on such an endeavor would be something completely new. The situation resembled the firm's first years in the early 1970s when it had struggled to establish itself on Wall Street. What had aided the investment bank to rise was its interest in Cocoline Chocolate Company, which supported it through its troubling times. That was not the case two decades later.

Shortly before Bell's death in 1988, the company had lost a major account when Nabisco merged with RJR. When the recession of the early 1990s hit, Cocoline was unable to cope with the crumbling economic conditions and eventually filed for Chapter 11 relief in 1992. This development made the asset management venture an all-or-nothing venture; if it failed, there was nothing to fall back on.

Things became more complicated when two of Bell's sisters and his second wife Laura, filed a lawsuit against Darryl Bell and Travers J. Bell Sr., the executors of his will, for payments they had not received. In their suit, the women charged that Darryl Bell had misspent company money and asked that he repay the estate and give them their due monies. The judge ruled that their claims were baseless stating that the cash-poor estate was the result of mismanagement rather than intentional wrongdoing.

Still, the lawsuit generated a wave of publicity that essentially sealed the fate of what had become a desperate situation at the Daniels & Bell offices. Money management had not taken off. Revenues were dwindling. The only real money coming in was from its work for remaining clients, and from work as a two-dollar broker. When word of the lawsuit reached the media, it suddenly put Daniels & Bell back on the newspaper pages, but not for positive reasons. What propelled the situation to great prominence was Darryl Bell's other job. He was a star on the NBC hit, *A Different World,* a spin-off of

The Cosby Show. Articles appeared in publications from *Jet* to the *National Enquirer*. Perhaps the most damaging was an article on the front page of the *Wall Street Journal,* the world's leading financial publication.[10] The negative publicity undermined all the attempts that were being made to save the company. The inexperience at the top made it impossible for the firm to overcome these factors and continue on, although they valiantly tried. Some say that even if an experienced hand had taken over, it could have never been the same as when Travers Bell ran the firm because he tended to keep strategies and thoughts about the business in his head.

In response to the bankruptcy judge's order to liquidate all assets of the estate to pay off remaining debts to the Internal Revenue Service, Cocoline Chocolate was sold as well as other holdings. Daniels & Bell sold its seat on the New York Stock Exchange for $750,000 to Spears, Leeds & Kellogg, agreeing to lease back the seat to maintain its member status. This move only postponed the inevitable, and the mounting bills forced Daniels & Bell to close its doors in December 1994 ending over two decades of African American participation on the floor of the New York Stock Exchange.

Sadly, the outcome of Daniels & Bell was not a solitary tragedy but was a portent of things to come in the black financial community. Daniels, the firm's co-founder, also encountered problems as the crackdown on the municipal market took hold. In the early 1980s, Daniels founded United Daniels Securities, a small firm that did muni underwriting, sales, trading, and research. The firm proved unable to cope with the rotten economic conditions and fell below the minimum capital required to maintain a National Association of Securities Dealers (NASD) license. It voluntarily surrendered the license in March 1995. Yet, after its withdrawal, United Daniels Securities continued to sell more than $100 million worth of bonds in Florida for agencies such as the Leon

County Finance Authority. There was one key thing they neglected to tell the county's officials: They didn't have the necessary registration to do business!

Perhaps in a different time and context, such oversights would have been missed, but with the crackdown came immediate suspicion and action. After investigations by the NASD, which works under the SEC, an agreement was reached between Willie Daniels and the government in 1997. In addition to fines totaling more than $100,000, "United Daniels Securities was expelled from NASD membership and Daniels was barred from association with any NASD member in any capacity."[11] The agreement was reached without determination of guilt or innocence, but it ended another era of participation in the securities industry.

One of the saddest sagas of this period was that of W. R. Lazard. Whereas many financiers mourned the loss of their businesses, this firm had to deal with the tragic circumstances surrounding the loss of its founder. In May 1994, Wardell Lazard, was found dead in a Pittsburgh hotel room at the age of 44. Kenneth Glover, who served as vice chairman and oversaw investment banking, remembers how he heard the news from Dwight White, whom Lazard was in town to meet. The four words would change the course of the firm and its employees: "Bad news, Wardell's dead."

Like Daniels & Bell, the firm had to deal with the calamity of the founder's sudden death. However, the circumstances that surrounded Lazard's passing made this situation all the more daunting. His body was found next to a nearly empty bottle of vodka and a tray with traces of cocaine. Investigators quickly concluded that his death had resulted from an accidental drug and alcohol overdose. The news came as a complete shock to friends and colleagues. "In my years with him, I never saw him touch one drop of alcohol," says former Salomon Brothers boss Dale Horowitz.[12] "Every time we went out to a social club, if he ordered a drink, he would still be drinking that same drink four hours later," says former employee Martin Everette.[13] Others close to the situation were in such disbelief that they wondered if foul play was involved, but that extreme scenario was never proven. Word soon came out that Lazard had had previous problems with narcotics in 1991 but after a stint in rehab was thought to have overcome them. To complicate things even further, it was soon revealed that the firm was under investigation by the New York City District Attorney's office. The deal in question was a transaction it did for the New York Job Developmental Authority that critics argued should have earned W. R. Lazard around $80,000 in fees, but actually earned more than $500,000. As this drama played out before the public eye, those left at the firm struggled.

Despite the cynicism that surrounded the firm because of these events, it was Wardell Lazard's initiative that helped to stabilize the firm in the months following his death. After reading the 1993 *Wall Street Journal* article about the problems Daniels & Bell was having after the death of its founder, Lazard had undertaken to clearly divide management responsibilities. Kenneth Glover, Mel Eubanks, and Chief Financial Officer Steven Cate were named to lead each of its core businesses. Such distinctions led to a smoother transition once grave adversity struck. Eubanks was named chairman and chief executive officer. Glover was named co-CEO a week later. Wardell's wife, Betty Lazard, who now owned 83 percent of the equity in the firm, took her seat as vice chairman.

With management in place, the objective was clear: Weather the storm. In a meeting at its New York headquarters shortly after the death of its founder in 1993, nearly all employees were gathered to discuss the future. According to people close to the situation, the general feeling was that the firm could go on and do well, but would never reach the full promise that it had before that night in Pittsburgh. To achieve success, a plan was hatched to meet with each of the firm's clients and challenge the allegations head-on.

The firm's leading executives met with each one of their clients, sometimes for hours, to answer questions, address concerns, and resell W. R. Lazard's capabilities. Their discussions often were calming and encouraging, but were not always successful. "Here we were with somebody involved with drugs and we are running money for a university or a police benevolence association," says Eubanks. "The guy would call us in and say, 'Look I can't have you manage our money with you in the papers as a result of a drug overdose.'[14] What could we say? We couldn't say anything." As a result, the firm had some defections, institutional investors who had to be especially careful about appearances and publicity.

Changes were not just occurring outside the firm, but inside the offices at 14 Wall Street as well. In the summer of 1994, some of the firm's most respected talent left the firm for reasons that are still unclear. Jack Gantly went to Cowen & Company, taking $1 billion in assets managed with him. At the time, he said that his decision had nothing to do with the accusations against the firm but those left at the firm felt differently. "He left because his clients told him that if he didn't leave, they would leave," says Eubanks. Whatever the cause, the tangible result was that a great deal of business was gone, leaving the firm with $1.7 billion in assets and stripped of the title of the nation's largest black money manager.

In the face of adversity, W. R. Lazard held together remarkably in the year following the death of its founder. Despite the assets lost and the *Wall Street Journal*'s estimate of a 63 percent drop in municipal underwriting in 1994, the firm made money. In fact, W. R. Lazard did so not despite the terrible marketplace but *because of it*. "We had one of our most profitable years because it forced us to build our other businesses," says Glover. The majority of revenues came from its municipal sales and trading operation, a business that Glover says was not affected during the period. This was coupled with a major effort to reduce debt and expenses including the firing of one fifth of the staff and the restructuring of its real estate liabilities. All moves combined to lead to black ink.

Yet, a classic disagreement over ownership led to a management shakeup, beginning a tense period of constant change in the top ranks at the firm. Glover, who already had a small percentage of equity in the firm, led a group in a buyout offer that was rebuffed, reputedly by Betty Lazard. He then left in late 1995 to form a company called Lintz Glover White. One of the partners was now former W. R. Lazard vice president, Dwight White. Both eventually left for Mesirow Financial.

The final chapter in W. R. Lazard's story is a record of confusion. From 1994 to 1998, the firm had four CEOs. The board of directors was constantly changing both in size and personnel. They were constantly fighting off rumors of lawsuits and an inevitable fate. What many find interesting, however, is that this fight would not have been necessary if Lazard had been willing to sell the management company. Throughout the post-Wardell era, offers were coming from would-be buyers most notably Maceo Sloan and Hedge Fund genius Alfonso Fletcher with bids ranging from $5 million to $9 million. The firm rejected all offers in the hope of "preserving Wardell's legacy."

In 1995, W. R. Lazard bought Luther Smith & Small, a Los Angeles firm that specialized in corporate finance. The goal of the buy was to branch out its investment banking business beyond its municipal bond roots. This broker/dealer arm never took off, and W. R. Lazard soon fell out of *Black Enterprise*'s top 10 Black Investment Banks. Sources say that an offer by new president, Michael Luther, to acquire the remaining stock was shunned prompting him to leave and vacate its top spot.

That year, W. R. Lazard made its last stand: Superstar municipal banker Marianne Spraggins took the helm as CEO after buying a 41 percent stake in the firm in 1996. Spraggins, who had been out of the business for three years, decided to help out the struggling firm that bore her former Salomon colleague's name, even though the situation that lay before her was unlike anything that she had ever encountered. She had never been the number one person at a financial services company, and the toughness that had helped her trailblaze a path for black women in bulge-bracket firms was often a detriment in this new setting. Some say that her brash management style offended many of the remaining employees. Yet, most of these same people credit Spraggins with a valiant effort to overcome what one called "the anchor" that was dragging the firm down.

By the time its new CEO took over, the broker/dealer arm was generating next to nothing: its revenues were coming mostly from its asset management business. This dramatic shift was punctuated when W. R. Lazard let its NASD license expire later that year, shutting down that end of the business.

Yet, even as its money management kept it alive, the cracks were widening. In February 1997, the firm acquired Pecksland Associates, which managed $193 million. Its international equity operations were meant to complement and add balance to W. R. Lazard's fixed-income management style. But, these plans were jeopardized as the broker/dealer arm wound down and its salesmen left. According to *Pensions & Investments,* these employees were to have sold research to fund much of the price.[15] Without the cash to pay for the new firm, all of the Pecksland employees were fired and followed by its founder, Pheobe Zaslove, who served as W. R. Lazard's chief investment officer for four months as well.

This disturbance was the final straw for many clients, who after years of enduring changes were now concerned about

W. R. Lazard's future. Some accounts left, and those who remained requested that the firm be audited to determine its health. The results of that audit were devastating: The firm had a negative net worth, some sources even estimating that it owed approximately $6 million to hundreds of creditors. In addition, Betty Lazard faced myriad lawsuits for millions of dollars from former employees who were suing for back pay and wrongful termination.

The mounting problems forced Spraggins to look hard for buyers. In September 1997, after her search reportedly generated some interest from other brokerage firms, the other two members of the board of directors, Betty Lazard and Jerome Shuman (a professor from Howard University who had joined a few years earlier) asked Spraggins to leave. Just days after her abrupt departure, W. R. Lazard lost its two largest accounts: New York City's nearly $500 million in pension assets and Los Angeles City Employees Retirement Fund's $182 million.

In four years, W. R. Lazard was stripped of business and confidence. A brief stint with James Williams as CEO didn't produce the miracle it needed. He was forced to resign in April 1998 and the firm dissolved.

The fates of both Daniels & Bell and W. R. Lazard were partly written in the obituaries of their founders. Although varied problems sealed their demise, their respective declines were rooted in the disappearance of the vision with which these founders built their firms. For two of the Street's other prominent black investment banks—the two that battled for supremacy in the early 1990s—the problems took place not in the field of finance but in a court of law. These legal problems would wipe out one and leave the other a shell of its former self.

Despite the downturn in the municipal market, Grigsby Brandford managed to make a profit in 1995; in fact, it was one of its best years. The previous year had been slow—the senior firm managed just $400 million worth of bonds, more than all other minority-owned firms combined, but less than in its booming years. It also used up a great deal of its capital reserves to invest in a subsidiary company called GB Derivative Products.

As the municipal market crumbled and many firms, both big and small, dropped out of the business, Grigsby Brandford's ambitions were higher than ever. Its goal was to be number one in negotiated deals.

However, all of its hopes, momentum, and accomplishments came to a screeching halt in the fall of 1996. On September 17, Calvin Grigsby announced to the press that he was resigning as CEO because "it was time to move on." The sudden and unexpected move sent shock waves through the industry. As the days passed, his reasons for leaving became clear when it was revealed that Florida officials were probing Grigsby's activities. The major accusation: He had been videotaped discussing potential kickbacks with Dade County Commissioner James Burke in return for bond assignments. Another charge that surfaced was that he had used $50,000 of the public's money for personal expenses related to Grigsby's restaurant.

Grigsby's departure led him to a separate firm, using the original name, Grigsby Associates. Those left at his previous company had little reason to stay around as it had no future.

Meanwhile, Grigsby was successfully defending himself against all accusations. The first bit of good news came in the summer of 1998 when a judge dismissed all charges against him and his codefendants. While the judge criticized them for the set up of the municipality and Grigsby Fiscal Operations, the prosecution failed to prove that the money ever belonged to the government.[16] A few months later, more good news came as he was acquitted in the bribery case involving Florida officials. The only conviction resulting from the probe was that of James Burke, who was convicted of taking money from an informant.

Overall, Grigsby Brandford's principals came out of the disaster relatively unscathed. Siebert Brandford Shank continues to succeed in the municipal market. In 1999, it ranked number one making Napoleon Brandford the first person ever to head two different *Black Enterprise* top investment banks. In 2001, it also broke the record for senior managed deals. Grigsby is now cleared of all charges and is free to devote his full time to Grigsby Associates. Still, some express regret when thinking of what could have been. "It was very sad," says Cliff Graves. "Grigsby Brandford had the potential, if it was played right, to get in the big leagues, the triple A and stay there."[17] But, Brandford has chosen to look toward the future, rather than ponder what could have been. As for his former partner? "I think we will hear from Grigsby again," says Glover.

More than any other black investment bank, Pryor McClendon Counts has been the symbol of excessive politicking. That label can be attributed to several developments. Certainly, they were more public and outspoken about their opposition to G-37 than anyone else. Their discord manifested itself in a business section, front-page story in the *Washington Post* entitled "In the Minority and Mad: Black-Owned Investment Firms Say SEC's Pay to Play Curbs Are Unfair."[18] Pictured in this article were the three partners sitting in their Atlanta offices, and the newspaper quoted them stating their strong opposition to the change of rules that had existed for so long. As a result of their public outcry, they became associated with the pay-to-play game. Some attribute such steadfast defiance to the firm's fall from grace. "I personally think that when people like Ray McClendon are so successful and so arrogant about it, that it pisses white people off and makes them marked men," said one investment banker.

What such sentiment is referring to are the legal problems that McClendon's activities brought to the firm. The attention and negative publicity weighed down his firm with problems beyond the deteriorating bond markets. The problems all stemmed from the city of Atlanta, where McClendon had established himself as an energetic power broker. In addition to being vice-chairman of PMC, he also operated and worked out of the firm's Atlanta office. Soon, stories emerged that the investment bank was engaging in unusual activities for the municipality.

The allegations were that McClendon had secured business with the city because of making payments to its treasurer. McClendon and the treasurer's wife, Theresa Stanford, had a long-standing relationship; the two had worked together in Atlanta's finance department. In return for giving a reported $350,000 to Stanford's husband, PMC received approximately $9.8 billion worth of securities business from government officials. The firm executed roughly 90 percent of the city's STRIPS transactions, netting a reported $15 million in commissions.

In 1997, McClendon left the firm he had helped propel to the top only a few years earlier. He joined Mesirow Financial, Incorporated, a white-owned firm that had a growing presence in the capital markets. At the time, he denied that his move had anything to do with the SEC investigation. PMC closed down their Atlanta office.

Once prosecutors assembled enough evidence, McClendon and Theresa Stanford were charged with more than 20 counts of mail fraud. The accusations resulted from a probe that discovered that the supporting documents mailed with each trade were illegal because of this scheme. Despite a vigorous defense, they were both convicted in an Atlanta courtroom after a three-week trial in 2000.[19]

With all the turmoil and controversy, the firm McClendon had left, now named Pryor Counts & Company, fell into hard times. The lurid headlines combined with the now depressed municipal bond market in which they had thrived, left the firm a shell of its former self. Just seven years after reigning at the top of *Black Enterprise*'s Investment Banks list in 1993, it had fallen to the fifteenth spot with no senior-managed deals. That it is still on the list at all is proof of the remaining partners' resilience. Unlike its peers W. R. Lazard and Grigsby Brandford, it remains in business. Although the firm's future is uncertain, it is trying to develop and expand new businesses, as well as come to terms with its past. In 1999, it sold its municipal finance division to Rice Financial Products for an undisclosed sum. At present, it is focusing on sectors like corporate finance with the goal of recapturing its former glory.

Thankfully, all of the prominent symbols of black high finance did not fall under such tragic circumstances. In 1999, the stockholders of TLC Beatrice International Holdings decided to liquidate its assets, ending its reign at the top of *Black Enterprise*'s 100 list and an era of achievement at the highest level.

TLC's driving force, Reginald Lewis, was diagnosed with brain cancer in the winter of 1992. In the spring of 1993, Lewis died at the age of 50.

Lewis left his stock to his family. However, in contrast to Lazard and Bell, both of whom died suddenly, he was able to initiate the transfer of succession, naming his half-brother Jean Fugett Jr. as CEO.

After a year on the job, Lewis's wife Loida, felt ready to take control of the company and became chairman and CEO in 1994. In appearance and style, Loida Lewis was the opposite of her husband. Born in the Philippines, her calm and warm demeanor would never be confused with Lewis's aggressive, demanding business style. But, underneath her disarming charm lay a financial savvy that would serve the firm well. A successful lawyer, she had participated in her family's businesses in the Philippines. Managing this billion-dollar company was as great a challenge as she would ever have. Other matters relating to the business also needed her attention, most notably legal problems. A group of Drexel Lambert executives who owned a 22 percent stake in TLC Beatrice through a company called Carlton Investments, filed a lawsuit against the company. They asked that $22.1 million that Reginald Lewis paid himself in bonuses and other monies be returned to the stockholders. Although Loida Lewis vehemently defended her husband's actions because she believed that his hard work and astute management made him deserving of the pay, the two sides settled the lawsuit in 1997 for $15 million so that Lewis could concentrate on the future.

Despite the ancillary circumstances that surrounded her conglomerate, Loida Lewis remained committed to Lewis's vision. Her husband was a businessman pure and simple and sought to enhance the value of stock for all TLC Beatrice shareholders. Just as her husband did in 1989, Loida Lewis looked to the capital markets as a means to this goal. "Naturally we looked at an IPO again," says Lewis. However, like the failed attempt of a few years before, that avenue was tainted by uncertainty and ill prospects.

With that option closed, the firm sought other measures to unlock the value of the company's assets and soon zeroed in on the possibility of selling them. The sale of a company's assets after an LBO is common. TLC's acquisition of Beatrice's International arm came shortly after Kohlberg Kravis Roberts bought the whole company for $6 billion.

At TLC Beatrice's peak in 1996, the company earned revenues of $2.2 billion, 85 percent of which came from its French food division. France was experiencing a period of consolidation making TLC's French food division more valuable and after a solicitation of bids, the group agreed to sell the division to Groupe Casino. The purchase would make Groupe Casino the second biggest retailer in France. In return, TLC would receive $576 million, roughly $4 per share when the deal was completed in September 1997.

Because the division was the main component in the TLC Beatrice machine, it fell from its throne of supremacy to third place in *Black Enterprise*'s 100 list for 1998 with over $300 million in revenues as the liquidation process continued. In May 1999, it sold its Spanish ice cream division for $191 million. A few months later, TLC completed the sale of its final major business, Tayto, an Irish snack food maker, for $120 million. The history of Reginald Lewis's fabled buyout came to an end.

Whatever lies in the TLC Group's future, it will always be remembered for its pioneering spirit, which originated in the late 1980s and lasted until its end. Others like Lazard will be remembered for their work but have acquired a taint that overshadows their legacy. With the end of this period of finance, whether it was a planned successful end, or a conclusion forced by adversity, the disappearance of these firms left a vacuum for others to fill.

10

THE NEW BREED

I T WAS NOW THE PERCEIVED TWILIGHT OF THE camelot period for most of the pioneering black investment banks. Their myriad afflictions tainted many of the articles that were written about them. Too often, journalists branded them with outlandish or unfairly dismissive adjectives when describing their achievements. Fueling these perceptions was the constant contrast between them and a younger generation of entrepreneurs who emerged during this period. These men and their firms would participate in deals and areas where no African Americans had been before, especially in the well-guarded Fortune 500 corporate finance area. Their success in these markets would be celebrated by some. Others would criticize the methods used to get this business and challenge the definition of a minority-owned firm with questions about the degree to which its purpose in business was financial or social.

Utendahl Capital Partners, the first of these newly constructed firms, started up in 1992. Its leader, John Utendahl, was a 36-year-old bond trader who had left Merrill Lynch to strike out on his own. A graduate of Long Island University with an MBA from Columbia University, he was a symbol of many of the attributes that this generation possessed: the almost mandatory Ivy League education as well as experience at the top firms and in businesses where the first minority-owned investment banks had yet to achieve success.

Utendahl bucked the trend to start his firm. That era was one of great conformity for minority-owned firms, not necessarily for pioneers like Grigsby, Brandford, W. R. Lazard & Co., and Pryor, McClendon, Counts, but for smaller, younger investment banks. There were a number of blacks, Asians, Hispanics, and women forming firms to cash in on the municipal opportunities, despite the lack of experience they had in the field or in the securities industry in general. Utendahl was smart enough to acknowledge that he did not know anything about the municipal bond business. "I didn't get into the municipal bond business because I wouldn't have known a muni-bond if it had bit me," he says. "One of things I learned from a marketing class in business school is that one should not get into a business that he or she cannot do themselves."[1] Certainly, such a decision, relative to those latecomers into the municipal bond game, was courageous. Utendahl was not the first to shun municipal bonds, but he was the one who first pulled it off in such a grand way.

He used the skills learned at firms like Salomon Brothers and Merrill Lynch, and his competitive spirit. Like most on Wall Street, he maintains an enormous love of the win and success. "I subscribe to that Vince Lombardi train of thought that if you show me a good loser, I'll show you a loser," he says. "I don't like losing but I am also appreciative of each opportunity I get. If it doesn't go to me, I hope the deal goes to a minority-owned firm."

Utendahl entered the securities industry in the early 1980s after graduation from business school. His first employer was Salomon Brothers which at that time was an imposing figure on the Street. It had always been admired and/or feared for its trading prowess, and it was in this unique environment that

Utendahl took his seat at the firm's trading desk. He quickly learned that despite conventional definitions that separate sales and trading departments, the skills needed in each field overlap in many instances. "I was fortunate enough to get there and took an interest right away in the traders. I like corporate bonds because there was a story there," he says. "What I learned right away is that to be a great trader, you had to be an even better salesperson. You had to sell not only people I was dealing with everyday, but to the salespeople who would sell my product."

Although he came into the business a few years after the first African Americans in the major firms, Utendahl still had to deal with the slow-changing social progress on Wall Street, especially in his early years. "The good thing about Wall Street is that money is the first thought and how much you can make for somebody," he says. However, the question that Utendahl and many others have had to confront is, "Will minorities get the chance to make that money? That's the challenge. And to do that, it's not just the results of exams, it's do you fit socially? Do you make people comfortable?"

Those walls came down and Utendahl did very well as a trader, both for himself and for the firm's bottom line. His trading philosophy served as the foundation for these gains as well as the motivation to move to Merrill Lynch. "The key to trading is to pack when you can, not when you have to," he says. Utendahl left with a group of traders to go to Merrill Lynch. Yet, by the early 1990s, he began to dream of possibilities outside of these major firms. "If you ever pick up the *Security Dealer Digest* in any given year, it's two to three inches thick with no more than three pages at best given to any individual broker/dealer," he explains. "At the time, I couldn't have named thirty broker/dealers so it became clear that there are companies out there that have found a way to make better than a living and actually create wealth for themselves, so I didn't need a lot of convincing that it could work."[2]

He now admits that if he had known how hard it would be, and how many situations would have to break his way in order to survive, he might still be trading at Merrill Lynch. At the time he opened Utendahl Capital Partners in 1992, he didn't know what he didn't know and set out on a mission to develop his firm along the lines of his experiences. They entered the market with a splash.

Within six months of its beginning, the firm landed a spot in a series of lucrative federal agency deals. These were high profile deals that became the subject of a C1 *Wall Street Journal* story.[3] These issuers included the Federal Home Loan Mortgage Corp. and the Resolution Trust Corporation. Its fellow minority-owned firms in the deal such as Doley Securities and Pryor McClendon Counts, had been in the business more than a decade, prompting some to question how Utendahl Capital Partners was able to enter so quickly.

To Utendahl, this was an acknowledgment of the strength of his strategy and business plan. "They included me in the top four or five (black) organizations of the time and I think the statement that the *Wall Street Journal* was making was that people need to think about their existing organizations and the things needed to stand storms and continue to grow," he says. "Such things as human capital which obviously leads into preparing for succession, diversification of product, and the ability to do different things without shooting yourself in the foot—that's what I think the *Journal* was saying." To others, the *Wall Street Journal* article was the start of a debate focusing on the source of the firm's capital.

∞

To understand what would become a debate drawn along generational lines, one must first understand the issues that caused so much public and private discourse. The first, as always in issues related to Wall Street, surrounded business and strategy. Toward the end of the 1990s, a longtime insider was heard saying "this is the beginning of the end" when reflecting on the activities in the financial community. His feelings derived from the formation of the so-called superpowers, the megamergers of Wall Street's biggest companies and the grandest examples of an industry trend. Wall Street has always been an industry dependent on capital, an assessment encompassed in the painful cliché, "It takes money to make money." It has rung true throughout the history of this business, but never more so than in today's climate when billion has become a commonplace word.

The changes that have occurred just with simple progress have made Wall Street a tougher place for small firms. Rapidly advancing technology has made the world smaller, and the global market has been an area of constant pursuit. Technology also has allowed firms to readily copy each other, creating an even greater demand for financial and technical innovation. As venture capitalists and technological heroes achieved godlike status, it became harder for investment banks to keep their top talent without significant compensation packages. These are just a few factors that put more pressure on every dollar in capital reserves held by securities companies. And in response, many of these firms sought to build capital so that they not only could survive the current times, but also make enough investments to develop potential new businesses.

To illustrate just how far investment banks had advanced in the 1990s environment, one need look no further than the revered Morgan Stanley. In 1970, when it was competing against fellow bulge-bracket rivals as Kuhn Loeb, First Boston, and Dillion Reed, it operated with just $8 million in capital. Twenty-eight years later, after merging its global and institutional strength with Dean Witter's massive retail distribution capabilities, the combined firm had a market capitalization of $23 billion! And Morgan Stanley was not alone. Salomon

Brothers merged with another retail brokerage house, Smith Barney. Donaldson, Lufkin & Jenrette merged with Credit Suisse First Boston. The largest of them all was the merger of Citicorp with Travelers to create the biggest financial services company in the world, Citigroup.

With all of the consolidation and positioning occurring at the highest levels of Wall Street, it was predictable that such developments would occur throughout the industry, including black-owned investment banks. However, such positioning would often take the form of selling equity, which is where Utendahl Capital Partners fits in. Like many in the period, Utendahl saw the chance to create a niche for a potential company, decided to break out on his own, and procured enough capital to do so. While he and many others viewed such strategy like any other deal, the background of hardships suffered by African Americans raised inevitable questions that would complicate the perception of such measures.

Utendahl Capital Partners was unique in its conception for black investment banks because it engaged in a partnership with Merrill Lynch. It was reported that in exchange for 25 percent of equity, Utendahl received $3 million and a $9.9 million line of credit. This money translated immediately into tangible results. They were able to draw top talent from bulge-bracket firms, including a former managing director at Salomon Brothers, to help carry out its business. Another key member of this initial team was Ronald E. Blaylock, a former PaineWebber salesman of mortgage securities, who would later achieve prominence in his own right. To clients and others, that was a reassuring attribute that many other start-ups could not boast. With criticism surrounding all small companies and the limitations of their staffs, the number of capable bodies with long-standing relationships helped to get business.

The strategy focused immediately on taxable bond deals; municipal finance was never in the equation. Within their first few years, the firm landed substantial deals with the Resolution Trust Corporation (RTC) and Fannie Mae. It co-managed a $750 million deal with RTC, offering single-family mortgage-backed securities deals. It also co-managed a $500 million Freddie Mac deal.

As soon as Utendahl emerged in the RTC deal, there were whispers about its structure. Those whispers came to a head around 1994 when other firms with similar partnerships emerged. Unspoken rumblings developed into outspoken criticism about the intentions of such firms. When the issue first came out, it did so in newspapers without any people going on the record. In 1994, other firms with a similar structure emerged. Co-founder of Utendahl Capital, Blaylock struck out on his own to form Blaylock & Partners. Bear Stearns owned a 25 percent stake for a reported $10 million. Williams Capital Group was also formed in that year by Christopher Williams, a former Lehman Brothers derivatives salesman, with Jeffries & Company owning 49 percent of the firm.

Around this time, many critics spoke out about these partnerships, questioning their intent. The most vocal was Harold E. Doley, chairman of the 100 percent black-owned Doley Securities, who said simply but firmly, "These are not black-owned companies."[4] At one point during the public discourse, he referred to these setups as being similar to Wedtech, the famous scandal in which minority firms were set up as fronts by whites to cash in on Affirmative Action business. Others who were less harsh, but joined in the criticism included Napoleon Brandford, Muriel Siebert, and Donald Rice of Rice Financial Products. "We were all 100 percent black-owned," says Brandford.[5]

Just why was this setup such an issue? The definition of a minority-owned firm at that time stated that 51 percent must be owned by a minority. So what was the big deal? The main part of the argument against these newer firms was that their appointment into slots reserved for minority-owned firms was defeating the original intent of inclusionary policies. Although they technically fit the definition of a minority-owned firm, many people argued that it was unfair that a big firm like a Merrill Lynch be able to profit from a spot designated to offer blacks and other groups the chance to do business. Should firms like Merill Lynch and Bear Stearns be able to cash in on diversity efforts? That question would cause the great debate.

Utendahl has argued that such criticism is unwarranted, in fact, he is proud of his capital structure pointing to the other firms who have cropped up behind him with similar structures. "You have the creation of two or three other firms that have since built themselves from the prototype structure that we put up," he explains. "Having some alliance with a larger, juggernaut, financial institution, a borderline limited partnership, helps with capital and access to supply and base. I was not any smarter than those individuals who ran those [older] firms, in fact, I still hold many of them in high regard as far as their financial acumen is concerned. But what has that got to do with the price of eggs? In general, Wall Street can change at any given moment and just like one could be a big winner, they could be a big loser, and it could have nothing to do with them,"[6] just the market conditions.

Without hesitation, Utendahl admits that he aims to mold his company into a Lazard Freres and has used many lessons from that history to shape his current plan. Arguably the firm's most influential person, Andre Meyer, was a pioneer in the mergers and acquisitions field. He also used the firm to do merchant banking, using its capital to be substantial investors in companies or other ventures. "True greatness as far as any of the great players out there, at some point has got to have played in real estate," Utendahl says. The result of this ambition is Urban America, L. P., a fund that invests in commercial real estate throughout inner cities. The fund's hope is to use these investments to attract businesses and jobs to areas that traditionally have lacked economic growth. This goal has also translated into the United Enterprise Fund that helps to finance the acquisition or expansion of chains like fast-food restaurants throughout these areas. It is Utendahl's belief that these two companies will have a greater impact as far as creating opportunities for others than his broker/dealer or asset management companies.

In addition to capital, such alliances provided these new companies with access to a network that ensured its ability to perform on larger scales. While standouts of the older guard like Pryor McClendon Counts and Grigsby Brandford had tremendous salesforces, most of the lower tier companies had only a few traders and could not take on large amounts of bonds. Many of the investment banks that have hooked up with white-owned firms boast about the capabilities that the two sides provide each other. When Ward & Associates, a small black firm in Atlanta joined with J. C. Brandford from Tennessee, they freely acknowledged that they did so to gain access to more deals and give Ward more channels to sell bonds.

Whatever one thinks about the new firms' structure and exact intent, they have racked up prestigious tombstones and can brag about participation in the capital markets in ways that no African American investment bank had previously achieved. To some extent, this was the result of strategy because small investment banks can only commit their resources to a few businesses, and the new banks chose to do so in areas other than municipal bonds. "I have always avoided businesses I don't understand,"[7] says Blaylock. "We did not choose to set up to pursue business earmarked for minority-owned firms,"[8] says Williams.

There are also many defenders of these firms who claim that Utendahl and Blaylock are smart for being willing to give up equity in a business more concentrated on green than black and white. "These firms are colorless and because of their strategy did something we could never do, make the transition from an investment bank to a financial services company," says one of the older investment bankers. Others expressed no feelings about the subject. "I never had a problem with it,"[9] says Bernard Beal.

In a capital-intensive game where partnerships are often vital for survival, some blame the pioneering firms for their failure to link up with each other to create one super black-owned firm. "I think ego got in the way a lot," says Ken Glover. "Wardell and Pryor McClendon Counts had a deal to get together but he pulled back because he didn't like the name of the proposed new company."[10] Wardell Lazard also pulled out of another almost sealed deal with M. R. Beal. Even Harold Doley acknowledges a failure to create a super-firm with Travers Bell because of personalities; "In hindsight we should have gotten together but he was hard to get along with and so am I."[11]

So if African Americans have traditionally failed to join together, many of them recognize that these new entrepreneurs have linked with major firms, not because those firms are white, but because they have deep pockets. The older investment banks operated with, at most, a few million dollars in capital. There are many who view this as restricting, not allowing them to expand into other businesses, or participate in areas where the barriers to entry require more money. Although investment banks like W. R. Lazard almost succumbed to the loan given by Drexel, these new firms were able to escape such calamity because they were willing to give up ownership. They have tried to build financial services companies involved in businesses like taxable securities, corporate finance, and convertible securities. Such diversification was possible because of the capital reserves they maintained, a failure evidenced by older firms. "Presently, the Utendahls, the

Williams, and Blaylocks are where the Pryors, Lazards, and Grigsbys should have been," says Glover. "Instead, they, like selected firms including M. R. Beal, reinvented themselves."

The story of M. R. Beal is one of survival and change. Of the older guard, the firm has adapted with the most success to the differing opportunities. In its beginning, 100 percent of its revenues derived from municipal finance. At the turn of the twenty-first century, its chief executive officer claimed that only 40 percent came from the municipal area. The majority of the balance came from the increasing participation of its fledging corporate division. Most notable was its co-manager role with firms like Bear Stearns and J. P. Morgan in the $10.62 billion offering from AT&T's wireless group in the year 2000.

Nobody would have dared predicted this a few short years before when the firm was on life support. Like many other minority-owned firms, it was on the verge of oblivion. From the municipal heyday in 1993 through 1997, M. R. Beal lost approximately $3 million in capital. For a primarily public finance investment bank, that was a tough period. "1994 was a correction. 1997 it tanked completely," Beal remembers.

However, market conditions were only half of his problems because Beal and his company soon were battling to clear his reputation. The problems stemmed from an investigation into the financing activities of the state of Wisconsin. The allegations were that a state senator, Gary George, accepted money in exchange for municipal bond business. All of the prominent black firms were looked into: W. R. Lazard, Grigsby Brandford, Daniels & Bell, Pryor McClendon Counts, and M. R. Beal. In the end, no charges were filed because there was insufficient evidence of any wrongdoing. Although the episode created no legal setbacks, it hurt the general perception. Any hidden motives behind the investigation are now and will forever remain a mystery, still some can't help but wonder. "I don't know if they went after minority-owned firms but that's 100 percent!" Beal says. Quite a coincidence!

The troubles for Beal continued as rumors about his firm began to hit the printed page. He believes that somebody was out spreading rumors about his firm, a practice that may or may not have led to what was the killer, a story in the *New York Daily News*.[12]

Clients became edgy. Nobody, especially public institutions, likes to do business with people associated with newspaper scandal and impropriety. In response, Alan Hevesi, then New York City Comptroller, took M. R. Beal out of the city's underwriting roster in 1996. Soon, others began to do the same, and Beal was on the brink of collapse. With some of his biggest clients gone and more looking as if they might bolt, he received a vote of confidence from a key institution. "The reason I was able to stay in business was because of Carl McCall, who refused to exclude me from any of his deals." McCall, the former New Your state senator from Harlem, and then New York State Comptroller, allowed M. R. Beal to continue to participate until any of the charges were proven true. That never happened.

As the allegations cleared like clouds disappearing on a sunny day, the company emerged with a newfound attitude and strategy. Clients began to come back; M. R. Beal was reinstated in the New York City roster. Although the new era was almost a second chance for the firm, M. R. Beal did not proceed without incorporating some of the lessons learned from its brush with finality. As soon as they were exempted from wrongdoing, Beal hired an administrative staff to watch all activities. The purpose is to keep all business as clean as possible so that nobody could ever construe ill intentions from their actions. "I told my staff to be as careful as possible," Beal explains. "The head could be cut off a major firm and they can go on. If we get a paper cut, we will be out of business."

With the turmoil in the municipal market, Beal began to reexamine corporate possibilities. The firm had made a run at that exclusive market before. In 1991, Beal made a public statement about his intent to enter corporate finance. So bold was his statement that it appeared on the front page of the *New York Times* business section.[13] As it turned out, the publicity greatly surpassed the results. Although they made inroads with a few issues from companies like Philip Morris and General Motors, the results fell far short of his efforts. His grand plan went unfulfilled. "That was a mistake," Beal would joke later. "We got slapped around." The major investment banks maintained a stronger control over syndicates than the municipal area, and M. R. Beal's contacts with corporate officers were simply not as strong. Yet, in his reincarnation, the firm was able to crack into that long-elusive arena, topped by the position in the AT&T Wireless deal, the largest offering ever.

Another group of people who reinvented themselves was Napoleon Brandford and Suzzanne Shank who left the clouded Grigsby Brandford to escape any misperceptions. The transition was not as difficult as one may have imagined after such grave circumstances. Although Brandford freely admits that Grigsby was "Mr. Outside" and the face of the firm, he later revealed that business within Grigsby Brandford was quite different. In an article with the *Bond Buyer,* he admitted that the two named partners maintained a strained relationship in the firm's last years.[14] Consequently, they and Shank, a then unnamed partner, worked with their own clients exclusively. So when the turmoil hit, it was time to consider alternative options.

In the days following Grigsby's resignation, the remaining partners were inundated with offers to leave it all behind. One such proposal was submitted by Muriel Siebert, founder and head of Muriel Siebert & Company. She asked that Shank and Brandford fly to New York and discuss a possible venture together.

Siebert, often referred to as the "First Lady of Finance," was the first woman to buy a seat on the New York Stock Exchange. She also pioneered, and made many unhappy, when she declared herself as a discount brokerage firm after the end of fixed rates. In a long career that was only interrupted by a stint as New York banking superintendent, she had built her firm into a formidable retail company including online trading and some underwriting. Although she had participated in a few offerings with other minority-owned firms, most notably the Conrail Corporation deal, she was seeking to increase her municipal bond business despite the depressed markets and looked at Brandford and Shank to do it.

In a meeting at the Post House in New York City, the two sides got together to discuss a possible venture, and soon the possibility translated into probability. "We thought that our capabilities would fit well with her retail distribution," says Brandford. With Siebert's more than 80,000 retail accounts, a newly formed company would enhance a distribution network beyond the two firms' existing clients. In addition, it would be a good selling point to potential issuers who have historically questioned the ability of minority-owned firms to sell the large allotment of bonds needed to lead a offering. For Siebert, the pairing would allow her to increase the financial products she could provide to these clients and include tax-exempt securities. After measuring the pros and cons, the two sides formed Siebert Brandford Shank in late 1996 with 51 percent owned by Brandford and Shank, and the balance by Siebert.

The transition would not be smooth. The two partners left what had once been the premier minority-owned investment bank in the nation with nothing but their own clients. That insufficiency did not last for long: The new firm soon rose to fifteenth place, as a senior manager of all underwriting, totaling about $2.5 billion in senior managed deals. It was the only firm consistently ranking in the top five of *Black Enterprise*'s Investment Banks list from 1996 to 2001 that concentrated solely on municipal finance. In 1999, Siebert Brandford Shank was number one on that list, making Brandford the only person to top the list with two different companies. It did so by landing several big deals. That year, it led a $295 million offering of general obligation bonds for the Detroit School District. The deal earned the firm profits as well as strengthened its reputation. Furthermore, it highlighted the talents of Shank who has developed a significant presence in the Motor City's financial community. Heading the Detroit office, she has also helped bring in deals like a $265 million capital improvement program for the Detroit Water and Sewage Program and other financing for the city's infrastructure including Tiger Stadium.

Such success in different cities has helped Siebert Brandford Shank develop what Brandford calls a "national presence," allowing them to do deals in a variety of regions. They have expanded to 10 offices with more than 40 employees and are receiving praise for the niche they have carved out in a game that was written off as passé.

Just when Utendahl, Williams, and Blaylock landed key spots in monumental deals in the late 1990's, a movement developed in some organizations to promote diversity throughout the capital markets: The Securities Industry Association began its diversity committee in 1997; Cromwell, Miller, Greer began their annual "Building Wealth Conference"; *Black Enterprise* started its "Black Wealth Initiative." But, none were bigger and more notable than the Rainbow/PUSH Wall Street Project, which began in 1998. The focus and attention received by this project reflected the enormous star power of its face and voice, the Reverend Jesse L. Jackson.

In the United States as well as many other parts of the world, Reverend Jesse Jackson has developed and maintained a titanic presence as a champion of civil rights. So, it was inevitable that he would turn his attention from the poorest of people to the richest as a means of bridging the gap. Such an attempt came in the form of the Wall Street Project whose efforts would be applauded by some and criticized by others.

The launch of the Rainbow/PUSH project was as lavish and on as big a stage as there can be—the floor of the New York Stock Exchange. As fate would have it, the event coincided with the NYSE's first recognition of Martin Luther King Day. For years, people grumbled because the Big Board continued its trading activities while other industries and governments honored the day by closing shop. So the symbolism of the Exchange's closed doors was profound as it played host to some of the most important people in the world. There to embrace the launch of this three-day conference were President Clinton, Federal Reserve Chairman Alan Greenspan, and then Travelers Chairman Sandy Weill.

Beyond the symbolism, the Wall Street Project took some real steps to influence the policies of Fortune 500 companies by purchasing equity in some of the most recognizable companies, such as Ford Motor Company and PepsiCo. These blocks were far from significant equity, as the buys were usually in the area of 50 shares of each stock but they were assets adding leverage to the Jackson force for change. That change effort first came in the form of national dialogue. Because either these companies agreed with the merits of his arguments, or just to save face, many of them put forth efforts for diversity. Whether these efforts were serious or show differed as time went on but the new attitudes did occur at around the same time that black-owned investment banks won roles in some big corporate offerings.

The firm that received the majority of headlines around this period in the late 1990s was Blaylock & Partners. So successful were they during this period that *Business Week* described the firm with the headline, "A Minority-Owned Firm Hits the Major Leagues."[15] What prompted the article as well as the accolades was Blaylock's being named as a senior manager of the historic AT&T $8 billion corporate debt issue in 1999. In that year, it would be far and away the leader of minority-owned firms in terms of senior-managed deals, about four times the number two firm, Utendahl Capital Partners according to *Black Enterprise*.

The AT&T debt issue was part of a string of extraordinary deals for what was a young and a relatively unknown firm. The areas in which they were working were unexplored for a black firm. They were the first black investment bank to finish in the top 20 in corporate debt. The firm began its climb in 1996 when it participated in its largest deal to that date, a $300 million offering for the Tennessee Valley Authority (TVA) in a syndicate exclusively comprising minority-owned firms including Muriel Siebert and Pryor McClendon Counts.

Then it became the first black investment bank to underwrite a corporate bond offering for a Fortune 500 company. A wall that has stood so strong for so long does not usually come down unless there are some special circumstances. This was the case in 1996 when Texaco became engulfed in controversy. It all started when a group of black middle managers filed a racial discrimination lawsuit against the oil giant. The plaintiffs claimed that the pay and promotions were far from meritorious, and sometimes were given according to preference instead of performance. The matter persisted sluggishly as only the legal system can, but a tape emerged in 1996 of a meeting that had taken place two years earlier. The tape horrified many but revealed attitudes that some knew were always there beneath the surface. Top Texaco officials, including its treasurer, were heard using racial slurs and negative characterization to refer to African Americans. After employees were fired and apologies offered, many wondered, what next? Then New York State Comptroller H. Carl McCall threatened to sell the more than one million shares of Texaco stock in the state's pension fund. Reverend Jesse Jackson threatened a boycott until significant changes were made. Soon, the company announced a diversity effort and then settled with the plaintiffs in the initial lawsuit for $176 million.

Although it was disturbing to see just how strongly ancient prejudices still existed within some of the highest offices, there was an interesting irony because these raciest Jim Crow attitudes actually provided an opportunity for African Americans. Shortly after the situation in January 1997, Blaylock & Partners was named as the lead underwriter of a 10-year note offering for Texaco. Blaylock acknowledged that the turmoil at the company certainly opened the doors to discourse between his firm and the financial officers at Texaco. However, all parties point out that the firm walked into the offices and presented the idea of the deal, and executed it well. So in demand were the bonds, that the offering was increased $50 million from the original amount of $100 million, with Blaylock & Partners selling most of the bonds.

Such success was not unusual for Blaylock. He is, by most accounts, an extremely likable guy whose warm demeanor and friendly gestures are enamouring and disarming. A tall, well-dressed man, he was a member of the famous Georgetown championship teams of the early 1980s. Those experiences have been absorbed in the way he handles himself. Basketball memorabilia hang on the walls of Blaylock's Fifth Avenue office, and he often talks in terms of sport calling clients "coach." From the windows of his office one can survey the fast-paced action of the city, and within that office business is often pressured—an enormous contrast from his childhood. He grew up in the sunshine and slow pace of Winston-Salem, North Carolina. Such different lifestyles are not as far apart as they seem; in fact, he credits this background with some of his success saying, "It reminds me to always step back, take a look, and evaluate, so it has served me well."[16]

Bolstered by its runaway success with the Texaco deal, the firm embarked on a magnificent run of work with huge corporate institutions. But, it was also the genesis in what became a public and closely watched association with Reverend Jesse Jackson. Some attributed the increasing opportunities for minorities to the dialogue that Jackson was able to generate about diversity and commitment to equal opportunity. Perhaps the best example of this commitment came from AT&T Chairman C. Michael Armstrong who boldly declared at the first Wall Street Project in 1998 that a minority-owned firm would have a significant role in their upcoming massive bond offering. Out of the firms that bid for the spot, Blaylock & Partners emerged victorious. As to their role, Armstrong said at the time, "We were impressed with the number of highly qualified minority-owned firms who applied. Blaylock & Partners did a superb job with the offering, helping AT&T tap new investors and surpass our original financing projections." This was a big move and garnered a great deal of attention including the *Business Week* article and the headline in *Black Enterprise,* "History Is Made."[17]

A series of high profile deals followed that would be associated with the Jackson influence, but the feelings surrounding these offerings were more critical and complaining. In question were the IPOs of the elite Goldman Sachs and the Pepsi Bottling Group. Articles in financial publications like the *Wall*

Street Journal and *Investment Dealers Digest* reported that the inclusion of minority-owned firms in these deals was done more out of fear than policy or business.[18] The fear was the threat of protest from the Rainbow/PUSH organization if these firms were not included, even linking such efforts to contributions received from African Americans on Wall Street. One investment banker at the time said "I'm all for Affirmative Action, but this is ridiculous!"

However, supporters of the organization's efforts attribute such rumblings to the mere fact that people do not like change. "Of course some are going to be upset because nobody likes to lose business," says Wall Street Project Director Chee Chee Williams. "But the Blaylock transaction was a success because they added value."[19]

"If you sit back and look and look at investment banking, we have had more corporate deals in the last five years than the previous fifty," says Maceo Sloan, who served as chairman of the Wall Street Project for its first two years. "Our argument was not 'give me what I want or I will boycott you,' it was 'let us sit down at the table together.' You do business with people you know and like. If you don't know me, you can't like me! So let us all sit down at the table together and learn each other."[20]

As of the writing of this book, the jury is still out on the lasting effect of the Wall Street Project in terms of changing the attitudes of corporate America. Will this initiative and others like it alter institutionalized systems and policies that have stood for centuries? Or are the increasing opportunities unrelated to the Wall Street Project and other initiatives like it? Some point to the heights that capable and accomplished black executives such as Ken Chenault, Franklin Raines, Lloyd Ward, and Ann Fudge have reached as the reason for these new opportunities. "I am seeing the same thing now in the corporate area that occurred in the political side two decades ago," says Hayden.[21]

Of the well-known new firms capitalizing on these oppor-tunities, Williams Capital Group is the unlikeliest simply be-cause it didn't aspire to be what it has become. "Unlike many African Americans who started their firms on Wall Street, mine took an interim step because I was not planning on start-ing an 'African American' firm," says Christopher Williams.[22] "What I wanted to do is to basically take the exact same de-rivatives business I was responsible for at Lehman Brothers, and then we set up as a division of Jeffries & Company, using them primarily for their financial strength." The new division was called Williams Financial Markets and did not purse busi-ness set aside for African Americans because there was no such designation in the derivatives market.

By all accounts, the new venture was doing well, but Williams was soon confronted with the reality that Wall Street always changes, and it often occurs in a heartbeat. When the Federal Reserve began to raise interest rates in 1994, and consequently Orange County, California, filed for bankruptcy in large part because of their investments in de-rivatives, the market imploded. The very foundation the company had set for itself was no longer there, and suddenly they had nothing but themselves and their talents. Faced with the decision to reenter the workforce as an employee or go out on his own, Williams and his team decided to found Williams Capital Group (WCG).

The firm was not completely independent at first. Because of a contractual agreement, Jeffries was allowed to buy 49 per-cent of the stock. Over time, equity was bought back by WCG and sold to its employees, many of whom are now partners. Jeffries's interest in the firm ceased in late 1998. The firm was able to do that after building from scratch. They were now en-gaged in a broker/dealer business, underwriting bonds and eq-uities. They had gone from knowing a lot about derivatives, a little understood secretive security, to knowing little about a business that is a Wall Street mainstay. "That was a tough period for us because we had no distinguishing characteristics." They soon discovered that businesses like executing orders, and investment banking is a much more competitive field; it took a while for the firm to prop itself up. Its early focus was on the commercial paper market which finally broke for the firm in 1996 when it was named as a dealer for Colgate Palmolive. Since then it has won several high-profile deals; as of the writing of this book, the biggest was being named a co-manager of a $11 billion Fannie Mae benchmark note, helping it to lead in the ranking tables when compared with other minority-owned firms. Williams estimates that his revenues at the turn of the century were between $25 million and $50 million. It also has hired a capable research staff and has expanded overseas. The move abroad was physically represented with their London office. An equity infusion from HypoVereinsbank, the second largest bank in Germany, helped their move abroad. "It provided us with sufficient capital to underwrite bond issues and they gave us a revolving door of credit," Williams says. It also helps them expand into the global markets. HypoVereinsbank did not have much of a capital market effort in the United States, and they viewed Williams Capital Group as a way to break in. Last, the firm became a member of the New York Stock Exchange in the year 2000, after agreeing to lease a seat for $250,000.

While these firms who have given up equity have become the capital structure of note, one firm has increased his firm's resources another way, a public offering. In February 1998, the Chapman Company became the first black-owned investment bank to go public. It was an extraordinary deal, because of its difficulty and success. At the time, Chapman had been pulling in revenues of approximately $3 million dollars, yet was able to sell the deal at $8 dollars a share, giving the firm a market capitalization of $8 million at the close of the day. Its founder,

Nathan A. Chapman, who formed his business in 1986, after working as a stockbroker for Alex Brown & Sons, spearheaded this achievement. Much of the Chapman Company's work revolves around a concept that they have labeled the Domestic Emerging Markets (DEM), which represents unrecognized opportunities in America, as much of the industry sought to expand abroad. "I thought there was a tremendous need on Wall Street because nobody had ever focused on companies controlled by women and minorities (in America) and compared them to traditional ways in which people looked at the international market," Chapman says. "Out of that came DEM and we were able to get a number of investment products approved by the SEC based on creating a portfolio exclusively controlled by minorities."[23] Chapman argues that those who concentrate solely on foreign opportunities are overlooking the potential in these underserved markets. His strategy has two purposes: One, invest in concepts and people who have traditionally lacked access to capital. Two, provide above-average returns because of the risk of investing in these smaller companies.

As they promoted their concept beginning in the late 1980s on through the 1990s, they also built their investment banking and brokerage services, the idea of raising capital soon confronted them in the era of megamergers. Up until 1998, almost all of the major firms had gone public with the exception of Goldman Sachs and Lazard Freres. As other black firms chose to give up equity to acquire this capital, Chapman decided against that route. "There are all kinds of things that go on with this minority-controlled universe that having seen it and really wanting to create a company that was truly minority-controlled, the only way to do it was the traditional way, to go public," he says. No black financial services firm has ever gone public before although some, like W. R. Lazard, has seriously considered it. However, to Chapman, the capital markets were a frontier they sought to break and did so in February 1998. In August of that year, the group tapped into the capital markets again by offering shares of its asset management company, the Chapman Management Capital Holdings, Inc., to the public. It was also around this period that its DEM Equity Fund scored its biggest success by being named one of the 100 mutual funds Aetna offers to its customers.

However, being public does have its drawbacks and Chapman had to adjust his managerial style to accommodate the new status. "We need to show ourselves every quarter," Chapman explains. "When you are a private entity, you are all right as long as you end up the right way by the end of the year. Even if I am building for something (long term), I have to figure out how it is going to affect me each quarter."

The negatives of the public marketplace soon hit the company after it embarked on another ambitious plan to roll all of the existing companies including the brokerage, asset management firm, and insurance company into one entity called eChapman.com. This decision was made during the height of the Internet gold rush, when other companies knee deep in red were valued in the billions by the marketplace. The goal was to extend the reach of its financial services to the online community, although most of the revenue would not be derived through the medium. However, in the Internet euphoria, Chapman related shares zoomed 300 percent higher once the announcement was made that the brokerage and asset management company would be included in the new online venture. Yet, the cold reality of the market soon hit as the pendulum swung back in the other direction. After a June 2000 IPO price of $13, eChapman.com was trading around $2 one year later as the halo around the word Internet became tarnished.

Such progress is not just occurring in the minority-owned investment banks, or the boardrooms of large Wall Street clients with the Frank Raines and Ken Chenaults, but in the largest Wall Street financial services companies as well. As far back as the mid-1990s, the highest African Americans had ever climbed within the big investment banks was senior managing director or partner; there had never been one in the chosen seats—those few in a firm who set the tone and make the decisions. Such positions are hard to earn because as one rises in the pyramid, the space becomes smaller. Throughout most of this history, African Americans have had to start their own firms to obtain that kind of power and influence. About his decision to leave Lehman Brothers in 1994 to found Williams Capital Group, Williams says, "I think my experience was similar to many African Americans on Wall Street in that up to a certain level you rise in the early stages when performance is measured by objectively determined standards. Standards in terms of work ethic knowledge, understanding of business matter, and effectiveness. I think one does reach a point when one's promotions, levels in an organization and compensation start to be determined more subjectively. In that case, there are a number of factors, and I'm not going to say they are racially motivated, but factors such as the socialization of a firm. Having mentors or close relationships with those in senior positions who tend to be more supportive and I saw opportunities where I could have gone up, but those opportunities were not presented to me."[24]

While this work on the entrepreneurial front was occurring, two pioneers in particular, however, E. Stanley O'Neal and Tom Jones were able to break through such barriers by the end of the twentieth century, landing top spots in some of world's biggest financial services companies, and in doing so proved that even those seats were now obtainable.

Jones's career is a study in contrast. From the grand office sitting up top the Citigroup headquarters in New York, many blocks away from the New York public school he attended, one could not have matched his current appearance how he was pictured in the late 1960s. Back then, his national identity was a photograph of Jones carrying a gun during a Civil Rights rally at his school, Cornell University. A bright, and intelligent young adult, he entered the institution at the age of 16 and soon became heavily involved in the protests and rebellions captured in that photo. Years after the unrest, Jones was a quick learner and high riser working at Arthur Young and then John Hancock Mutual Life Insurance Company. After successful stints at other institutions, most notably as president of Teachers Insurance and Annuity Association College Retirement Equities Fund, he was named to Travelers board of directors in 1997 and joined as vice chairman of the firm only a few months later. His ability to acquire such a high position in what would become the biggest financial services company in the world, and then perform well there is a beacon for other African Americans.

The other high-ranking black member on Wall Street is E. Stanley O'Neal. There are similarities in the roots of the two executives' backgrounds. Each had a childhood and young adulthood that gave little indication of the careers they were to choose, although for very different reasons. O'Neal was born in a little town in Alabama named Wedowee. It had all the classic symbols of poverty. No indoor plumbing, a one-room schoolhouse with just a woodstove to heat it during cold weather. In his young adulthood, he was forced to confront the realities of the world under extreme circumstances: He was one of the first black children to attend an integrated Atlanta high school and did so under great duress and conflict. From such primitive beginnings with limited resources, O'Neal graduated from school academically unchallenged and entered the General Motors Institute, now known as Kettering University. While studying there, he worked the late shift in the trenches, as part of the assembly line team for each of the company's cars. Such work bought him time until he figured out his next move, a step that would come in the form of higher education. It was then that he got the opportunity to maximize his abilities when he left for Harvard Business School. Within a few years, he returned to General Motors, but this time in a suit, behind a desk, and in New York. He worked in the accounting end of the company until he decided to switch careers and entered the investment banking field in 1986 at the age of 34.

His interest in Wall Street came from the inevitable dealings with investment bankers as a fiscal officer of a multinational corporation. He was recruited by Merrill Lynch former chief financial officer, Courtney Jones. After five successful years serving as a vice president in this field, O'Neal was selected to head the firm's high-yield division. He took the reins shortly after the Drexel Lambert scandal as a result of the insider trading by its head, Michael Milken. Confidence in securities was low, the market was not what it had been, and in this tough environment, O'Neal led Merrill Lynch to the number one spot.

From there he rose to other positions, first in the firm's capital markets group and then as head of institutional sales. By 1998, O'Neal entered the big time when he was named Merrill Lynch's chief financial officer. In that role, he was in charge of many departments and categories relating to the company's fiscal responsibilities. Things became even more complicated once Wall Street became engulfed in the Long Term Capital Management hedge fund crisis in the fall of 1998. Merrill Lynch, like many of Wall Street's notables was invested with the fund, and it was largely O'Neal's responsibility to settle the firm's financial liabilities.

Such abilities and other successes led to the spring of 2000 when O'Neal was appointed to head Merrill Lynch's brokerage division, which at the time consisted of more than

14,000 account executives. The move was significant in the context of O'Neal's life, the business, and the history of African Americans on Wall Street. The mere fact that O'Neal is now in charge of nearly 20 times the number of people in his hometown is a fitting snapshot of the journey he has taken to the top. The symbolism of O'Neal's appointment to head the brokerage division is historic considering that Merrill Lynch practically made the modern retail market. Charles Merrill's vision to bring Main Street to Wall Street in the mid-twentieth century propelled the firm that bears his name to the top; and decades later, an African American was now in control of those operations. As far as the future is concerned, the appointment signaled that he was one of a select few people in the running for the top spot presently occupied by Chairman David Komansky. Never before has an African American held such a position with a major financial services company and in July 2001, O'Neal was appointed as the heir apparent to the CEO, a position he is expected to take over in 2004. It, without question, signaled a new era of opportunity for African Americans and is the starting point for this history's next chapter.

A black man in position to run the largest brokerage house in the world was nothing but a far, distant dream when Harvey Thomas, Forrest Tomlinson, and George King Jr., arrived at Merrill Lynch in 1965. It was even harder to picture when Norman McGhee and Philip Jenkins founded the first black broker/dealers in the 1950s. Yet, the progress in the past century for African Americans on Wall Street was accomplished by a group of talented individuals who were able to use their intelligence and abilities to perform and succeed in the toughest business in the world. While they have all had to deal with other social factors that complicate their daily activities, the essence of this history is performance. African Americans have proven that if given the opportunity, they can execute and deliver the necessary goods and solutions to win.

Although some of this history's most important figures suffered sad setbacks and ungraceful tragedies, their body of work should not be relegated to the single sentence they receive in many articles. Although Wall Street is a "now business" predicated on the present and future, this history has many valuable lessons that extend beyond any limits of eras and periods.

John T. Patterson Jr., came more than half a century before today's players. His brokerage business never made millions or participated in billion-dollar deals. Yet his firm, Patterson & Company, was full of the hopes and dreams of future generations. The wisdom and effort he put forth when he began in 1952 are still relevant today as are words he uttered later in the decade about the importance of African American participation on Wall Street:

> It must be done because equality means responsibility. Responsibility takes dollars. We say you can't be a first-class citizen without being a first-class capitalist. In the future, when Negroes are graduated from business schools and from courses in finance, they'll be able to go into businesses besides the now restricted areas of government and the few Negro insurance companies we have today. Patterson & Co. is just one of the few companies we hope will offer the new Negro his golden opportunity.[25]

Notes

Many of the references in the Notes section came from the New York Stock Exchange Archive. This source does not use page numbers.

Introduction

1. Maynard H. Jackson, interview with author.
2. Ibid.
3. Brian Garrity, "The Voice of Experience," *Investment Dealers Digest,* August 16, 1999, pp. 14–15.
4. Fonda Marie Lloyd, "Footprints in Time," *Black Enterprise,* August 1995, p. 108.

Chapter 1: The Beginning

1. The New York State Freedom Trail Commission Report.
2. "Negro Wall Street," *Ebony,* October 1950, pp. 75–78.
3. "75 to Get Dividend Checks From Negro Brokerage Firm," *Amsterdam News,* December 7, 1935.
4. "Wall Street Firm Hires Tan Agent," *Afro-American,* June 4, 1949, p. 1.
5. "Negro Wall Street," *Ebony,* October 1950, pp. 75–78.
6. Ibid.
7. Ibid.
8. Norman L. McGhee Jr., interview with author.
9. Dorothy Horton, interview with author.
10. Ibid.
11. Robert Seltzer, "McGhee & Co. First Negro Brokerage Office Directs Investment of Workers Dollars," *Cleveland Press,* January 14, 1957, p. 23.
12. Norman L. McGhee Jr., interview with author.
13. Dorothy Horton, interview with author.
14. McGhee & Company booklet, "Integration on the Economic Front."
15. Dorothy Horton, interview with author.
16. Terry Robards, "Brokerage Firm Is Run by and for Negroes," *New York Times,* September 6, 1967, p. 63.
17. D. Hepurn, "The Wizard of Wall Street," *Sepia,* January, 1961, pp. 30–32.
18. Terry Robards, "Brokerage Firm Is Run by and for Negroes," *New York Times,* September 6, 1967, p. 63.
19. "Brotherhood-Also Business of Investors, Patterson & Company," *New York Age,* February 21, 1959, p. 14.

20. Carol Patterson Lewis, interview with author.
21. Lula Powell-Watson, interview with author.
22. Chuck Stone "Patterson & Co., Young Brokerage Firm Offers Financial Opportunities for Negroes," *New York Age,* May 30, 1959, p. 19.
23. "Brotherhood-Also Business of Investors, Patterson & Company," *New York Age,* February 21, 1959, p. 14.
24. "Woman Passes NY Stock Exchange Exam," *Jet,* May 7, 1953, p. 18.

Chapter 2: Cold Calling

1. Anonymous source, interview with author.
2. George W. King, interview with author.
3. Ibid.
4. Ibid.
5. Harry Jacobs, interview with author.
6. Anonymous source, interview with author.
7. Vartanig G. Vartan, "A Girlhood Dream Is Realized," *New York Times,* February 5, 1965, p. 39.
8. Terry Robards, "Brokerage Firm Is Run by and for Negroes," *New York Times,* September 6, 1967, p. 63.
9. Ibid.
10. June L'Rhue "Women's Day on Wall Street Highlights Mutual Funds," *New York Amsterdam News,* October 28, 1961, p. 8.
11. "N.Y. House to Finance Negro Firms," *Pittsburgh Courier,* September 2, 1961, p. 10.
12. "First Negro-Owned Brokerage House Opens on Wall Street," *Wall Street Journal,* July 22, 1955.

Chapter 3: The Big Time

1. Franklynn Peterson, "First Black Firm in Stock Exchange," *Sepia,* June, 1972, pp. 67–70.
2. Jim Greene, interview with author.
3. Franklynn Peterson, "First Black Firm in Stock Exchange," *Sepia,* June, 1972, pp. 67–70.
4. "Travers Bell," *Institutional Investor,* June, 1987, pp. 219–220.
5. Author.
6. Timothy Tegeler, interview with author.
7. "Travers Bell," *Institutional Investor,* June, 1987, pp. 219–220.
8. Bill Jordan, "Daniels & Bell, Inc. Had Rocky Road to NYSE," *Atlanta Journal Constitution,* December 6, 1971, p. C1.
9. Myron Kandel, "Moneyline with Lou Dobbs," *CNN,* commentary given on January 19, 1998, 7:23 P.M.
10. "Travers Bell," *Institutional Investor,* June, 1987, pp. 219–220.
11. Dan W. Lufkin, interview with author.

12. "Muriel Siebert," *Institutional Investor,* June, 1987, pp. 89–91.
13. Arthur Levitt, interview with author.
14. Vartanig G. Vartan, "Negro Proposed for a Seat on Exchange," *New York Times,* January 31, 1970, p. 1.
15. Joseph Searles, interview with author.
16. Jerome Becker, interview with author.
17. Joseph Searles, interview with author.
18. Ibid.
19. Ibid.
20. Vartanig G. Vartan, "Negro Stockbroker Is Starting Over Alone," *New York Times,* March 19, 1971, p. 53.
21. Joseph Searles, interview with author.
22. "Crispus Attucks Comes to Wall Street," *Black Enterprise,* October 1970, pp. 17–21.
23. Charles Elia, "Negroes Are Urged to Study Finance," *New York World-Telegram & Sun,* March 23, 1965.
24. Stephen Fields, interview with author.
25. Ibid.
26. Alger "Duke" Chapman, interview with author.
27. Gerald C. Fraser, "Broker's Plan for Harlem Office Is Criticized by CORE Leader," *New York Times,* July 27, 1968, p. 25.
28. Ibid.
29. Alger "Duke" Chapman, interview with author.
30. Ibid.
31. Melvin Eubanks, interview with author.
32. Earl Andrews Jr., interview with author.
33. Jim Greene, interview with author.
34. Harold E. Doley Jr., interview with author.

Chapter 4: A Dry Husk

1. Philip Greer, "Despite Setbacks in First Year, Black Brokers Confident," *Washington Post,* June 5, 1972, p. D10.
2. Earl Andrews, interview with author.
3. Clarence O. Smith, interview with author.
4. Jim Greene, interview with author.
5. Ibid.
6. Earl Andrews, interview with author.
7. Martin Everette, interview with author.
8. Robert D. Hershey Jr., "Black Broker Finds Action in Wall Street," *New York Times,* June 26, 1972, p. 49.
9. Gregg Harris, "Taking Stock on Wall Street," *Black Enterprise,* March 1980.
10. Dan Dorfman, "Heard on the Street," *Wall Street Journal,* January 27, 1972.
11. Clarence O. Smith, interview with author.

12. Ibid.
13. "First Blacks on NYSE Have Turned the Corner," *Boston Globe,* March 11, 1973.
14. Philip Greer, "Despite Setbacks in First Year, Black Brokers Confident," *Washington Post,* June 5, 1972, p. D10.
15. Ibid.
16. Ibid.
17. Harold E. Doley Jr., interview with author.
18. Baunita Greer, interview with author.
19. Philip Greer, "Despite Setbacks in First Year, Black Brokers Confident," *Washington Post,* June 5, 1972, p. D10.
20. Harold E. Doley Jr., interview with author.
21. Philip Greer, "Despite Setbacks in First Year, Black Brokers Confident," *Washington Post,* June 5, 1972, p. D10.
22. Robert E. Dallos, "Black Broker Stung by Blacks' Prejudice," *Los Angeles Times,* June 13, 1976.
23. Anonymous source, interview with author.
24. Baunita Greer, interview with author.
25. Quoted from "Pinnacle, *CNN,* March 1985.
26. Howard Mackey, interview with author.
27. Earl Andrews, interview with author.
28. Alger "Duke" Chapman, interview with author.
29. Earl Andrews, interview with author.
30. Melvin Eubanks, interview with author.

Chapter 5: Rising in the Ranks

1. Maynard H. Jackson, interview with author.
2. Ibid.
3. Ibid.
4. "White Business Balks at Sharing Work," *Business Week,* November 17, 1975, p. 47.
5. Melvin Eubanks, interview with author.
6. Henry E. Parker, interview with author.
7. Gedale Horowitz, interview with author.
8. David C. Clapp, interview with author.
9. Gedale Horowitz, interview with author.
10. Napoleon Brandford, interview with author.
11. Bernard B. Beal, interview with author.
12. William H. Hayden, interview with author.
13. Maynard H. Jackson, interview with author.
14. William H. Hayden, interview with author.
15. Ibid.
16. Maynard H. Jackson, interview with author.

17. Jeffrey Humber, interview with author.
18. "Who Are the Blacks at the Top of the Money Industry?" *Ebony,* November, 1979, pp. 158–163.
19. Ernest G. Green, interview with author.
20. Kenneth E. Glover, interview with author.
21. Franklin D. Raines, interview with author.
22. Napoleon Brandford, interview with author.
23. Gedale Horowitz, interview with author.
24. Ernest G. Barefield, interview with author.
25. Franklin D. Raines, interview with author.
26. Kenneth E. Glover, interview with author.
27. Napoleon Brandford, interview with author.
28. Franklin D. Raines, interview with author.
29. Jeffrey Humber, interview with author.
30. Franklin D. Raines, interview with author.
31. Ibid.
32. David C. Clapp, interview with author.
33. Gedale Horowitz, interview with author.
34. Milton Irvin, interview with author.

Chapter 6: The Building

1. "Travers Bell," *Institutional Investor,* June 1987.
2. Ibid.
3. Earl Andrews Jr., interview with author.
4. Kenneth E. Glover, interview with author.
5. Henry E. Parker, interview with author.
6. Ibid.
7. Ibid.
8. Ibid.
9. Harold E. Doley Jr., interview with author.
10. William H. Hayden, interview with author.
11. Anonymous source, interview with author.
12. Harold E. Doley Jr., interview with author.
13. Napoleon Brandford, interview with author.
14. Bernard B. Beal, interview with author.
15. Gedale Horowitz, interview with author.
16. Bernard B. Beal, interview with author.
17. Earl Andrews Jr., interview with author.
18. Eric Pianin, "Barry Friend Quits Bond Advisor Job," *Washington Post,* December 17, 1987, p. B1.
19. Gedale Horowitz, interview with author.
20. Earl Andrews Jr., interview with author.
21. Melvin Eubanks, interview with author.
22. Gedale Horowitz, interview with author.

23. Melvin Eubanks, interview with author.
24. James White, "W. R. Lazard's Rapid Growth Proves Risky," *Wall Street Journal,* June 24, 1991, p. C1.
25. Napoleon Brandford, interview with author.
26. Clifford Graves, interview with author.
27. Dennis Cauchon, "GBP's Giant Ambitions; 'Success Is Color Blind' for Black Investment Firm," *USA Today,* June 20, 1989, p. B7.
28. Kenneth E. Glover, interview with author.
29. Kieran Beerm, "Q&A: Grigsby Seeks to Transcend Minority Firm Status," *The Bond Buyer,* August 1, 1995.
30. Napoleon Brandford, interview with author.
31. Fran Hawthorne, "Is the Muni Market Color-Blind?" *Institutional Investor,* June 1988.
32. Howard Mackey, interview with author.

Chapter 7: Money Managers

1. Maceo K. Sloan, interview with author.
2. Ibid.
3. John W. Rogers, interview with author.
4. Ibid.
5. Caroline V. Clarke, *Take a Lesson: Today's Black Achievers on How They Made It and What They Learned Along the Way,* New York: John Wiley & Sons, 2001.
6. Maceo K. Sloan, interview with author.
7. Bill Atkinson, "Manager Is as Golden as His Picks," *Pensions & Investments,* September 15, 1997, pp. 44–45.
8. "BE Asset Managers," *Black Enterprise,* June 2000.
9. Maceo K. Sloan, interview with author.
10. Christine Philip, "NCM Capital Leads Pack," *Pensions & Investments,* July 18, 1991, p. 17.
11. Gerald B. Smith, interview with author.
12. Bernard B. Beal, interview with author.

Chapter 8: The Breakthrough

1. Fran Hawthorne, "Is the Muni Market Color-Blind?" *Institutional Investor,* June 1988, pp. 43–47.
2. Napoleon Brandford, interview with author.
3. Douglas Blackmon, "Round Trip: Black Muni Bond Firm Scaled the Heights, Fell Back to Earth," *Wall Street Journal,* August 28, 1996, p. A1.
4. Howard Mackey, interview with author.
5. Mark Sherman, "Lucrative City Bond Sale Goes to Mayor's Friends: Aides Say He Just Has Many Contacts in the Field," *Atlanta Journal-Constitution,* September 17, 1990, p. B1.

6. Ibid.
7. Maynard H. Jackson, interview with author.
8. Howard Mackey, interview with author.
9. Melvin Eubanks, interview with author.
10. Edward Iwata, "Bond King Admired, Resented: Calvin Grigsby Driven to Succeed," *San Francisco Chronicle,* March 31, 1996, p. A1.
11. Clifford Graves, interview with author.
12. Ibid.
13. Ibid.
14. Loida N. Lewis, interview with author.
15. Ibid.
16. Daniel Cuff, "90 to 1 Return for Investor," *New York Times,* July 10, 1987.
17. Anthony Bianco, "The King of Wall Street," *Business Week,* December 9, 1985, p. 98.
18. "Beatrice Deal a Landmark for Black Business," *USA Today,* August 11, 1987, p. B2.

Chapter 9: The Turmoil

1. Leah Nathans Spiro, "The Trouble with Munis," *Business Week,* September 6, 1993, p. 94.
2. Michael Schroeder, "Affirmative, Yes—But Is It Fair?" *Business Week,* July 4, 1994, p. 74.
3. Phyliss Berman, "The Set-Aside Charade," *Forbes,* March 13, 1995, p. 78.
4. Ibid.
5. Ibid.
6. Laurie P. Cohen, "SEC Expands Investigation of Muni Bonds," *Wall Street Journal,* June 3, 1993, p. C1.
7. William H. Hayden, interview with author.
8. David C. Clapp, interview with author.
9. Kenneth E. Glover, interview with author.
10. Constance Mitchell, "A Piece of History: First Wall Street Firm Owned by Black Sinks After Founder's Death," *Wall Street Journal,* May 11, 1993, p. A1.
11. National Association of Securities Dealers disciplinary actions reported for April 1997.
12. Gedale Horowitz, interview with author.
13. Martin Everette, interview with author.
14. Melvin Eubanks, interview with author.
15. Terry Williams, "New Woes Hit W. R. Lazard," *Pensions & Investments,* June 23, 1997, p. 2.
16. David Dietz, "S. F. Financier Acquitted in Miami Theft Trial," *San Francisco Chronicle,* June 8, 1999, p. A4.
17. Clifford Graves, interview with author.

18. Benjamin Weiser, "In the Minority and Mad: Black-Owned Investment Firms Say SEC's Pay to Play Curbs Are Unfair," *Washington Post,* January 29, 1995, p. H1.

19. Bill Rankin, "Two Guilty of Bilking Atlanta's Portfolio," *Atlanta Constitution,* August 9, 2000, p. A1.

Chapter 10: The New Breed

1. John O. Utendahl, interview with author.
2. Ibid.
3. Constance Mitchell, "Black-Owned Investment Banks Gain Ground Even as Big Fees Prove Elusive," *Wall Street Journal,* November 18, 1992, p. C1.
4. Harold E. Doley, interview with author.
5. Napoleon Brandford, interview with author.
6. John O. Utendahl, interview with author.
7. Ronald E. Blaylock, interview with author.
8. Christopher J. Williams, interview with author.
9. Bernard B. Beal, interview with author.
10. Kenneth E. Glover, interview with author.
11. Harold E. Doley, interview with author.
12. "Probe Black Broker Bribes," *New York Daily News,* January 25, 1995.
13. Diana B. Henriques, "Piercing Wall Street's Lucite Ceiling," *New York Times,* August 11, 1991, p. 31.
14. Shelly Sigo, "Siebert, Shank, and Brandford Lash Out at 'Ludicrous' Lawsuit," *The Bond Buyer,* September 11, 2000, p. 1.
15. Joan Oleck, "A Minority Firm Hits the Big Leagues," *Business Week,* April 19, 1999, p. 6.
16. Ronald E. Blaylock, interview with author.
17. Advertisement, "History Is Made," *Black Enterprise,* June 1999.
18. Brian Garrity, "Breaking the Mold," *The Investment Dealers Digest,* August 16, 1999, pp. 12–19.
19. Chee Chee Williams, interview with author.
20. Maceo K. Sloan, interview with author.
21. William H. Hayden, interview with author.
22. Christopher Williams, interview with author.
23. Nathan A. Chapman, interview with author.
24. Christopher Williams, interview with author.
25. Chuck Stone, "Patterson & Co., Young Brokerage Firm Offers Financial Opportunities for Negroes," *New York Age,* May 30, 1959.

Index